DATE DUE

GAYLORD

PRINTED IN U.S.A.

D0992455

EDUCATIONAL POLICY:
An International Survey

EDUCATIONAL POLICY

AN INTERNATIONAL SURVEY

EDITED BY J.R.HOUGH

CROOM HELM
London & Sydney

ST. MARTIN'S PRESS
New York

© 1984 J.R. Hough
Croom Helm Ltd, Provident House, Burrell Row,
Beckenham, Kent BR3 1AT
Croom Helm Australia Pty Ltd, First Floor, 139 King Street,
Sydney, NSW 2001, Australia

British Library Cataloguing in Publication Data

Educational policy
   1. Educational planning
   I. Hough, J.R.
   379.1'5   LB2805
   ISBN 0-7099-1270-6

Library of Congress Cataloging in Publication Data
Main entry under title:

Educational policy.

   Includes bibliographical references and index.
   Contents: Australia / D. Berwick and G. Harman –
France / J.R. Hough – West Germany / W. Schwarck and
A. Wolf – [etc.]
   1. Education and state – Addresses, essays, lectures.
2. Educational surveys – Addresses, essays, lectures.
3. Comparative education – Addresses, essays, lectures.
I. Hough, J.R.
LC71.E34   1984   379.1'54   83-40627
ISBN 0-312-23804-5

Printed and bound in Great Britain

CONTENTS

PREFACE

The idea for the present book arose out of discussions with the publishers early in 1982. That it has been possible to produce the completed volume so quickly is due in no small part to the active support and co-operation I have received from the publishers throughout the period of its preparation. My grateful thanks are due to all the contributors of the individual country essays for agreeing to be involved with this book and for responding so readily to the many queries I had to raise with them when they were preparing their contributions, particularly when these were at the first draft stage. Above all, my gratitude is due to Dr Grant Harman for kindly agreeing that his work on conceptual and theoretical issues could be included, in somewhat revised form, as Chapter Two. As will be seen, the coverage of this chapter is general and international in nature but in its later pages is illustrated with specific examples (printed in italics) drawn from developments in Australia.

I am grateful to Mrs Gloria Brentnall who typed almost all the final typescript, with her usual cheerful efficiency, and to Ms Janice Oselton and Mrs Avril McNamee who assisted, particularly with earlier drafts. The Department of Education at Loughborough University readily provided various other facilities and the staff of the university library were helpful in checking sources and references.

Finally, I am unable to express on paper how much I owe to my wife and family. Doubtless each of the contributors would wish to acknowledge similar debts of gratitude and I can only assume proxy to do so here on their behalf.
Loughborough,

One

INTRODUCTION

J.R. Hough

Although there are in existence many books which
describe and/or analyse the educational systems of
different countries, in general they tend to make
rather little reference to educational policy as
such. And there appears to be previously no one
volume which brings together a collection of recent
studies of educational policy in the countries
covered by the present book, namely, Australia,
France, Japan, Sweden, The United Kingdom, The
United States of America, and West Germany (the
Federal Republic). Hence one motivation for this
book: to fill an important gap in the existing
literature. A second motivation stemmed from the
experience of recent years (say, approximately the
last decade) in which, it can scarcely be doubted,
profound changes have occurred in the economic and
social systems in very many, perhaps most, of the
countries in the world, certainly including all of
those covered by this volume - changes which have
given rise to major re-orientations of educational
policy in every one of these countries.

THE CONTEXT

In the wake of the successive oil crises the
historical trend towards greater economic prosperity
appeared to come to a halt as rates of economic
growth declined, sometimes reaching zero or even
recording negative values. The long-standing notion
that a country's economic policy could broadly
choose a trade-off between a higher rate of unemployment or a higher rate of inflation gave way to a
series of years, in all the countries covered by
this volume, in which unemployment and inflation
were positively correlated and both reached

1

unprecedently high values. Although rates of
inflation eventually abated and returned to single
figures, unemployment continued to rise in all the
countries in question, despite such off-setting
tendencies as earlier retirements, reduced overtime,
typically a shorter working week, and longer periods
spent in education.
     Gradually both governments and public opinion
came to accept that unemployment, at very high
levels, was here to stay and might not significantly
decline before the end of the century, especially as
computerisation, which signified the replacement of
man's (or woman's) labour by automated machine
processes of varying degrees of sophistication,
continued to accelerate. By the 1980s even punch-
card operated computers were everywhere being broken
down for scrap as they gave way to the newest fully
interactive computers which could do all the same
operations, and more, many times faster. At the
time of writing, the latest generation of word
processors in the USA will 'read' input from any
typed or printed page, manipulate this as desired
with a few commands from an operator, and produce
an output of whatever style, size, or quantity as
required, all within a matter of minutes. The
present book is being produced via camera-ready typescript which eliminated almost all the human labour
previously required for type-setting, checking and
proof-reading. In the very near future authors
will, after doing much of their work of authorship
at the video screen, merely send to publishers the
magnetic disk output from the word processor. It
is small wonder that the pace of change in modern
technology has been described as quite frightening.
     The same economic hiatus produced massive
balance-of-payments deficits, on a scale not
previously known, in all non-oil-producing countries,
and these were the immediate cause of the governments of all the countries in question adopting
deflationary economic policies of varying degrees of
severity. One prime instrument of retrenchment
policy consisted of cuts in government expenditure,
one result being that, either directly or indirectly
and either immediately or at some future date, the
educational sector found itself deprived of the
often rather generous levels of funding that it had
come to expect. This was not always revealed in
significant changes in the central government's
budget because education was not always a prime
responsibility of the central government, particularly in federal states such as Australia, the USA,

and West Germany. In every country, however,
education was one of the very largest spenders of
public funds in total and so could not hope to
escape unscathed from the effects of the deepening
economic depression.

THE EDUCATIONAL CLIMATE

The same years of economic gloom saw the blossoming
of doubts about education: was more and more
education really the universal Good that educators
had long proclaimed and that society at large had
generally accepted? If so, why were increasing
numbers of young people apparently increasingly
alienated by the educational system? Why did we
read of, and see on our television screens, student
riots in every one of the countries considered here?
Why, in every one of these countries, was there
official concern, howsoever expressed, at the
apparently growing numbers of young people leaving
school functionally illiterate and/or functionally
non-numerate for a complex modern society? Why did
the percentages of young people opting to remain in
education beyond the age of compulsory schooling
largely cease to rise in the mid-1970s before being
bolstered again by the young people desirous of
leaving school but unable to find work? Why were
unemployed young people apparently ill-equipped by
their long years of full-time education to use
profitably or even enjoy the enforced leisure which
confronted them and which others might envy? Why
had education apparently done little to reduce
inequalities in society or even within education
itself - so that, for example, in every one of the
countries dealt with here, higher education remained
largely dominated by the middle-classes, with the
less fortunate strata of society being represented
only rather minimally? Why were curricula in
schools and colleges increasingly accused of being
irrelevant to the needs of modern society,· as most
symptomised by the large numbers of young people,
in every one of the countries, opting to study arts
subjects rather than science, whereas national needs
were apparently for more scientists, engineers, and
technologists?
    Such questions as these did not arise overnight
and did not all arise in all the countries at the
same time. But they do typify some of the problems
which led to official policy relating to education
becoming a major focus of interest. Increasingly at

all levels of government more **time and resources**
came to be devoted to educational policy issues, and
this was reflected by and concomitant with much
increased attention to matters of educational policy
in the mass media. At the present time such trends
show no signs of abating. It has been said that
certainty has given way to uncertainty and optimism
has given way to pessimism.

It would, however, be easy to over-exaggerate
the 'doom and gloom' approach: educational policy
has also had to deal with the upsurge of numbers of
students, more than ever before in every one of
these countries, with rising standards required in
many fields, and with adaptation and re-training to
meet the requirements of new technologies, and for
much of the time in most countries appeared to cope
with remarkable success. By the late 1970s or early
1980s each of the countries in question had
experienced reduced birth rates and therefore
smaller student populations, initially in the
nurseries or kindergartens that were increasingly a
feature of the educational scene and then in the
primary schools. Although this reduction in numbers
would everywhere mean that fewer teachers would be
required (and hence the work of educational colleges
or training institutions would be severely curtailed)
there would be pressure on some school staff to
retire early and some schools and colleges would
have to close completely, it should also, was and
is the hope, pave the way for increased opportunities in terms of easier access to education, less
pressure on places and on space, fewer financial
constraints, and new incentives to adapt and
diversify. At the time of writing the reduced
numbers are approaching their secondary years and
some of the more traumatic changes, for good or ill,
at the secondary or higher education levels, still
lie ahead.

AIMS

The aims of this book are not merely to describe
educational policy within each of the seven
countries but to focus on the development of that
policy over time, as related to its setting within
the relevant national society and economy, and to
explore comparable and contrasting trends and
influences between them. In the modern world
characterised by apparently instantaneous communication flows and by rapid transmission of

information of all kinds it is increasingly impossible for any one country to remain isolated from developments that are influencing other countries which are frequently faced with similar problems. If this is true in respect of many fields, it is particularly so in the case of education and educational policy. An important theme in this book will therefore relate to the common factors which have affected a number, and sometimes all, of the countries in question. At the same time significant national and even sub-national differences remain as each country sets any new development within the context of its own esoteric historical, political and social setting. It is now over 80 years since Sir Michael Sadler wrote:

> a national system of education is a living
> thing, the outcome of forgotten struggles and
> difficulties and of 'battles long ago'. It
> has in it some of the secret workings of
> national life. It reflects, whilst seeking
> to remedy, the failings of national
> character[1].

Reflections of such thoughts are certainly to be found in each of the contributing essays that make up this book.

COMPARATIVE STUDIES

Within the field of education, there is nothing very new about comparative country studies and in such studies there is nothing very new about a focus which takes a keen interest in the interaction between educational institutions and the wider society, and the forces which the latter may exert on the former. To quote Sadler again, writing at the turn of the twentieth century:

> in studying foreign systems of education we
> should not forget that the things outside the
> schools matter even more than the things
> inside the schools, and govern and interpret
> the things inside[2].

The theme of the interaction between the educational sector and society at large, which finds repeated expression in all the essays included in this book, was one which may be said to have preoccupied early writers in the field of comparative educational studies. Mallinson concluded the fourth edition of his seminal work[3] with the words:

> the highest goal of comparative education studies must be to describe, explain and compare educational systems in terms of their cultural totality

which may be taken as a fair reflection of what has usually been seen as his major emphasis, namely the importance of understanding a country's 'national character' to be able fully to appreciate its system of education. Similarly, an early emphasis was on the uniqueness of educational systems rather than on their commonalities[4], whereas in the essays included in the present volume the twin aspects of uniqueness and commonality will be found to be so intertwined that they can scarcely be separated. Educational policy, and policymakers, will be seen to react both to national trends and to international influences.

Comparative educational studies inevitably reflect trends within such fields of study as history, sociology, politics and economics, and in particular they could not be unaffected by what has been called the 'soul-searching in the social sciences'[5]. In what is now usually seen in retro-spect as the structural-functionalist era, national educational systems tended to be depicted as (relatively) static, as broadly serving society well and responding without difficulty to its (rather slowly) changing influences, and as produc-ing the manpower and skills the national economy required in (approximately) the right numbers and proportions. The notion of reform was always present, in that increasing layers and quantities of education were seen as liable over time to amelior-ate the ills of society as expressed in ignorance, want, ill-health and inequality, but the concept of reform would have about it nothing radical, dramatic, or volcanic, and certainly nothing Marxist. A prime aim of studies in this field was to aid educational decisionmaking and policy-formation - and hence their direct relevance to a volume of comparative essays on educational policy - along the road towards planned and gradual change.

If serious doubts were expressed about any ideological or theoretical underpinnings to the many comparative studies that were published in the field of education they might refer to 'cultural borrow-ing'[6]: the issues relating to, for example, the raising of the school-leaving age would differ in every one of the countries included in the present book.

It is now possible to look back at such earlier writings (up to, say, twenty years ago) and find within their pages traces of what only later were clearly identified as the phenomenological, ethnomethodological, neo-Marxist, conflict, or other radical labels that came to be taken as symptomatic of the 'new' sociology, which profoundly affected this as other fields. Or perhaps we might say this more than most other fields in view of its essentially eclectic nature. The newer emphases led to the formation of quite distinct 'schools' or points of view, with stances which developed and changed over time, were at times not clear to external observers, and which frequently overlapped with each other. One survey[7], for example, distinguished between the positive, neo-positive, Marxist, neo-Marxist, relativist and neo-relativist schools, in such terms as 'deductive- nomological analysis', 'verisimilitude', 'critical rationalism' and 'theories that support capitalism as being ideologically infused'. Perhaps it was small wonder that observers, or even ordinary participants in educational systems or educational policymaking, were liable to become confused.

Few serious critics would now deny the importance of attention to ideological, philosophical, and conceptually critical approaches to educational studies and such reflective aspects will certainly appear in this book. When, however, the newer schools of thought go on:

> to argue that educational systems are directly affected by international currents and that national school systems and the relations between school and the nation are no longer worthy subjects of analysis

it is probably time to part company[8]. That the development of educational policy is profoundly interlinked with the specific national context appears repeatedly in every one of the essays included in this book and it is perhaps comforting to find that Professor Torsten Husen of the Stockholm Institute of International Education could write[9] in 1982 that the main purposes of comparative studies were 'to arrive at greater generalisability' and to consider 'how educational phenomena are related to each other and to society at large'.

It may also be salutary to note at the outset that, after more than 30 years of development, comparative education as a field, i.e. simply the study of education in other countries,

> has failed to develop one single, widely
> accepted method of inquiry; moreover it has
> not established a unitary body of knowledge.
> Rather, comparative education remains a field
> characterized by methodological debates and
> diversity of opinion as to what constitutes
> its subject matter and orientation[10]

or, in even more pessimistic vein,

> The final conclusion is that there is hardly
> any cumulative empirically based knowledge
> in the field of comparative education.
> Neither do we find a systematic application
> or testing of theories, nor does the available
> evidence without considerable effort
> contribute much to the inductive development
> of generalisations and theories. These facts
> raise serious obstacles to approaching the
> aims of comparative education[11].

If, however, a crucial aim of comparative research remains 'aiding problem-solving or policy-making'[12] and if few up-to-date studies, and even fewer collections of studies, of educational policy currently exist, then the motivation for the present volume becomes clear.

POLICY TASKS FOR THE 1980s

The conclusions of a recent major intergovernmental conference[13] on policies relating to higher education, held at the Organisation for Economic Co-operation and Development (whose membership includes all the countries covered by this book) were expressed in the following terms:

> At the beginning of the 1980s the overriding
> concern ... seems to be how to sustain public
> confidence in and support for a system which,
> in most countries, is no longer growing in
> such a way as to ensure its continued dynamic
> evolution ...
> In many countries there appears to be a crisis
> of confidence which is approaching alarming

dimensions. Unless new policies are rapidly conceived and implemented there may be a real danger, over the longer term, that the potential of higher education for supporting countries' economic vitality and the welfare of their citizens, through cultural, scientific and technological development, could be seriously and perhaps irretrievably compromised ...

... there are clear signs that in the period ahead, governments will be led to adopt more active roles and explicit policies in the development of higher education. A major policy concern will be how to mediate between the pressures arising from ... external factors (and also linked to the pursuit of broader social, economic and technological policy objectives) and those stemming from higher education institutions themselves, including the consequences of the rapid expansion of higher education in the past. It is equally clear, however, that the way in which these policy concerns will be expressed will vary from country to country, so that generalis-ations are even more difficult now than they were in the past.

The same conference went on to specify the tasks with which education policy would have to deal in the 1980s, at the higher education level, i.e. to:

(a) respond to new needs at local and community level;

(b) contribute to revitalising the economy by producing the 'right' kinds of highly qualified manpower and contribute to the further training of the labour force in the context of rapidly changing technologies;

(c) sustain adequate levels of technological innovation through scientific research progress;

(d) help to promote greater social equity, at a time when the more deprived sections of the population are hardest hit by the economic situation.

From a reading of these extracts it can scarcely be doubted that they apply to every one of the seven countries included in this volume and that they apply to levels of education other than higher education, i.e. certainly to secondary schooling and in at least some respects to primary schooling and even (in terms, for example, of the equity criterion quoted) to pre-primary.

Such a 'practical' emphasis may perhaps be seen as usefully complementary to the more theoretical or ideological considerations referred to above and the two together may be seen as forming a suitable back-cloth to the individual country essays that follow.

STRUCTURE OF THE BOOK

The choice of which countries to include within the compass of this book followed on from two previous volumes published by Croom Helm in which the present editor was involved as a contributor[14]. It would, of course, be easy to criticise the choice or to argue the case for the inclusion of one or more other countries (Italy? Canada?). The constraints of space and size limited the number of countries that could be covered and, apart from expediency, the seven chosen are all developed countries with highly developed educational systems and a complex mix of educational policies and problems. Further, to assemble a panel of contributors to provide the essays that form the core of this book was no quick or easy task and was aided by the fact that the countries in question are ones that the editor had either visited in person or with which he had some other contacts.

Each of the authors can claim to be an expert on educational policy in the country studied and six out of the seven are resident participants at very senior level in the country's educational system, mostly in a prominent university. The seventh formerly resided and studied in, and has subsequently made frequent visits to, the country under consideration, namely France, and was able to obtain detailed comments on an earlier draft of his paper from a senior representative of that country's Ministry of National Education.

It could especially be argued that the most crucial problems of educational policy in the world today are to be found in the developing countries and it might therefore appear particularly regrettable that no Third World countries could be included. The editor would have considerable sympathy with such sentiments but to attempt to include such countries would clearly have entailed major changes to both the size and the nature of the book. The problems of

educational policy in the poorer countries of the
world are clearly so acute and so different from
those considered here, from every point of view,
that they surely require exmination in a separate
volume, or, more probably, more than one.

The task of editorship of this book has
entailed endeavouring to achieve a reasonable degree
of homogeneity in terms of coverage and approach
whilst leaving each contributor sufficient freedom
and flexibility to develop his essay as he considered most appropriate. Therefore, a common outline
structure for the essays was suggested and at least
elements of this may be discerned in each but, as
may be seen, each contributor has felt free to
diverge from this as necessary. Only by such a
compromise approach was it possible to avoid
imposing a straitjacket on the contributors, which
would have been liable to mar the quality of the
final product. To cite just one specific example,
it was agreed that earlier historical coverage would
be kept to a bare minimum in order to concentrate on
current and recent educational policy developments;
at times, however, current educational policy could
only be fully appreciated if set in the appropriate
historical context.

No neat summary of the various strands referred
to in this Introduction will be attempted here but
the following quotation may serve to bring together
a number of the points made above:

> The comparative argument is that various
> profiles of educational purpose and function
> exist ...   These profiles differ according to
> specific national or regional ideologies
> which are in turn closely related to varying
> Epistemological Styles. As such they are
> temporary but locally satisfactory solutions
> to what is otherwise an insoluble puzzle,
> namely, how to square a triangle made up of
> the conflicting needs, wants, desires,
> interests, etc. of (1) individuals
> (2) society - and all this in relation to
> (3) varying definitions of worthwhile, useful
> knowledge[15].

Before turning to the studies of educational
policy in the seven individual countries which make
up the core of this book, the reader is first
invited to read Chapter 2 which deals with major
conceptual and theoretical issues common to all
seven. Finally at the end of the book in Chapter 10

the editor will seek to bring together a number of conclusions which emerge from the essays.

NOTES

1. M. Sadler, *How Far Can We Learn Anything of Practical Value from the Study of Foreign Systems of Education?* (Guildford, 1900), quoted in V. Mallinson, *An Introduction to the Study of Comparative Education*, Fourth Edition (Heinemann, 1975).

2. *Ibid.*

3. V. Mallinson, *An Introduction to the Study of Comparative Education*.

4. D.F. McDade, 'The Things that Interest Mankind: A Commentary on Thirty Years of Comparative Education', *British Journal of Educational Studies*, Vol.XXX, No.1, February 1982.

5. *Ibid.*

6. *Ibid.*

7. E.H. Epstein, 'Currents Left and Right: Ideology in Comparative Education', *Comparative Education Review*, Vol.27, No.2, February 1983.

8. *Ibid.* To avoid misunderstanding, it should be made clear that the words quoted are Epstein's categorisation of 'the new' methodological perspectives', not (necessarily) his own views. The article was based on his Presidential Address to the Comparative and International Education Society, meeting in Chicago.

9. In his Forword to M. Niessen and J. Peschar, *Comparative Research on Education* (Pergamon, 1982).

10. G.P. Kelly, P.G. Altbach and R.F. Arnove, 'Trends in Comparative Education: A Critical Analysis' in P.G. Altback, G.P. Kelly and D.H. Kelly (eds), *International Bibliography of Comparative Education* (Praeger, New York, 1981).

11. Niessen and Peschar, *Comparative Research on Education*.

12. *Ibid.*

13. Reported in: *Policies for Higher Education in the 1980s* (OECD, 1983). The first extract quoted is from the Concluding Remarks of the Chairman, Professor Peter Karmel.

14. W.P.J. Maunder, *Government Intervention in the Developed Economy*, and E. Owen Smith, *Trade Unions in the Developed Economies*.

15. E.J. Nicholas, *Issues in Education: A Comparative Analysis* (Harper & Row, 1983).

Two

CONCEPTUAL AND THEORETICAL ISSUES

Grant Harman

POLICY

The term 'policy' is an elusive one and demands
some clarification. Even a brief investigation will
reveal that the word 'policy' is used in many
different ways to refer to a highly diverse set of
phenomena. This is the case, both in everyday
language and in scholarly writing. In a single day
in many countries, one might well hear a Prime
Minister announce changes in the nation's foreign
policy, a city mayor discussing an aspect of city
traffic or parking policy, and a shop assistant
explaining to a customer that, because of company
policy, particular goods cannot be returned or
exchanged. The same lack of a precise agreed meaning is true in the world of scholarship. Policy is
sometimes used in a narrow sense to refer to formal
statements of action to be followed, while others
use the word 'policy' as a synonym for words such
as 'plan' or 'programme'. Many writers too do not
distinguish clearly between 'policy-making' and
'decision-making'.
    Here there is not space to systematically and
critically review both everyday and scholarly usage
of the term[1]. Instead we will suggest one view of
policy, and how policy can be distinguished from
related concepts. Here, we will use policy to refer
to the implicit or explicit specification of courses
of purposive action being followed or to be followed
in dealing with a recognised problem or matter of
concern, and directed towards the accomplishment of
some intended or desired set of goals. Policy also
can be thought of as a position or stance developed
in response to a problem or issue of conflict, and
directed towards a particular objective. Policy
conveniently can be distinguished from related

13

concepts, some of which we define as follows:

Goals:	desired ends to be achieved.
Plans or proposals:	specified means for achieving goals.
Programmes:	authorised means, strategies and details of procedure for achieving goals.
Decisions:	specific actions taken to set goals, develop plans, implement and evaluate programmes.
Effects:	measurable impact of programmes.
Laws or regulations:	formal or legal expressions providing authorisation to policies.

Policy, then, is focused on purposive or goal oriented action or actively rather than random or chance behaviour. It refers to courses or patterns of action, rather than separate discrete decisions; usually policy development and application involves a number of related decisions, rather than a single decision. Policies may vary greatly in orientation, purpose and whether they are explicitly stated. Policies may be either positive or negative in the sense that they can have as their basis decisions to take particular action in response to a problem, as well as developing simply from failure to act, or from decisions to delay action. Policies include substantive policy as well as procedural or administrative policy. For example, a national government will have a number of substantive policies related to Tertiary Education including e.g. the provision of means-tested living allowances to tertiary students. Such policies will include details about eligibility criteria and the operation of means test. But in addition within the same government's Department of Education procedural policies will guide officers in processing claims from individual students. Policies also include unwritten as well as written policy; for example, in universities quite a deal of procedural policy may be unwritten, yet be clearly understood and followed by key administrators. Our analysis will be concerned mainly with positive, substantive written policy, and with public policy which, unlike policy in private organisations, is generally based on law and is certainly authoritative; it is the authoritative and potentially coercive quality for a society as a whole that distinguishes public policy from other policy.

Public policy in any field including education can take different forms of expression and can be directed towards different ends. Some policy finds expression in ministerial statements or white papers, some policy is authorised through legislation or regulations, while other policy takes the form of a directive issued by a minister or senior official. With regard to ends, some policies aim to regulate or control activity (e.g. compulsory schooling legislation), while others are directed to the provision of a new service or benefit (e.g. provision of scholarships, or a programme to assist disadvantaged groups), the establishment or control of an organisation (e.g. setting up a new university) or the transfer of resources and wealth from one group to another (e.g. means-tested living allowances for students)[2]. Some policies aim to introduce change, while others are meant to defend the *status quo* or to achieve return to an earlier set of conditions.

In terms of content, public policy for education can be grouped conveniently into four categories. First, there is policy concerned with the essential functions of schools and tertiary education institutions. A large part of this relates to curriculum, but it includes policy related to setting objectives and goals, recruitment and enrolment of students, student assessment (whether by internal or external means), award of certificates, diplomas and degrees, and student discipline. Second, there is policy concerned with the establishment, structure and governance of individual institutions and the whole education system or parts of it. A third area relates to the recruitment, employment, promotion, supervision and remuneration of all staff, but particularly different categories of professionals. A fourth category is policy related to the provision and allocation of financial resources and the provision and maintenance of buildings and equipment[3]. Some categories of policy tend to be of greater concern and importance at system-level than others.

Policy Process
Our discussion will pay some attention to how policy problems are characteristically handled, as well as

to the nature of particular policy problems and
their origins, and the responses developed. In
doing this, we will emphasise the notion of a
'policy process' rather than the more traditional
concept of 'policy-making', since we believe that
public policy is essentially about the transformation of group conflict over public resources and
values into authorised courses of action concerning
their allocation. Thus, while the concept of
'policy-making' concentrates attention almost
exclusively on the decision element of policy at the
point of formulation, the concept of 'policy process'
is based on the notion that the handling of policy
by any department or agency generally involves a
series of sequential stages or phases, covering a
span from when a particular programme has run its
course and is terminated, or takes on some new form.
Each stage is different, both in terms of what
happens to the political actors and their policy
efforts, and of results. These sequential stages
can be defined in different ways, but for the purpose of this essay we will use the schema set out
in Table 2.1[4]. The process begins with quiescence
on a particular issue, with most of the participants
being satisfied. Then dissatisfaction or disturb-
ance develops and the issue is recognised as a
problem and finds a place first on the public policy
agenda, and perhaps later on the agenda of official
actors. If the process continues, efforts are made
to explore possible solutions, a new policy is
formulated and an authoriative endorsement and
authorisation is made. Thereafter follows the
implementation of the new policy, later efforts to
review and evaluate its success and impact, and in
some cases eventual termination or replacement by
another policy. Generally new policies in education
more often emerge out of the variation, adjustment
and termination or variation of old ones, rather
than by a government entering a new field of policy
endeavour. Hogwood and Peters argue that this is
true generally of policy development in Britain and
the United States. Thus, they write, 'most policy-
making is actually policy succession: the replacement of an existing policy, programme or organisation by another'[5]. At each stage there is often
disagreement and conflict and not all policy
efforts result in all five stages being reached.
Often activity at each stage acts as a stimulus
(either immediate or delayed) to new pressures for
change or redirection.
    As already indicated, education in a narrow

Table 2.1: Stages in the Policy Process

(a) <u>Issue emergence and problem identification</u>
     (recognition of a problem or matter needing
     government attention; problem gains place on
     the public agenda and the official agenda;
     early mobilisation and support for particular
     strategies).

(b) <u>Policy formulation and authorisation</u>
     (exploration of various alternatives;
     formulation of preferred course of action;
     efforts to achieve consensus or compromise;
     formal authorisation of particular strategy
     such as through legislation, issue of
     regulations or publication of directives).

(c) <u>Implementation</u>
     (interpretation of policy and its application
     to particular cases; development of a programme
     or programmes).

(d) <u>Termination or change</u>
     (termination because the problem has been
     solved, the policy was unsuccessful or the
     outcomes were thought to be undesirable;
     alternatively major change in direction
     resulting from feedback, or replacement by
     new policy).

---

sense refers to formal education in institutions
rather than the whole process of rearing, upbringing
and the development of people of any age. We are
restricting attention to such activities only within
primary and secondary schools, and within tertiary
education institutions. This means that even quite
a range of formal education is excluded, such as
education in pre-school centres and in post-school
institutions other than those in what is now
regarded as the tertiary education system.

The Policy Context
Policy does not emerge within a vacuum. Rather it
is developed within the context of particular sets
of values, pressures and constraints, and within
particular structural arrangements. It also is a
response to particular problems, needs and

aspirations.

POLICY DEVELOPMENT AND APPLICATION

To appreciate more fully why key policy problems
have been tackled in particular ways, it is helpful
to have some understanding of the main policy actors
involved and of the characteristic ways in which
education policy is developed and applied[6].

Policy Actors

Within any community, divergent and often conflicting
views are held about where the real power lies in
terms of education policy decisions. One extreme
may be that the role of government is essentially
passive and that the evolution of policy is
dependent on the interplay of pressure from
teachers' unions, parents' associations, employers
and other interests. At the other extreme, there
may be the view that education policy depends
essentially on the personal whim of the Prime
Minister, Minister of Education or other powerful
official. Both views are exaggerations, though they
contain elements of truth. The reality is that a
wide range of actors share in policy formulation and
that even the formal powers of authorisation are
shared between a number of participants.

The actors involved with education policy fall
readily into two groups, the official and non-
official. Official actors are individuals or
organisational entities which have legally-based
responsibilities, while the unofficial actors comprise mainly interest groups, political parties and
the media. While this distinction between official
and non-official actors has utility, there is some
blurring of the boundaries; for example, teachers'
unions will operate as pressure groups communicating
demands to various points of official decision-
making, while at the same time they may have
representation on different official committees and
statutory boards. Hence in some senses they can be
regarded as being both official and unofficial actors.

The official actors conveniently fall into five
sets. The first comprises actors at the senior
levels of government: the Head of State, Parliament,
Prime Minister or Premier, Cabinet, and the
political party or parties in government. At the
pinnacle of executive authority, the Head of State
may rarely exercise independent authority and will

normally act on the advice of Ministers. The other actors in this group are much more important, and have the capacity to take an even greater part than they often do in determining education policy. All new policies needing a legislative base, for example, are subject to debate in Parliament and require the successful passage of bills to become acts. Since many education programmes each have their separate acts and since various grants legislation may have to be passed each year in order to provide new government funds for particular institutions and programmes, the Parliament will often have a more important role in education policy at national level compared with the greater executive role at local, state or regional, level. But at all levels in many countries there is a marked tendency in recent years for Cabinet and the party leaders to take a larger role. All major policy initiatives will require Cabinet approval, and on controversial issues the Premier or Prime Minister is likely to become actively involved. Often the broad lines of policy direction for any government are laid down by party platforms and may have to be approved by members of the parliamentary party.

The second set of official actors comprise the Minister for Education and the major education agencies and their senior officials. Ministers hold the formal authority for the administration of the education portfolio within particular jurisdictions, though in practice a great deal of authority is delegated to senior officials. *[In Australia, at both federal and state levels there has been a tendency to more activist ministerial styles; in Victoria, for example, over the period 1979-82 the Minister for Education, rather than his senior officials, initiated major restructuring of the Education Department. Senior officials, particuarly permanent heads, have a pivotal role, but this role is changing. In the past, at state level Directors-General or permanent heads were often extremely influential and to a large extent dominated their respective education departments and school or TAFE systems. But their power is being challenged from all sides. An American scholar recently reported after extensive interviews that Directors-General and their senior colleagues*

> *... believed their influence is being eroded - and that is bad. Politicians are getting too involved in administrative matters. Parents are challenging professional prerogatives.*

19

> *Militant teachers want autonomy but not*
> *responsibility. The federal government is*
> *meddling with state priorities. Taxpayers*
> *want more education for fewer dollars. In*
> *this view, the good old days of centralised*
> *professional leadership are over, and the*
> *rough days lie ahead[7].]*

The third set of official actors comprises other education agencies, which may be responsible for such tasks as conducting public external examinations for final-year secondary students, curriculum development, and fixing teachers' salaries.

The fourth group are government agencies outside the education portfolio which play a part in developing and implementing education policy. These may include Premiers' Departments (which provide advice to the Premier on education policy), Public Works Departments (which usually handle school building contracts and building maintenance) and Public Service Boards (which frequently determine or influence decisions about staffing levels and organisational structures).

The fifth and last set of official actors are intergovernmental bodies *[- the Australian Education Council and its associated Standing Committee, and the Conference of the Directors-General of Education. Formed in 1936, and now comprising the Commonwealth, state and Northern Territory Ministers of Education, the Australian Education Council is a non-statutory consultative body that meets for full sessions every six to eight months. Since a separate secretariat for the Council was established in the late 1970s in Melbourne, it has become an increasingly important vehicle for developing national policy on a range of problems. It is used by the state and Northern Territory Ministers to put pressure on the federal government and by the Commonwealth Minister to bargain collectively with the states. Working parties of officials have addressed problems such as school statistics, national assessment of achievement and educational research, while the Council has begun to commission major national research projects on topics such as school enrolment trends and their implications.]*

The main informal actors, as already indicated, are interest groups, political parties and the media. Of the interest groups, the key players are the teachers' unions, the associations representing tertiary education teachers and students, committees representing heads of universities or colleges, but also important are associations representing parents, employers, and trade unions. Each of the major teachers' unions is particularly important as at any time it will be exerting pressure about a wide range of topics on a variety of pressure points, including the Premier or Prime Minister, the Minister of Education, the permanent head of the Education Department, and other senior officials. While the teachers' unions often portray an image of militancy and antagonism towards ministers and senior officials, they will be closely involved in day-to-day negotiations with senior officials and are represented on official government committees and boards. The non-partliamentary components of each of the major political parties sometimes develop particular stances on education questions, which they seek to implement when the party gains office; otherwise, the political parties are usually content to let their parliamentary leaders act within the framework of broadly expressed aims. In many countries the mass media has taken an increased interest in education policies in recent years, and provides a mechanism for different interests to publicly explain their policy proposals and try to attract support. But, apart from a small number of leading newspapers, the media tends to be surprisingly ill-informed and often reflect community feelings and education experiences of an earlier era.

The Policy Process in Practice

At any time in any education policy system there are dozens, perhaps hundreds, of potential issues that could become recognised as policy problems and so provide the stimuli for education policy responses. Yet over a limited period of time only a relatively small number will become public issues, and even fewer still will be seriously addressed by official actors. This raises the important question of what mechanisms operate to determine which potential issues are transformed into policy problems to receive attention.

Cobb and Elder define issues which find a place on policy agendas as 'conflict between two or more identifiable groups over procedural or substantial matters relating to the distribution of positions or resources'[8]. They suggest four main means by which issues are created:

(a) Manufacture by one or more contending
parties who perceive an unfavourable bias
in the distribution of positions or
resources. (They label such initiators as
'*readjustors*'.)
(b) Creation of an issue by a person or group
for their own gain ('*exploiters*').
(c) Initiation through an unanticipated event
('*circumstantial reactors*').
(d) Generation by persons or groups who have
no position or resources to gain for themselves ('*do-gooders*').

Various triggering devices help shape issues that
will be defined by initiators; these include natural
catastrophes (fires, floods), unanticipated human
events (riots, strikes), technological changes,
imbalances or bias in the distribution of resources,
and 'ecological' changes such as population movements or changes in attitudes. The formation of an
issue is dependent on the dynamic interplay between
initiator and the trigger device.
    This theory has utility with regard to under-
standing the education policy process. Many
different actors can play the part of initiator -
Prime Minister, Minister of Education, the teachers'
union, a parents group. Such initiators can be
defined as '*readjustors*' (such as when teachers see
themselves falling behind in salary levels and take
industrial action, or when on gaining office a
political party attempts to vary an established
policy, such as that relating to government support
for non-government schools), '*exploiters*' (such as
when a Minister creates an issue for personal or
party publicity), '*circumstantial reactors*' (when
policy activity is spurred by a change in the
economy, or in population numbers or distribution),
and '*do-gooders*' (where group self-interest yields
to altruism). Over the past two decades in many
countries particularly important trigger influences
have been demographic changes, especially those
affecting student enrolments, employment and the
ethnic composition of the population; the influence
of economic and social policy in other areas of
government activity; changing social attitudes and
political climate, particularly relating to
education and young people; changing employment
prospects and particular demands from employers and
professional groups relating to preparation of
young people for employment; and changing social and
educational ideas in circulation particularly among

élites. But another trigger not provided for by the
Cobb and Elder theory is administrative difficulties
and the potential for trouble; a great deal of
policy effort is initiated by senior officials who
spot potential problems long before they produce
open conflict, or find a place on public agendas.
    There are other problems too with the framework;
three in particular deserve mention. First, some
initiators do not appear to fit neatly into any one
of the four categories for issue creation. Second,
sometimes it is hard to identify a single initiator,
since some issues emerge out of a new climate of
opinion with a range of different actors being
involved. Third, political problems addressed by
official actors do not always arise from open conflict. For example, especially at the national
level a great deal of education policy is developed
in conjunction with annual budgetary or triennial
planning exercises. Fourth, *Cobb and Elder*'s list
of trigger devices is somewhat limited. Other
trigger events, for example, may be publicity about
major education developments elsewhere, or the
impact of other education policies.
    With regard to policy formulation and authoris-
ation, the characteristic style is for the chosen or
agreed alternative course of action to emerge out of
a process of extensive consultation. Such consultation may take place within education departments or
agencies, between different agencies or government
at different levels, and between formal and informal
actors. Sometimes consultation is informal. At
other times, the setting is a working group within
a department, an inter-departmental committee, an
advisory committee, a statutory board, an *ad hoc*
working party or a special committee of inquiry
which often would include senior officials, outside
professional experts and interest group representatives. This consultative style differs from the
style of earlier decades, when both Ministers and
permanent heads tended to make more independent
policy decisions. *[In Australia, at federal level,
as Smart has noted, the committee of enquiry
frequently has been used as a device by both Labor
and non-Labor governments for developing detailed
policy recommendations for a new area of new
endeavour as well as for dealing with problems or
concerns related to on-going activities[9].]*
    Whether Ministers or public servants are
taking the lead in consultations, characteristically
there is concern about political feasibility as well
as technical, professional and social considerations,

for only in exceptional circumstances are Ministers or public servants prepared to choose a policy option likely to lead to political trouble. The result as *Lindblom*[10] has noted is usually a strong tendency towards an incremental style of policy development, rather than sudden shifts in policy direction.

Associated with this consultative and incremental style normally is a search for a broad-based consensus, acceptable both to government and key interest groups. This does not mean that conflict is absent. Conflict, in fact, often is necessary before a problem can get detailed attention, but comparatively rarely is conflict allowed to develop into prolonged confrontation between the main actors. *[As Hogan and West report with regard to the Teachers' Federation and the policy process in New South Wales, Australia, 'militant rhetoric is normal, but almost always serious negotiations are very quickly begun'*[11]*.]*

We know less about the other stages of the policy process. The design of new policies, formulating them in words and suitable slogans and securing their authorisation through legislation, new regulations or Ministerial approval is by no means an easy task. But it is often harder still to translate such policies successfully into government action. The experience of the last two decades in many countries demonstrates that high sounding education policies do not always work well when converted into particular programmes, and that outcomes may be very different from those intended. Often implementation produces the classic symptoms of under performance, delay, and escalating costs. *[In Australia the implementation problem in primary and secondary education is made more difficult by the sheer size of the larger state-wide school systems, by the complications of federalism in translating Commonwealth policies into action within state institutions, and by the separation between state independent school systems.]*

Implementation often places considerable pressure on senior officials, particularly when a government wishes to have a promised programme well in place before it must face another general election. *[A good example of this was the pressure placed on officers in the Department of Prime Minister and Cabinet in 1963-64, following the election promise of November 1963 by Prime Minister Robert Menzies to provide financial assistance to both government and non-government secondary schools*

*for the building and equipping of new science
laboratories*[12]*.]*

Success in implementation basically depends on
four factors. First, there is the policy design.
An ideal policy is one that is clear with unambiguous goals; a policy will have a reduced chance of
success if it is based on a defective theoretical
conception, or if the objectives are unclear or
unrealistic. *[In Australia, some of the recent
programmes of support for isolated children are good
examples of well-targeted policies, based on clear
and modest policy objectives.]*

A second factor is the implementation strategy.
Generally simple straightforward programmes that
anticipate accurately likely problems and that
require minimal management effort have the best
chances of success. *[The policy of the Holt Government in Australia in the late 1960s of unmatched
grants for building and equipping new teachers'
colleges, for instance, worked well because of the
clear, realistic goals and because the detailed
administrative arrangements were left largely to
state governments.]* On the other hand, it is not
difficult to produce examples of programmes which
have encountered difficulty when application has
been dependent on co-operation of separate bureaucratic agencies at different levels of government.
*[The innovations programme and the disadvantaged
schools programme of the Australian Schools
Commission during the years of the Whitlam Government
1973-75 ran into troubles of this kind.]*

A third factor affecting success with implementation is the commitment and capacity of the bureaucratic system; capacity includes the political
resources available and means available to secure
compliance. *[In the higher education area, the
Australian Commonwealth Government has considerable
power to secure compliance with many policies because
it is able to legislate for compliance as a condition
of its grants to states.]*

Fourth, there are environment factors,
particularly the degree of support or opposition
encountered in the community, and the ability of
those likely to benefit to be able to build effective
coalitions of on-going support and political pressure.

Evaluation takes different forms. Sometimes
policies or particular programmes are formally
evaluated using outside personnel. *[The Australian
Commonwealth Department of Education and Youth
Affairs and the two Commonwealth Commissions have
funded a number of evaluative studies of Commonwealth*

programmes, or of aspects of educational services delivered[13].*]* But often, especially at state level, the evaluation process is more in the nature of incidental 'feedback' to officials or the Minister. Sometimes education policies are openly and deliberately terminated, but more commonly policies are repeatedly adjusted, modified, refined or replaced with other policies.

NOTES

1.   For a discussion of definitions of policy, see T.R. Dye, *Understanding Public Policy* (Prentice-Hall, Englewood Cliffs, 1975); R. Rose, *Policy Making in Great Britain* (Macmillan, London, 1975); and C.O. Jones, *An Introduction to the Study of Public Policy* (Duxbury, North Scituate, 1977).
2.   Lowi suggests that the political processes differ according to the different kinds of policy and their purposes.   See T. Lowi, 'Decision Making *vs* Policy Making: Towards an Antidote for Technology', *Public Administration Review*, Vol.30 (May-June 1970); 'American Business, Public Policy, Case-Studies and Political Theory', *World Politics*, Vol.XVI (July 1964); and 'Four Systems of Choice', *Public Administration Review*, Vol.32 (July-August, 1972).
3.   We are indebted to Gareth Williams for some aspects of this categorisation.   See, G. Williams, 'Continuity and Change in British Educational Policy', paper presented at the annual conference of the Australian College of Education, Hobart, 1982.
4.   For a discussion of slightly different ways of conceptualising this process, see Jones, *Introduction to the Study of Public Policy*; J.E. Anderson, *Public Policy Making* (Holt, Rinehart and Winston, New York, 1979); and R.E. Jennings, *Education and Politics: Policymaking in local education authorities* (Batsford, London, 1977).
5.   B.W. Hogwood and B. Guy Peters, *Policy Dynamics* (Wheatsheaf Books, Brighton, 1983), p.1.
6.   For a detailed discussion of policy actors and processes, see G. Harman and F.M. Wirt (eds), *The Policy Process for Education: A Comparative Study of How Public Policy for Schools is Handled at State Level in Australia and the United States*, forthcoming.
7.   J.T. Murphy, 'School Administrators Besieged: A Look at Australian and American Education', *American Journal of Education*, Vol.89

(November 1979).

8.   R.W. Cobb and C.D. Elder, *Participation in American Politics: The Dynamics of Agenda Building* (John Hopkins University Press, Baltimore, 1972), p.2. See also, R. Cobb, J.K. Ross and M.H. Ross, 'Agenda Building as a Comparative Political Process', *American Political Science Review*, Vol.70 (March 1976), pp.128-138.

9.   D. Smart, 'The Pattern of Post-War Federal Intervention in Education' in G. Harman and D. Smart (eds), *Federal Intervention in Australian Education: Past, Present and Future* (Georgian House, Melbourne, 1982).

10.   C. Lindblom, 'The Science of Muddling Through', *Public Administration Review*, Vol.XIX (1959); and *The Policy-Making Process* (Prentice-Hall, Englewood Cliffs, 1968).

11.   P. West and M. Hogan, 'Making Policy in a Changing Context' in Harman and Wirt, *The Policy Process for Education*.

12.   D. Smart, *Federal Aid to Australian Schools* (University of Queensland Press, St Lucia, 1979); and P.N. Gill, 'The Federal Science Grants Scheme: An Episode in Church-State Relations 1963-1964' in E.L. French (ed.), *Melbourne Studies in Education 1964* (Melbourne University Press, Melbourne, 1964).

13.   See, for example, D.S. Anderson *et al.*, *Students in Australian Higher Education: A Study of their Social Composition since the Abolition of Fees* (Australian Government Publishing Service, Canberra, 1980); and D. Beswick *et al.*, *Evaluation of the Tertiary Education Assistance Scheme: An Investigation and Review of Policy on Student Financial Assistance* (Australian Government Publishing Service, Canberra, 1983).

Three

AUSTRALIA

David Beswick and Grant Harman

INTRODUCTION

This chapter aims to provide an introduction to
aspects of education policy in Australia. More
specifically it seeks to

(a)   describe the context in which education
       policy emerges, paying particular
       attention to some of the major influences
       and constraints which operate;
(b)   distinguish some of the main policy
       actors, and the characteristic ways in
       which policies are developed and applied
       in different settings; and
(c)   outline some of the major policy problems
       that have received attention over the
       past two decades, explain some particular
       policies that have been formulated,
       authorised and implemented to resolve
       these problems, and comment on some of
       the outcomes.

Because of the constraints of a single chapter, the
treatment of many aspects and topics must be
relatively brief.
     The analysis concentrates on public policies
or, in other words, policies developed by governments, or government departments and agencies. This
means that particular policies developed by interest
groups or non-government schools, for example, will
not be the main concern. Little attention too will
be given to policies developed by political parties,
except in so far as such policies have become public
policies at either state or federal levels, or major
topics of political discussion. Throughout the
discussion the emphasis will be on policy and policy

processes at national and state system level, rather
than at regional or local institutional levels.
Further, the discussion will be limited mainly to
educational policies related to formal education,
particularly in primary and secondary schools, and
in tertiary education institutions.

STRUCTURE AND ORIGINS OF THE AUSTRALIAN EDUCATION
SYSTEM

Two of the most striking characteristics of the
Australian education system relate to the mix of
public and private responsibility, and to the roles
of state and federal governments. Tertiary
education is provided almost entirely in public
institutions which operate under state or federal
legislation and are responsible directly to a
Minister and/or to a particular Parliament (i.e.
federal or state legislature). Almost all tertiary
education institutions were established by government action and today they are publicly financed and
publicly co-ordinated. This is in marked contrast
to education at school level, where 18 per cent of
pupils in primary and secondary schools are enrolled
in Roman Catholic schools, 5 per cent in other non-
government schools, and 77 per cent in government
schools.
     Constitutionally, education has been regarded
in Australia as a state rather than a federal
responsibility. The current state systems of public
education were reasonably well developed at the
primary level before the six Australian colonies
united using a federal structure in 1901 to form the
Commonwealth of Australia, and in the discussions
which preceded federation it was assumed that
education would be a state responsibility. As a
result, education was not one of the powers handed
over to the Commonwealth. Indeed, the federal
constitution made no reference at all to education
and so, by implication, education was regarded as a
power reserved for the states. However, over the
years the Commonwealth Government gradually developed interests in education. These interests
increased dramatically during the Seond World War
and the three decades which followed. The result
is that today the Commonwealth Government has a
major interest in all levels of education, from the
pre-school to post-graduate education. It provides
over 40 per cent of the total costs of all public
education and bears full responsibility for

providing regular recurrent and capital funds for
all universities and CAEs (*colleges of advanced
education*), and provides substantial amounts for the
support of TAFE (*technical and further education*),
pre-schools and government and non-government
schemes, but particularly under the Tertiary
Education Assistance Scheme which is the main form
of public financial assistance available to
tertiary students. Commonwealth expenditure on
education (of about $3 billion per annum) accounts
for almost 9 per cent of total Commonwealth outlays.
As a result of its educational involvements, the
Commonwealth established a full ministerial department and other agencies to provide policy advice and
to administer programmes. These bodies in turn have
enabled the Commonwealth to assume even greater
power in determining national priorities and policy
directions. Thus today the Commonwealth Government
is a major force in Australian education, and
education policies are influenced to a major degree
by federal initiatives and directions. Policy is
also influenced by the complications and tensions
which arise from having both federal and state
participation in the financing and control of
educational enterprises and programmes[1].

Commonwealth involvement in education sprang
largely from the need to take national approaches to
particular policy problems and because the Commonwealth's superior financial resources enabled it to
undertake new responsibilities and to develop
initiatives to meet new widely identified needs.
Constitutionally, the substantial federal role in
Australian education was achieved through powers
given to the Commonwealth Parliament in Section 96
of the Constitution 'to grant financial assistance
to any state on such terms and conditions as the
Parliament thinks fit', and in the Social Services
Amendment of 1946 to make laws 'with respect to the
provision ... of benefits to students'. Section 96
is used to channel funds through state grants acts
via state treasuries to institutions and programmes,
while the benefit to students amendment is the legal
basis for programmes of direct financial assistance
to individual students[2].

School attendance is compulsory throughout
Australia between the ages of 6 and 15 years,
except in Tasmania where compulsory attendance
extends to 16 years of age. In each state and
territory legislation requires that all children
between the prescribed ages must attend either a
government school or some other recognised

educational institution[3].

Primary and secondary education in government schools is organised and controlled through ministerial departments in the six states and in the Northern Territory, and by a statutory authority in Australian Capital Territory. Formal responsibility lies with the respective Parliaments and Ministers of Education, though much of the initiative for policy lies with senior officials. Especially in the larger states, the government school systems are large by world standards (the New South Wales system, for example, has almost 800,000 students and 45,000 teachers) and are still highly centralised, even though in most cases deliberate attempts have been made to decentralise and to involve teachers and parents in policy development, especially at school level. Teachers are centrally recruited and employed. Education is free and each state and the Northern Territory provides the major portion of funds for its own system from its general revenue funds. However, substantial funds also come from federal sources through the Commonwealth Schools Commission. Primary education and secondary education generally takes place in separate institutions and most state schools are co-educational.

The non-government schools sector is more diverse and includes parish and diocesan Catholic schools (especially primary schools), Catholic schools operated by religious orders (especially at the secondary level), and schools operated by a wide range of other groups including other churches and religious organisations, and charitable and educational associations. Non-government schools must meet specified minimum standards to secure registration, and all registered schools are eligible for grants for recurrent and capital expenditure from both state and Commonwealth sources.

Both government and non-government schools had their origins in the early days of settlement. In most states a dual system of publicly-assisted private schools and public schools developed, but in the late nineteenth century financial support to private schools was discontinued with the establishment of the present-day systems of free, compulsory, and secular public education. From then on until about two decades ago non-government schools were denied any form of substantial public financial support[4].

In current Australian usage, '*tertiary*

education' consists of three sectors: universities,
CAEs and TAFE[5]. The university sector is probably
the strongest and certainly has the most prestige.
There are nineteen universities, most of which are
located in capital cities. In 1982 they enrolled
167,400 students, of whom 100,358 were studying
full-time. They were all established under state
legislation, except for the Australian National
University in the national capital of Canberra, but
are wholly funded by the federal government, except
for relatively minor levels of endowment income,
gifts and research grants from other than Commonwealth sources. They are also largely co-ordinated
at that level, and view themselves as part of a
national and international system. Most students
(about 80 per cent) are enrolled at undergraduate
level, but in relation to other educational
institutions the universities have a special role
in research and post-graduate study. The
universities vary in size and in the range of
courses they offer. The larger institutions, such
as the University of Sydney or the University of
Queensland, have almost 20,000 students and offer
courses in a wide range of professional fields as
well as in arts and science, while some newer
'suburban' universities like Murdoch University in
Perth or Griffith University in Brisbane have less
than 3,000 students and a restricted range of
fields. The first universities were established in
colonial times in the early 1850s in Sydney and
Melbourne. From then until the Second World War
the rate of development was slow; it was not until
1911 that all six states had a university and in
1939 total enrolments amounted to only slightly over
14,000 students.
    The *college of advanced education* sector was
created in the mid-1960s by Commonwealth initiative
on the recommendation of the *Martin Committee*. This
committee, chaired by Sir Leslie Martin, Chairman of
the Australian Universities Commission, recommended
further expansion and diversification of post-
secondary education and the establishment in each
state of an Institute of Colleges to co-ordinate and
stimulate the development of colleges offering
advanced level courses. Only in Victoria was the
Institute model followed strictly, but soon in each
state existing senior technical colleges, agricultural colleges or other non-university institutions secured recognition as CAEs and so
qualified for Commonwealth funding distributed on a
matching state-federal formula. In addition, a

small number of new CAEs were created and then in mid-1973 thirty-two state government teachers colleges and private kindergarten teachers colleges were absorbed into the sector. Following numerous amalgamations, today there are forty-four CAEs, which enrol 168,588 students, or slightly more students than in the university sector. The CAE sector is still growing faster than the university sector. However, compared to the universities, a higher proportion of CAE students are enrolled as part-time students. Although the CAE sector was established to provide mainly middle-level courses leading to the award of certificates and diplomas, now almost 70 per cent of students are enrolled in bachelors degree and post-graduate courses. CAEs are much more dispersed geographically than universities, and less homogeneous in character. Although now funded entirely by federal authorities, they are subject to a much greater degree of government control, especially at state level.

The TAFE sector offers a variety of vocational and non-vocational courses in a network of approximately 450 colleges with almost 800 annexes or branches. In 1982 approximately 950,000 students were enrolled of whom only about 6 per cent were studying full-time. The largest enrolments tend to be in trades and apprenticeship courses, other skilled courses, preparatory work (often similar to the final years of secondary education) and adult or leisure education. The administration of the TAFE system within the states is in the hands of separate government departments or boards in New South Wales, South Australia and Victoria and of branches of state education departments elsewhere. Although the Commonwealth Government now provides substantial financial assistance, especially in capital funds, the main burden of recurrent funding continues to be borne by the states. The origins of the TAFE system go back to private adult education such as in mechanics institutes established last century and to technical schools and colleges established early this century, but the sector's identity as TAFE is less than a decade old and stemmed from the 1974 *Kangan Report* - a report of a Commonwealth committee chaired by Mr Myers Kangan and appointed by the Whitlam Labor Government to make recommendations on the financial needs of technical education.

AUSTRALIAN SOCIETY AND ECONOMY

The Australian nation inhabits a large island
continent adjacent to South-East Asia. Its nearest
neighbours apart from New Zealand are Papua, New
Guinea, Indonesia and the numerous new nations of
the South Pacific. Yet in cultural terms Australia
is essentially a European-based society, isolated
from the lands of its origins and from those
societies that still influence its thinking most
today. Melbourne or Sydney are twenty-four hours by
regular jet service to London, or about sixteen
hours to California. Australian education arrangements to a large extent are derivative. The school
systems and the older universities were influenced
to a major degree by nineteenth century European
social thought and by English, Scottish and Irish
models. More recently the United States has become
another major source of educational ideas.

In terms of size, the Australian continent plus
the island of Tasmania is similar to continental
United States without Alaska. Thus Australians have
faced similar problems of distance and transport to
Americans. As Blainey[6] has shown, 'the tyranny of
distance' had a major influence on the pattern of
Australian development. But despite the size of the
land mass, Australia has a relatively small population - a mere 16 million people - concentrated
mainly in the south-east corner and in the west
around Perth. The highly centralised government
schools systems were one attempt to cater for the
needs of such a widely scattered population in
colonial times. Other more recent responses include
various off-campus modes of delivery for tertiary
courses, various state correspondence schools,
special 'isolated students' programmes, and the
extensive use of radio for primary and secondary
education. With a small population and being
isolated from the main centres of European culture,
it is not surprising that Australians often feel a
sense of cultural isolation and go to great efforts
to keep in touch with current developments in
technical, scientific or educational fields in
Europe and North America. This means for education
that often senior officials in state education
departments or university specialists are as well
informed about educational developments in London or
California, as they are about new currents in
neighbouring states in Australia. It has sometimes
been claimed that when a new problem of some
magnitude emerges in an Australian school system the

immediate response of officials is to think of send-
ing someone to London, New York or Stockholm to
find a solution, rather than relying on local
resources or seeking to learn from experience elsewhere in Australia. This is probably an exagger-
ation, but at the same time it underlines the
Australian habit of borrowing freely from abroad in
dealing with policy problems, and a tendency to
undervalue locally developed solutions.

Despite the image of being a land of farmers,
graziers and people who live 'outback', Australia is
a highly urbanised society; in fact, it is more
highly urbanised than Canada or the United States.
Further, a large proportion of the population is
located in the capital cities; the cities of Sydney
and Melbourne alone account for more than 40 per
cent of the total population. Over 80 per cent live
in urban areas. This urbanisation means that most
educational institutions are located in a small
number of major cities and that education policy is
often concerned to a major extent with problems of
delivering educational services in urban settings.
It also means that different and special approaches
often are needed in dealing with problems outside
the major cities.

The indigenous Aboriginal population is small
(less than 2 per cent of the total) and most
Australians are either recent immigrants or
descended from immigrants one or several generations
earlier. From the foundation of the first colony in
1788 until the Second World War, most immigrants
came from the United Kingdom or Ireland, but since
1945 immigrants have been drawn from a great number
of European countries and more recently from the
Middle East and South East Asia. Recent arrivals
include significant numbers of Vietnamese refugees.
Now about one-third of the population comprises
recent immigrants or their children, and particular
districts of the major cities are more likely to
have a majority of Greek or Italian speaking people.
Post-war migration has greatly affected Australian
society and its values. It has also influenced
education in various ways, but particularly by
contributing to population growth and so to
increased demand for student places in school and
tertiary education, by necessitating special classes
for students unable to speak English, and by leading
to pressure for 'multi-cultural' educational
programmes.

Australia became a nation in 1901 when the six
British colonies united under a federal structure,

influenced considerably by American and Canadian
experience. There are now six states and two
territories - the Northern Territory, and the
Australian Capital Territory. Since federation the
power of the federal or Commonwealth Government has
increased very considerably *vis-à-vis* that of the
states, and education is only one of many policy
areas where the Commonwealth has become involved
deeply in what was traditionally regarded as a state
responsibility. Both federal and state levels use
Westminster cabinet style parliamentary systems of
government. While there are three major political
parties and one minor party which currently holds
the balance of power in the upper house (the Senate)
of the Commonwealth Parliament, effectively the
party system operates as a two party system, comprising the Australian Labor Party on the one hand
and the Liberal Party and the National Party on the
other. In most states and at the federal level the
Liberal Party and the National Party have formed
coalition governments. In 1983 Labor was in power
in four states and the Commonwealth. While there
are substantial differences in policy between the
Labor and non-Labor parties, the areas of broad
agreement are much greater than the areas of disagreement. For education, especially at state
level, changes of government tend to mean changes in
emphasis and detail rather than substantial shifts
in policy direction, except perhaps for matters
relating to the employment and remuneration of state
school teachers.

Australia is a relatively wealthy country with
its export income being derived mainly from wool
and other agricultural products, and from coal,
natural gas, iron ore and other minerals. Despite
substantial tariff production, manufacturing
industries currently are in serious economic trouble
and unemployment nationally is over 10 per cent of
the work-force. These conditions have affected
young people especially, and in turn have had
various serious repercussions on the education
system. One consequence in the seventies has been
loss of confidence especially in the state school
systems and in tertiary education, but there has
been some recovery of interest in education in the
past year or so.

Developments to 1965
The period in Australia from the Second World War
until the mid-1960s, from where our analysis begins,

was one of rapid economic development and expansion which stemmed largely from high demand for farm products, a programme of government assisted immigration and large-scale overseas capital investment. During that period the total population increased from less than eight million to 11.5 million people. Investment was largely directed to manufacturing, mining, and urban development. These changes in turn affected education.

The expansion in population generated increased demand for new schools and new facilities. Moreover, with increased wealth and industrial expansion major developments took place in secondary education and as larger numbers of young people completed a full secondary course so demand increased for additional places in universities and other post-school institutions. Industrial and commercial development also created new demands for university and college graduates, with a wide range of specialisations. All this meant that in the two post-war decades a great deal of policy effort in education was directed to planning, and to achieving expansion and greater diversity of services.

A second theme has already been touched upon - that of the increase in the federal role. Because state governments and universities were unable on their own resources to cope with the rapid post-war expansion in student numbers, the Commonwealth Government agreed to continue to provide substantial financial assistance, begun during war years. In the late 1950s, on the basis of recommendations made by the *Murray Committee* and in response to pressure from the states and universities, the Government led by Sir Robert Menzies made a commitment to long-term financing of capital and recurrent university expenditure on a matching formula with the states. It also established the *Australian Universities Commission* as a specialist agency to provide advice on the detailed financial needs of universities. In 1965 the Commonwealth decided to assist the states to develop and fund CAEs on a similar basis, while two years earlier the first Commonwealth funds were provided for schools and for technical education throughout Australia.

A third theme of this period related to government and to non-government schools. It will be recalled that in the late nineteenth century government financial aid was discontinued in each colony with the establishment of free and compulsory public school systems. The post-war expansion of the school population placed great stress on non-

government schools, particularly those operated by
the Catholic Church. The result was renewed
demands for financial support. This met initially
with considerable opposition, especially from
sections within the Australian Labor Party, from
state school teachers, and from some spokesmen for
Protestant churches. But by 1965 financial 'state
aid' had begun to be provided by both federal and
state governments, though at first the extent of
such aid was not great. It is notable that no
constitutional challenge was mounted against 'state
aid' in the early period and that the High Court
finally determined the matter in 1982 when it found
that the actions of the Commonwealth did not
contravene the section of the constitution prohib-
iting it from establishing any religion.

Another dominant theme related to patterns of
school organisation. As the school systems
expanded and became increasingly complex, so the
traditional arrangements developed in the late nineteenth century often became less appropriate and
suitable. One development was to begin to provide
schools with greater freedom with regard to
curricula. Another was to rethink the structure of
secondary education in order to cater for a more
varied secondary school population. In New South
Wales, for example, major secondary school reforms
were implemented in the early 1960s on the
recommendation of a committee of enquiry chaired by
the then Director-General of Education, Dr (later
Sir) Harold Wyndam.

Finally, another trend was the development of
a view that teachers and parents should play a
greater part in policy development, and that the
administration of school systems should be considerably decentralised to regional administrative units
and to individual schools. This movement did not
achieve a great deal up to 1965, and much more
significant developments in terms of broadening
participation in policy development have occurred
more recently. Still, the movement goes back to the
post-war period and by 1965 some important moves
towards regionalisation had been made, especially in
New South Wales and Queensland.

EDUCATION POLICY 1965-1983

This section and the two sections which follow are
concerned with the key issues in education policy
from about 1965 to the present time. Attention will

be given to some of the major influences that have
affected education policy, and to some of the
particular problems that education policy has sought
to address. Examples of policy development and
application both for schools and for tertiary
education will be explored.

The period since 1965 has been one of a rapid
and extensive change, in terms of the composition of
Australian society and the economy, and also in
terms of the structure and direction of the
education system. To a substantial extent the main
developments in education policy over this period
can be understood in terms of responses to three
sets of factors: demographic changes and fluctuations in the economy; the growing power and
influence of the federal Government; and changes in
social and political values.

Demographic Changes and Economic Fluctuations

The ten-year period beginning in 1965 was characterised by a high rate population growth based on
natural increase and migration from overseas,
accompanied by sustained economic growth. Begun
immediately after the Second World War, the federal
Government's assisted migration scheme was
responsible for attracting to Australia large
numbers of new settlers, first mainly from the
United Kingdom and northern Europe and then in
increasing numbers from southern Europe and some
Eastern Mediterranean nations. Combined with
settlers who came independently this scheme resulted
between 1945 and 1975 in some 3.35 million immigrants arriving in Australia, of which an estimated
80 per cent settled. This immigration combined with
a fairly steady rate of natural population increase
meant that between 1965 and 1975 the Australian
population grew from 11.5 million to almost 14
million. This growth in turn stimulated rapid urban
development, in particular in the capital cities of
the mainland states, and provided the labour supply
to facilitate continued economic growth and
expansion. Prices for farm products remained high
and, while rural industries continued to provide
the bulk of export earnings, the importance of
minerals in overseas trade grew considerably and by
1975 accounted for 30 per cent of export income.
Ready availability of overseas capital assisted the
development of large-scale mining ventures and the
further expansion of manufacturing. Rapid economic
growth and increasing gross national product meant

a high demand for labour and low rates of unemployment. It also resulted in rising affluence, shared by a large proportion, but not all, of the population.

Sustained population and economic growth had various consequences for the education system and education policy. With an expanding school age population, considerable effort and investment went into planning the development of new schools and school facilities, and into teacher recruitment and training. Some school systems even made special efforts to recruit substantial numbers of teachers from abroad. As Table 3.1 indicates, school enrolments increased by almost half a million students or 20 per cent between 1965 and 1975. This growth placed heavy strains on non-government schools and especially Catholic school systems and intensified demands on both state and federal authorities for government financial assistance.

Table 3.1: Enrolments in Government and Non-Government Schools

	Government	Non-Government	Total
1960	1,612,281	512,657	2,124,938
1965	1,857,120	580,557	2,437,677
1970	2,160,177	608,056	2,768,233
1975	2,297,979	621,301	2,919,280
1980	2,318,077	666,485	2,984,562
1981	2,299,828	687,997	2,987,825

Source: Publications of Australian Bureau of Statistics.

The result was that within a decade government assistance to non-government schools expanded from small programmes of assistance with capital funds for building secondary school science laboratories and libraries and minor per capita grants based on student enrolments to programmes costing annually hundreds of millions of dollars. With a continuing shortage of teachers until almost the mid-1970s, teachers' unions became increasingly more militant and gradually expanded their demands from purely industrial questions of salaries and wages to matters such as minimum professional requirements for the employment of teachers, curriculum policy,

and policy related to final year secondary school
public examinations. Increased size and complexity
and growing pressures from interest groups put new
strains on the machinery for the administration of
the state school systems; the result was that in
most states major efforts at restructuring head
offices and devolution were attempted. With growing
community affluence, a strong belief in the
individual and societal value of investment in
education, and expanding needs for skilled and professional manpower for industrial development,
government employment and service industries, high
school retention rates continued to climb. This in
turn posed the same kinds of problems as those
experienced elsewhere, as an élite secondary school
system was expanded to cope with the pressures of
mass education. Thus, efforts were made to broaden
the secondary school curriculum, and to lessen the
influence of universities on curriculum and on final
year secondary education examinations.

Tertiary education also expanded at a relatively rapid rate as Table 3.2 indicates. University
enrolments increased from 83,320 in 1965 to 138,338
in 1975 and during that decade the last of the new
universities were founded. The CAE sector, which
was established as a result of Commonwealth
initiative in 1965, grew quickly and by 1975 there
were almost eighty colleges with a total enrolment
of over 122,000 students.

Table 3.2: Number of Students in Universities and
CAEs, and Enrolment in TAFE

	Universities	CAEs	TAFE
1965	83,320	n.a.	365,000
1970	116,778	20,656	387,812
1975	138,338	122,557	688,831
1980	163,156	159,476	955,767
1981	166,611	162,749	1,042,185
1982	167,400	168,588	n.a.

*Source: Publications of the Commonwealth Tertiary
           Education Commission and the Australian
           Bureau of Statistics.*

In the early 1970s, technical and further education
became recognised as the TAFE sector of tertiary

education and by 1975 TAFE colleges had almost
700,000 enrolments. Thus, to a large extent over
the decade 1965 to 1975 education policy was
concerned with the problems and effects of a growing
population, sustained economic development and
rising affluence.

In the mid-1970s, however, these trends which
had operated consistently for a long period changed
relatively sharply at least for most sectors of the
education system, and since then the educational
institutions and systems have been forced to cope
with reduced rates of growth in numbers of students,
and with the consequences of fluctuating economic
conditions and varying government economic policy.
The population changes stemmed from a quite sharp
and largely unexpected change in the birth rate and
from a substantial fall in immigration. The annual
migrant intake, in fact, fell from a peak of 185,000
in the year 1969-70 to a thirty-year record low of
52,000 in the year 1975-76[7]. The changed economic
conditions were associated with relatively rapid
inflation during the period of the Whitlam Labor
Government (1972-75) and with fluctuations in the
international economy, especially in the price of
and demand for oil, minerals and farm products.
But also important were the effects of dramatic
increases in interest rates, and changes in the
availability of overseas investment capital. In
Australia at the federal level from 1975 to 1983 a
Liberal-National Party government led by Malcolm
Fraser adopted a relatively conservative economic
policy, where a major goal was to reduce public
expenditure in order to control inflation and
stimulate growth in the private sector. Unemployment increased greatly during this period, but
inflation continued at about 10 per cent.

This new set of conditions soon had effects on
the education system at institutional level. The
rate of increase in enrolments in tertiary education
dropped first for universities and then for CAEs,
although in both sectors total enrolments have
continued to grow each year up to the present time.
These broad statistics, however, disguise the fact
that had not participation in higher education by
adults continued to grow, overall university and CAE
enrolments would have declined, and that quite sharp
drops have been experienced by particular institutions and by particular fields of study, such as
teacher education and engineering. Growth was
faster in the TAFE sector but the rate of growth was
only about 2 percentage points per annum higher than

in the CAE sector. Although favoured in funding
TAFE too suffered constraints on funds available,
especially for capital development. In the schools
area, total enrolments peaked at 2,992,628 students
in 1978, and since then have fallen. Secondary
school age groups have not fallen, but primary age
groups have declined and the retention rate for
male students in senior secondary education has
falled significantly. Government school systems
have been affected more than non-government schools,
with the worst affected states being South Australia,
Tasmania and Victoria[8]. Marked changes in the sex
ratio in senior secondary education took place as
participation rates for females passed and then
considerably exceeded those for males.

The impact of the new demographic and economic
conditions was felt first in terms of Commonwealth
rather than state policy, and it was Commonwealth
efforts that led to some of the sharpest changes in
policy direction. High capital costs, especially
for the rapidly expanding CAEs and for schools in
the early seventies, became a matter for concern in
1975 when the onset of the international economic
recession was posing other problems for the Whitlam
Government. At the same time lack of co-ordination
in the development of the three sections of tertiary
education (universities, CAEs and TAFE) made it
difficult for the federal Government to decide
priorities in a coherent manner. The triennial
system of funding was abandoned temporarily in 1975
by adoption of budgetary plans for any one year at
a time and at a level of funding which ended the
period of rapid growth. A new co-ordinating
authority for universities and CAEs was announced,
but the government of Mr Whitlam was dismissed in
November 1975 before the necessary legislation was
passed. The *Tertiary Education Commission* was,
however, established subsequently.

The policies of restraint and rationalisation
begun by the Whitlam Government were continued by
the Fraser Government which sought generally to
favour non-government schools at the expense of
government schools, to reduce the cost of higher
education, and to transfer resources to fields of
study it regarded as more closely related to
economic development priorities, especially to
technology and business studies and to the TAFE
sector. Mainly for demographic reasons the demand
for teacher education fell sharply. This decline
combined easily with changed priorities and cost
saving aims to encourage and eventually to force

institutional rationalisation. The forced amalgamations of a large number of CAEs were a major area
of dispute in public discussion of higher education
in the last two years of the Fraser Government
before it was defeated at the 1983 federal elections.
A further sharp deterioration in the economy
occurred in those years and attention was focussed
on the high rate of unemployment, especially among
young people. The new Hawke (Labor) Government has
made commitments to increased rates of participation,
to greater social equity and to raising the esteem
in which education is held, but budgetary constraints
are accepted as seriously limiting early action to
these ends.

The Expanding Role of the Commonwealth Government

The last two decades have witnessed a substantial
increase in the role and power of federal Government
generally, and perhaps no area of government policy
has been affected more than education. To a
substantial extent, Australian education policy over
the past two decades has been the result of federal
initiatives and action, or of complexities and
complications associated with a federal system in
which new structures were being evolved as instruments of Commonwealth and state Government interest.
Earlier in this chapter, we reviewed the
constitutional position with regard to the federal
Government and education and noted how the federal
role in education had developed from small beginnings prior to the Second World War mainly
associated with the work of universities and pre-
school centres, and accelerated greatly after the
war. The period 1965 to 1975 saw a major expansion
in the federal role, from providing merely matching
grants for capital and recurrent expenditure in
universities, funds for secondary school science
laboratories, and limited scholarship schemes to a
situation where the Commonwealth Government was
deeply involved financially in education at all
levels, and was supporting the full costs of normal
expenditure in all higher education institutions as
well as providing a comprehensive programme of
student financial assistance through the Tertiary
Education Assistance Scheme, as well as substantial
funds for TAFE, government and non-government
schools and pre-schools. Over this period, Commonwealth administrative machinery for education
expanded to match its growing policy involvement
and new agencies created included a *Department of*

Education and Science (renamed the *Department of Education* in 1972 and the *Department of Education and Youth Affairs* in 1983), the *Commission for Advanced Education*, the *Schools Commission* (now the *Commonwealth Schools Commission*), the *Technical and Further Education Commission*, the *Curriculum Development Centre* and the *Education Research and Development Committee*. Of particular importance was the three-year period from 1972 to 1975 under the Whitlam Government, whose enthusiasm for education was a response to the Labor Party's commitment to the ideal of equality of educational opportunity and to community demands and aspirations. In the late 1960s, the Labor Party had accepted the principle that the availability of a comparable standard of education to all was a means of achieving social equality, and that this would necessitate the Commonwealth providing substantial assistance to both government and non-government schools, based on an assessment of need. Thus, substantial sums were provided and use of the needs approach largely solved (at least for a decade) the vexed 'state aid' dispute, although the Fraser Government's subsequent policy of varying the allocation of federal funds gradually in favour of non-government schools produced increased antagonism among teachers' unions representing state school teachers and associations representing state school parents.

Since 1975 the pattern that emerged by the end of the Whitlam years has changed relatively little. The Fraser Government attempted to re-negotiate with state Governments to secure a change in federal and state responsibilities with regard to tertiary education, but when its proposals met with little support it then put its main energies into securing a greater degree of control over education policy and securing a greater measure of accountability. Policy areas in tertiary education where it took particular initiatives included manpower related planning of teacher education, engineering and medicine; modification of study leave provisions for academic staff in universities and CAEs; student financial assistance and tuition fees; the funding of research; the operation of a 'rolling triennium' in forward budgeting; and, as noted above, the amalgamation of institutions. In a number of cases the initative for policy change came from the Government itself, from members of Parliament and from senior officers in the central departments, rather than from the education commissions. This is well illustrated by the review of study leave for

academic staff, which was seen in academic circles
in the guise of a review of costs and perceived
privilege in an attempt to discipline, devalue, and
control institutions and their staffs. It thus was
viewed as part of a political process of 'talking
down' education which like the transfer of resources
between fields and the overall budgetary constraint
tended to discourage private as well as public
investment. Oversupply of teachers, the closure
and rationalisation of some engineering courses,
criticism of educational standards and publicity
given to the existence of (actually quite low)
unemployment among graduates also took place at the
time in the late seventies when retention and transition rates for young people in higher education
fell away.

Apart from this, the Fraser Government
attempted on a minor scale to reduce federal commitments to education and as a result the *Curriculum
Development Centre* and the *Education Research
Development Committee* were closed. Through a
variety of methods it also sought to lessen the
independence of its education commissions and so to
secure greater control over their operations. In
1976 the Government began the practice of specify-
ing guidelines for the commissions to follow in
preparing their recommendations. Such guidelines
generally specified total maximum limits of funding
available for tertiary education and for schools,
and in the later Fraser period often specified
amounts available for each tertiary sector and
particular policy objectives to be followed, such
as increased support in tertiary education for the
technologies.

After 1977, when the three tertiary commissions
were amalgamated, the *Tertiary Education Commission*
(now the CTEC) and the *Schools Commission* developed
the practice of making two sets of recommendations
with regard to each funding period, the first on
broad policy recommendations and the second on
financial allocations once the financial limits had
been set in the guidelines. Thus for the 1982-84
triennium the CTEC in February 1981 presented
Volume 1 of its triennial report entitled *'Advice
on Guidelines'*[9]. The title indicated that the
limits under which specific funding proposals were
to be made later in the year should be set in the
guidelines only after the Government had considered
its advice on the needs of the institutions and the
system as a whole in general terms, and in the
context of much detailed factual reporting of

previous developments and the plans and aspirations
of the institutions which had been reviewed by the
relevant Councils of the CTEC. The Commission was
not entirely successful in this move (to advise
about advice the Government should give it on advice
it wished to receive at the next stage) for the
Government acted in a somewhat unpredicted and
apparently uninformed way in the April 1981 *'Review
of Commonwealth Functions'* with decisions which
were carried over into the guidelines issued in
June 1981. Nevertheless, these processes of advice
and direction took place in the domain of public
discussion in the form of statements in the Parliament and published reports. Such openness tends to
further the interests and effectiveness of the
Commission as an expert and independent body, albeit
one which must operate in a political environment.

Changing Social and Political Values

The important influence of changing social and
political values on education policy is often not
fully appreciated. Here there is not space to
explore these changes and their influence in detail,
but mention should be made, for example, of the
growing ethnic diversity of the Australian population and public recognition of this fact, thus
prompting replacement of the migrant education
programmes of the 1950s and 1960s (which were
concerned mainly with teaching English) with 'multi-
cultural education' programmes and the teaching of
ethnic languages, and the inclusion of representatives of various ethnic communities on government
advisory bodies. There has been a trend towards
increased social and political pluralism, with
growing support for progressive educational ideas
and abandonment of many traditional values on the
one hand, but conservative reactions have occurred
on the other, fighting against so-called 'permissive-
ness' and opposing particular new policy developments, especially in the areas of social science
curriculum and human relations programmes. Then,
too, social and political conservatism combined with
concern about youth unemployment has prompted quite
savage attacks on the education system, particularly
in relation to teaching of basic skills and preparation for employment. Such attacks became particularly common in the second half of the 1970s. In
the weekly news magazine, *The Bulletin*, for
example, one leading journalist wrote in 1976:

The last five years have seen governments in
Australia of all political colours lavish
unprecedented and unparalleled amounts of
public money on education ... Yet this
upsurge in the application of community
resources in pursuit of better education
has been almost precisely matched by a
spreading fear that the schools are failing
as education institutions and that increase
in the cost and quantity of schooling has
somehow been matched by a decline in the
quality of their education[10].

Changes in public opinion about education and
changes in the general direction of education policy
are obviously closely related. This relationship
is well illustrated by the events of the last two
decades, with major changes of national policy
direction being preceded by clearly identifiable
shifts in public opinion. The education reforms of
the Whitlam years were made possible by the growing
climate of opinion strongly in support of education
that developed throughout the 1960s and early 1970s.
This was a time of strong faith in the value of
education, both as a means of achieving greater
equality and of contributing to increased wealth.
Thus, strong demands were made for increased funds
to be allocated to education activities and for
deliberate attempts to be made to increase the range
of education facilities, to widen access and to
improve the quality of the education offered. As a
consequence, both socially and politically,
education became a prominent, perhaps even a
dominant, public issue during that period.
    But by the last year of the Whitlam Government,
as the first effects of the international recession
and rising unemployment began to be felt, the public
mood changed quickly and, as we have noted, it was
the Whitlam Government rather than the Fraser administration which began the period of budgetary
restraint and contraction for education. From this
followed a long period, when education was severely
under attack and when the importance of education
dropped from being a top ranking issue in federal
election campaigns (as it was in the late 1960s to
about 1974) to being an issue of lesser importance,
and then in dropping almost out of sight altogether
until, perhaps, 1983. In these circumstances, the
relative influence at the federal level of the
specialised commissions declined somewhat as their

structures were refined and their relationship to government was more clearly controlled. Interestingly, the changes in relation between the federal Government and the commissions at least began before the Fraser Government came to power. In 1975, a few months before it lost office, the Labor Government rejected the advice of the *Schools Commission* and three tertiary commissions, reduced expected funding levels, and moved to rationalise the structures of bodies to provide advice. However, as noted above, its plans with regard to combining the *Universities Commission* and the *Commission on Advanced Education* were not realised when it lost office suddenly in November 1975. The Liberal-National Party coalition did not proceed immediately with this plan, partly because its members had criticised the Labor Government's proposals when in opposition. But in mid-1977 it combined the three tertiary commissions to form the *Tertiary Education Commission*, and then worked to reduce the influence of the new body in several ways. In one, it used a problem-solving device, common in Australia, when it set up a special committee independent of government under the chairmanship of Professor (now Sir) Bruce Williams to prepare a report on matters that might have been expected to fall within the advisory functions of the Tertiary Education Commission and the Schools Commission.

However, just as the restrictive and interventionist policies of the Fraser Government were foreshadowed by a change of climate before it came to power, so were the more expansionary policies of its successor anticipated in changed emphases in the last year or so of its term of office. The CTEC regained some initiative when it was asked to make a study of factors affecting participation rates after it had referred to declining rates being something of an anomaly in a time of rising unemployment in its 1981 triennial report. The *Learning and Earning*[11] (1982) report which resulted was well received by the Government as a basis for further discussion. The scheme of assistance for senior secondary students was expanded and an advertising campaign was introduced to encourage students to re-enrol for the 1983 school year. (For whatever reason, a substantial increase followed.) The implications of that report from the CTEC have not yet been fully explored, but it represented a return to well documented, rationally developed advice from specialised agencies somewhat removed from the immediate concerns of party politics, and

it tended to enhance education in public esteem in
place of the 'talking down' of the past six years or
so.

Problems of Structure and Purpose

It is very much easier to satisfy competing demands
and, especially, to experiment with new structures
in times of rapid growth than it is to manage
contraction. The influence of population growth
and its diversification through immigration was
noted above. At the same time rising retention
rates in secondary schools, and those changing
social and political values discussed in the
preceding section, gave added reasons for reconsider-
ation of curricula and the general social function
of schooling. During much of the period of growth
in the early seventies, optimistic social planning
was never far below the surface. Even under conservative governments, the idea that society could
be improved through changes to education gained
currency. The expansion of tertiary education and
the development of new types of institutions and
systems was one expression of such hopes. Equally,
the debate over the curriculum and organisation of
secondary education, especially in the post-
compulsory years, was seen to be a debate about the
kind of society Australia should become. Whether
education was objectively a means to an end in this
respect or merely another medium of expression for
social values is another matter.

The minimum school-leaving age in Australia is
15 years by law in all states except Tasmania, where
it is 16 years, save in exceptional circumstances.
Until the late sixties it was common for the great
majority to leave school soon after completing the
compulsory years. Thus all children received some
secondary education. The transition from primary
to secondary schools at about the age of 11 or 12
years was non-selective, and most secondary schools
were comprehensive both in offering a broad general
education at the junior secondary level and in
catering to all children within a geographic neighbourhood. There were, however, distinctions
between public and private schools which gave rise
to important policy questions discussed below in
relation to the establishment of the *Schools
Commission*. A few academically selective government
high schools existed in some of the larger cities
and were seen to offer a competing public alternative to those private schools with a reputation for

academic achievement. Decisions to close or change
the character of such schools in favour of fully
comprehensive institutions were points of conflict.
In addition, in the State of Victoria a separate
public system of junior technical schools was
operated by the state in parallel with its high
schools and this system was changed only recently as
a result of the restructuring of the Victorian
Education Department of which a case-study is given
below.

In most states the secondary schools cover the
age range from 11 or 12 to 17 or 18 years, except
that Tasmania has developed a system of senior
secondary schools for the last two years, and in
Western Australia there is a break at an earlier
point. Diversification of the curriculum, its need
to serve purposes of social integration and technological development, and increasing retention rates
have produced pressure for change. Awareness of
difficulties relating to the social structure of
schools and the attitudes of teachers in secondary
schools which include also pre-adolescent children
have led to some attempts being made to extend and
further develop the Tasmanian senior secondary type
of school in other states. This was done in the
seventies in the Australian Capital Territory after
research on students' attitudes and a study of
options by a government committee of inquiry:
Secondary Education for Canberra[12] of which later
evaluations are available[13]. The alienation
expressed by students in the schools prior to the
change of structure appears to have been overcome,
but the change was possible only in the unusual
circumstances of growth and acceptance of social
change in the early seventies. Teachers' unions
have tended to oppose such restructuring, fearing
the creation of an 'élite' corps associated with the
senior schools, and changes have taken place only
with their co-operation in the smaller systems[14].

There have been no serious moves in recent
decades to raise the legal minimum school-leaving
age, but the actual average age of leaving has
increased. Important policy questions, however, are
associated with the uneven nature of the increase in
retention. Since 1970 there has been a decline in
the proportion of boys remaining in the normal
secondary schools to year 12 (age 17 or 18 years).
At the same time the retention rate for girls
continued to increase so that from a position of
inferiority the girls have now moved to a superior
proportion of the final year of secondary school.

In parallel with these changes in the full-time
enrolments in the regular high school type of
education, part-time attendance at institutions of
technical and further education (TAFE) has grown
significantly. At the age of 18 years 26 per cent
of the age group in the population was enrolled in
TAFE in 1980, while the retention rate to year 12 of
secondary school was 35 per cent (making total
participation about 60 per cent). This is one of
the consequences of the earlier tradition of a
majority leaving school at about 15 or 16 years of
age. Recently, high unemployment rates among teen-
agers and signs of unproductive competition between
TAFE and senior secondary education have led to
discussion in both Commonwealth and State agencies
of new options for the mixing of work and study and
for the rationalisation of competing interests in
post-compulsory education. Some experiments have
failed, at least in part because of industrial
issues. A basic problem is the representation of
different traditions in TAFE and the more academic
senior secondary education. These differences
reflect social class differences in an otherwise
democratic egalitarian society. The resolution of
conflicts in this area will be another illustration
of the way in which questions of educational policy
raise for a society anxieties about its structure
and purposes in general.

CASE-STUDIES OF EDUCATION POLICY FOR SCHOOLS

Three case-studies in this section will illustrate
particular types of policy development and application with regard to education policy for schools
over the past two decades. The first relates to a
federal initiative, while the other two are drawn
from state and territory levels.

The Establishment of the Schools Commission

The establishment in 1973 of the *Schools Commission*
by the Whitlam Government illustrates well how a
federal initiative can have a major and continuing
impact at state level. It also provides an example
of a policy being developed to meet more than one
problem - in this case the 'state aid' controversy,
the financial plight of Catholic and other non-
government schools, and the demands from government
school interests for federal funds to up-grade the
quality of Australia schools.

We have noted already how the school expansion
of the 1950s and 1960s placed great strain on both
government and non-government schools, particularly
when associated with rising retention rates in
secondary education and, after Sputnik, demands to
up-grade science education. Catholic interests
mounted a long and sustained campaign for 'state aid'
and they were supported to some extent by interests
representing other non-government schools. Independently, state school interests were campaigning for
federal funds to aid government school systems. In
response, in 1963 Prime Minister Robert Menzies
announced during a federal election campaign that,
if re-elected, his coalition Liberal-Country Party
Government would provide funds to build and equip
secondary school science laboratories. This master-
ful tactic satisifed demands from both Catholic
school and other non-government school interests, as
well as from state school supporters. The result
was that following its return to office the Menzies
Government introduced legislation to implement the
scheme. Thus there was established 'a crucial
double-barrelled precedent, which not only initiated
Federal Aid to schools, but simultaneously re-
introduced *State aid* to church schools after more
than eighty years'[15]. Initially there was some
angry reaction about funds going to non-government
schools, particularly from Protestant church spokesmen and from teachers' unions, but by the time the
proposed legislation for the secondary school
science laboratories scheme was being debated in
1964 in the federal Parliament a national opinion
poll revealed that 65 per cent of the population
favoured the grants being shared between government
and non-government schools[16].
    State governments swiftly imitated Menzies'
bold and successful move so that by 1969 all states
were providing financial aid to non-government
schools, mainly in the form of per capita grants.
At the federal level, Menzies' successors developed
first a parallel programme to the science laboratory
scheme of grants for secondary school libraries, and
then went on to provide direct per capital grants.
By May 1972 Prime Minster McMahon had announced that
if his government was returned to office in the
general elections scheduled for late 1972 per capita
grants for non-government schools would rise to the
level of 20 per cent of the per capita costs
incurred in operating state schools. However, the
McMahon Government was defeated in the December 1972
poll and a Labor Government led by Gough Whitlam

took office.

The 'state aid' dispute had provided great difficulty for the Labor Party, particularly in view of its egalitarian outlook and the fact that it drew substantial electoral support from Catholics. In the end, the solution for the Party was to agree to provide federal funds to all schools, based on their needs. This policy strategy largely satisfied both Catholic interests, the demands of State school teachers' unions and notions of commitment to equality of educational opportunity. Thus, in his election campaign of 1972, Whitlam capitalised on the strong mood of public support for education and held up education as 'the great instrument for the promotion of equality'[17].

Almost immediately on the Whitlam Government assuming office an Interim Committee for the Schools Commission, chaired by Professor P.H. Karmel, then chairman of the Australian Universities Commission, was appointed to make detailed recommendations for the establishment of a *Schools Commission* and the level of funding required. Within five months, this committee presented its detailed report, *School Schools in Australia*[18], which was widely acclaimed by the education and wider community. This report sought to establish both present and future educational resource norms for schools, and to measure the needs of schools against these norms. It concluded that the great bulk of Australian schools had serious resource deficiencies and, therefore, recommended the virtual doubling of Commonwealth expenditure on schools to $660 million over the next two calendar years. It proposed that this expenditure should take place within seven major programmes (general recurrent grants, general building grants, primary and secondary libraries, disadvantaged schools, special education, teacher development, and innovations) and that levels of funds would vary according to needs of major categories of schools assessed by the committee. But apart from this, the report caught the education mood of the time, emphasising such themes as equality, diversity, devolution and community participation.

The recommendations of the *Karmel Committee* were accepted by the Government and given effect in late 1973, after a stormy legislative passage. A potential deadlock was averted when the Country Party reached a compromise agreement with the Government over amendments to the grants to élite independent schools and over the membership

composition of the Schools Commission. Thus in late
1973 there came into being a body which for a decade
has been a major force of support, initiative and
change in Australian education policy with regard to
schools. Each year large sums of federal funds are
channelled to schools (in 1983 total funds allocated
exceed $1,000 million), while through such means as
formal reports, publications, special programmes,
research, working parties and new ideas espoused by
Commission personnel it influences the direction of
policy for both government and non-government
schools.

Re-organisation of the Victorian Education Department

Over the past decade, each of the six state
education departments and two government school
systems in the Australia Capital Territory and the
Northern Territory has been involved in major re-
organisations of administrative and policy
structures. These changes have been triggered off
by different specific events in each case, but they
should be seen as similar responses to increases in
size and complexity of their respective school
systems, and to demands for increased accountability,
for more responsive structures incorporating a
greater degree of decentralisation, and for greater
community and teacher participation in governance.

In Victoria the current re-organisation of the
Education Department began on 17 May 1979 when,
immediately following a general election Mr Alan
Hunt was sworn in as Minister of Education, and
Mr Norman Lacy as Assistant Minister. The two
Ministers made a review of the portfolio and soon
concluded that major reform was essential. Alan
Hunt has recorded his views at that time:

> I was ... disappointed to find no clear
> statement of aims and objectives for the
> Department, for education generally or for
> the state system of education existed -
> although this is generally accepted as a
> fundamental starting point.
> During my initial review I received a
> number of papers purporting to explain the
> organization of the Department, but nowhere
> was its rationale explained. It also be-
> came apparent to me that there were in fact
> no clear lines of communication, that there
> was a high degree of duplication and

triplication, and indeed in some areas
replication, and that the fundamental maxim
that any organizational structure to be
effective must be simple had not been
applied to the Education Department. It
appeared to have grown like Topsy, and the
potential for misunderstanding or conflict
between various segments was obviously
great[19].

Thus a decision was taken to initiate a major
Ministerial review of management structures and
governance and to involve the public, professional
groups and schools in the process. Departmental
officers were enlisted to help and a Consultative
Committee, composed of prominent educators outside
the Education Department and lay persons, was
appointed. By late 1979 a detailed statement of
aims and objectives for the state school system had
been agreed upon and presented to Parliament, and
made available to schools and the public.
    Efforts were then directed towards the prepar-
ation of a 'Green Paper' on strategies and
structures, which was published and widely
distributed in May 1980 with a view to securing
public comment. The main inputs to this document
came from senior departmental officers, and the
Consultative Committee. Special efforts were made
to increase community awareness and to get a
substantial degree of response both from schools
and community groups. In all well over 5,000 submissions were received. Apart from this, seventeen
interest groups accepted the invitation of the
Ministers to form an *Organization Reference Group*
to be involved in consultations, while further
advice was sought from the Consultative Committee.
    Between 20 October and early December 1980 the
final *White Paper*[20] was prepared under the direction
of the two Ministers. This paper went through a
series of five drafts and at each stage comments
were received as a result of a consultative process.
Those involved in this final consultative process
included senior departmental officers, the Consultative Committee, the Cabinet, the Liberal Parliamentary Party Committee on Education, and the
Education Committee established by the State
Executive of the Liberal Party. The final paper
stressed the themes of devolution and decentralisation, increased participation and consultation,
economy and efficiency in administration, and the
need for adequate review mechanisms. It proposed

abolition of the existing head office structure
based on functional directorates as well as teaching
and service divisions, and instead a structure based
simply on four functional areas. It also proposed
substantial transfer of administrative responsibilities from head office to regional administrative
units and to schools, and devolution of policy
responsibilities to school councils and regional
education councils. On 10 December 1980 the White
Paper was tabled simultaneously in both houses of
the Victorian Parliament, where its policy thrusts
were welcomed by spokesmen for both the Labor Party
and the National Party.

The following year, after detailed advice was
received from a firm of management consultants[21],
the implementation phase began. This involved
creating a new head office structure and filling all
senior positions through open advertisement.
Following the election of a Labor Government in
April 1982, there was a brief pause in the implementation process while the new Minister, Robert
Fordham, reviewed progress and considered future
directions. But soon the process of re-organisation
resumed, basically along the lines outlined in the
1980 White Paper. Slowly the new arrangements and
appointees are taking over and by the beginning of
1984 it is anticipated that re-organised school
councils with considerably enlarged powers will be
in operation[22].

Managing Contraction

Some of the most difficult problems concerning
contraction in enrolments in combination with
budgetary constraint have been experienced in the
government school system in the Australian Capital
Territory, where administrative and policy responsibility rests with a statutory body, the ACT Schools
Authority, rather than with a ministerial department. Teachers and parents are represented on the
governing body of this Authority, and this factor
had added complications to the problem.

Almost all schools in the Australian Capital
Territory are located in the capital city of
Canberra, which experienced exceptionally high
annual population growth rates up to the mid-1970s.
Its schools also were particularly well supported
and in the Whitlam years were thought of as pace-
setters for Australian school systems generally.
In 1975-76, expenditure per pupil in government
schools in the Australian Capital Territory amounted

to $927 in primary schools and $1,605 in secondary schools, compared to national averages in the six states of $719 for primary schools and $1,182 for secondary schools. Teacher-pupil ratios were also substantially better than in most of the states[23].

Following the first effects of the international recession and the election of the Fraser Government in 1975, the situation for Canberra government schools quickly changed. With deliberate limits placed on levels of government employment and slowing down of the further transfer of remaining Commonwealth departments to the national capital, Canberra's growth rate soon dropped to less than 2 per cent per annum, compared with 11 per cent in 1971 or even 5 to 8 per cent over the period 1972-76. About the same time the birth rate declined in line with the national trend and the Fraser Government decided that funding levels for schools in the Territory would be brought as quickly as possible into line with those in the six states. But this was not all. Because of a decided drift of enrolments in Canberra from government to non-government schools, the government school system in fact did not expand at all after 1976, and between 1976 and 1981 the proportion of enrolments in government schools actually dropped from 74.5 per cent to 69.6 per cent. Further, because of the sequential pattern of urban development in Canberra, a situation developed where enrolments were decreasing significantly in older suburbs while at the same time they were increasing in new suburbs. Thus, at a time of no overall growth there was considerable re-adjustment of the enrolment distribution in government schools.

In 1979 the *ACT Schools Authority* faced a difficult decision. Three new secondary schools were completed and ready for opening, but resources to operate these schools could be secured only through rationalisation elsewhere. One of the new schools, Erindale College, represented a major capital cost of $8 million and also major achievement in terms of school-community interaction, since under one roof it included a college for Year 11 and 12 students, a library for the college and community, a swimming pool, other indoor sporting facilities, a hall, and some commercial facilities. Community and teacher groups pressed strongly for the new facilities to be utilised, but the Schools Authority knew that resources would not allow the new schools to become fully operational unless costs were saved elsewhere. A particular problem in

Canberra was a generous staffing formula which
allowed new government schools to open with a full
complement of teachers in promotion positions,
regardless of student numbers.

In April 1979 the Authority considered a paper
on *Planning for ACT Schools 1980-85*, prepared by
staff and recommending closure of three existing
secondary schools. Urged by interests representing
teachers and parents from the affected schools, the
Authority declined to make an immediate decision on
closures, and instead authorised the opening of
Erindale College and decided to publish a discussion
paper on closures, call a series of public meetings
to discuss the issue, and establish a working party
to review further the cost structures in secondary
schools. Over the next three years the Authority
was to receive a dozen or more reports from working
parties, committees and consultants before it
decided in late 1982 to close compulsorily the first
secondary school in an older suburb, Watson. In the
crucial vote, the six government nominees on the
Authority voted for closure. But with the election
of the Hawke Labor Government in March 1983 representation on the Authority changed, since the new
Minister declined to proceed with the confirmation
of two appointments announced just prior to the
election. Thus two new members were appointed to
the Authority, changing the balance on the Authority
and leading to reversal of the decision on Watson
High School since the Labor Party had undertaken
during the federal election campaign of early 1983
to review the decision if elected.

CASE-STUDIES OF TERTIARY EDUCATION POLICY

The three examples used in this section illustrate
aspects of tertiary education policy development and
application. Since the federal Government plays
such a major role in tertiary education it is not
surprising that each case provides an example of
federal initiative and action.

The Williams Committee
The Committee of Inquiry into Education and Training,
chaired by Professor Bruce Williams, reported to the
Prime Minister in February 1979[24]. Known popularly
as the *Williams Committee*, the Committee made
recommendations affecting all three sections of
tertiary education as well as schools and other

forms of education and training. Some of the
recommendations were addressed to the federal Government, some to state governments and other agencies,
and some to the educational institutions themselves
and to associated bodies such as the Australian Vice-
Chancellors' Committee. The report was a significant
achievement in documentation and analysis, with
particular attention being given to the funding of
tertiary education in relation to the national
economy. Some of the recommendations were acted
upon by the federal Government either directly or in
co-operation with the states through the Australian
Education Council, as for example in setting up a
research and development centre for TAFE. Other
recommendations were referred to the CTEC or other
bodies for further advice. Some recommendations,
such as those on student progress and attrition,
and on staff development which were taken up by the
Australian Vice-Chancellors' Committee, were acted
upon independently.

Apart from its specific recommendations for
action, the Williams Committee was significant for
its attempts to promote informed debate and to
introduce conceptual innovations. One such innovation was the idea of contracting between
institutions, especially between institutions in
different sectors, to provide a wider range of
courses than the limited capacity of individual
institutions could normally provide within the
limits of their charter as institutions of a
particular type and size. Staff and student union
leaders expressed fear that the purpose of the
Williams Committee was to assist a conservative
government to carry out large-scale rationalisation
and budget reductions. It did not have that effect,
although it did increase emphasis on vocational
education, favour commitment to continuing growth
in the TAFE sector and make some moves towards
rationalisation. It failed to deal with the
significant problems arising in Advanced Education
with the run-down of teacher education and its
threat to the viability of the smaller single
purpose colleges. It thus left open the possibility
of more severe rationalisation in the future.

The Razor Gang Decisions and Rationalisation

The propensity of the Fraser Government to act
independently of its education commissions is
illustrated most clearly in what became known as the
'razor gang' decisions of April 1981[25]. Following

the 1980 general election, the Commonwealth Government set up a 'Review of Commonwealth Functions', as part of its emphasis on 'small government'. This review was carried out by a small sub-committee of Cabinet under the chairmanship of the Deputy Leader of the Liberal Party, Phillip Lynch. As a result the Prime Minister reported to Parliament on 30 April 1981 the intention of the Government to dispose of a large number of semi-government authorities and committees of advice, to leave more reponsibility in certain fields, especially education and health, to the states, and to impose some specific cost saving measures. Among these specific measures were the abolition of the *Education Research and Development Committee* and the *Curriculum Development Centre*, a decision to close engineering schools at Deakin University and a number of CAEs and a determination not to fund thirty named CAEs, heavily or exclusively involved in teacher education, unless they entered into satisfactory amalgamations with other institutions.

The decision made by politicians to close the engineering school at Deakin University without the advice of the CTEC or the state concerned represented a degree of intrusion into the affairs of the universities which was unusual and feared as a precedent, although it had some justification in the review which had been made of engineering education in Victoria. The Commonwealth demonstrated its ability to impose its will by attaching conditions to States Grants Acts under which funds are granted to the states for distributions to the universities and colleges, according to schedules recommended by the CTEC. Normally the conditions are defined on the advice of the CTEC, but the Commission had been careful in the past to protect the autonomy of the universities by avoiding such direct instruction. It sometimes recommended specific purpose grants for new developments and always specified particular projects for major capital expenditure, but its advice on academic priorities was usually included in the published reports only in the form of suggestions or statements of preference or understanding. Universities were highly responsive to such guidance, even when not a strict condition of funding and they noted with alarm both the source and the directness of the 'razor gang' decisions.

The requirement placed upon thirty colleges to amalgamate with unspecified local institutions also had an unusual degree of directness and specificity

in the relations between government and the
educational institutions. It was not, however, the
same kind of intervention as the closure of the
Deakin engineering school, in that it did not enter
into the internal affairs of an institution without
the advice of the relevant authority. The CTEC
favoured such amalgamations and had given general
advice to that effect in the first volume of its
report for the 1982-84 triennium published early in
1981[26]. The amalgamations were required to take
place under a timetable which was regarded by many
of the administrators responsible as unrealistic
and without sufficient regard to the educational
desirability of particular mergers. They were
represented as a cost saving measure, but the
Commission saw also some administrative and
educational advantages in such a policy in general,
although it might have been doubted whether the
advantages would have been achieved in the particular circumstances of some amalgamations, which were
strongly resisted by state governments, the
institutions and their local communities. The co-
ordinating authorities established to advise the
state governments played a role in the amalgamations
by helping to arrange particular mergers and advising the states on legislation required to put them
into effect. The Commonwealth authorities were
consulted on what would constitute an acceptable
amalgamation, but the CTEC appears to have left the
detail to the state bodies. Indeed, the developing
capacity of the state co-ordinating authorites and
the larger, often multi-campus, institutions formed
by amalgamations can be seen to be desirable from
the Commonwealth point of view in establishing
structures within which further decisions for
rationalisation and transfer of resources could be
made, without a distant body unfamiliar with local
conditions having to arbitrate. The Commission
continued to hold this view in favour of amalgamation which led to political commitments being made
by the Opposition to placate local interest groups
in the federal election campaign of 1983. Two
mergers at Armidale and Newcastle, in each case
involving combination of a university with a former
teachers' college, have been halted by the new
Government. They remain however, subject to review
in the next triennium (1985-87). With these two
exceptions and two other cases (Milperra College of
Advanced Education and Hawthorn Institute of
Education), where the previous Government in the
end did not insist on mergers proceeding, all the

planned amalgamations have gone ahead.

Student Financial Assistance
Financial assistance to students illustrates
different processes in policy development for
tertiary education. Unlike the funding of institutions, Commonwealth programmes of assistance to
students are administered directly by the Commonwealth Department of Education and Youth Affairs.
This difference arises from the 'social services'
amendments to the Constitution in 1946 which, as
noted above, gave the Commonwealth power to make
laws with respect to 'benefits to students'. That
is, financial assistance to students is a federal
matter and does not depend on the states being
prepared to pass any necessary legislation or to
co-operate in administration of a programme. The
relevant federal Government department advises the
Minister and in administering the various schemes
it relates directly to members of the public such
as students, their parents and relevant personnel
of institutions. In contrast, although the Department might comment on its recommendations, the CTEC
has the right to report directly to Parliament and
its programmes for the funding of institutions are
administered by the Commission itself and the
relevant state government agencies operating under
state laws. The states are thus in a position to
have a significant influence in the funding of
institutions. They are always consulted in the
preparation of Commission reports and their
priorities can be decisive in such matters as the
founding of new institutions or the preference of
one institution over another for particular developments. The only point in matters of student
finance, however, where the state could play any
part is where the co-operation of the educational
institutions is necessary, as in the charging of
tuition or other fees by the universities and
colleges, or where the funding of students for a
specific purpose requires also the funding of
particular education programmes.
     Abolition of fees was part of the platform on
which the Whitlam Government was elected in 1972.
It was coupled with a commitment to funding
assistance to students on a basis of needs, rather
than merit. In this case policy was developed
initially by the political party while in
opposition, and later worked out in detail in the
relevant government department. Previously tuition

63

fees had been charged, but they were waived for
holders of Commonwealth Scholarships which were
awarded on the basis of examination results. Fees
were also paid or waived on behalf of those students
who held teacher education studentships. There were
some other similar schemes affecting small numbers.
Altogether about 60 per cent of university students
did not have to pay the fees themselves. Commonwealth Scholarship holders received in addition to
the value of fees a living allowance which was subject to a means test. There was no means test for
teacher education studentships. State education
department studentships involved a commitment to
teach in state schools for specified periods.
These generous state awards continued until the
late 1970s, but Commonwealth Scholarships were
abandoned in favour of the *Tertiary Education
Assistance Scheme* at the beginning of 1974. At the
same time the universities and colleges were forced
to cease charging tuition fees by making it a
condition of their receipt of grants.

The new TEAS allowances were subject to a means
test of parents or the students own income, but were
otherwise available to all full-time tertiary
students in approved courses. Less than half
actually received any assistance. Commonwealth Post-
graduate Awards continued to be made to research
students on a competitive basis. Other schemes were
introduced to provide special funding to disadvantaged groups including aboriginal students at all
levels of education and students from the poorest
families completing senior secondary education.
Subsidies to the employers of apprentices who are
enrolled part-time in TAFE colleges and a complex
range of other forms of assistance for students in
post-compulsory education were developed and
extended as the economic recession deepened and
youth employment became a matter of public concern.
Although providing direct financial benefits to
students in certain categories (mainly in TAFE) and
to educational institutions for specified training
purposes, those programmes conceived as assistance
to gain employment were administered by the Department of Employment and Industrial Relations.

At the same time unemployment benefits, administered by the Department of Social Security, were
available to young people who had left school and
were unable to find or hold employment. Unemployment benefits were not available to full-time
students, although a recent court case has allowed
an exception. Equivalent benefits, considerably in

excess of TEAS allowances and not subject to a means
test on parents income, are paid to some unemployed
youth in training programmes who might be sitting in
the same classes as the holders of TEAS allowances
and other students with no assistance. Anomalies
have developed and the cost of the special programmes and unemployment benefits considerably
exceeded the cost of TEAS by the end of 1982. An
evaluation of TEAS commissioned by the Commonwealth
Department of Education[27] found inadequacies in the
scheme, especially in its assumptions regarding the
dependence of students on their families. It also
found evidence of disadvantage to women and other
groups as the level of assistance had declined,
especially when coupled with the run-down of teacher
education studentships. An attempt was made by the
Fraser Government in 1981-82 to reimpose fees for
second and higher degrees and to introduce loans as
a supplement to and probably as a partial replacement for TEAS allowances. The reintroduction of
fees was defeated in the Senate and the loans
scheme was delayed with the result that it too was
scrapped when the government changed in 1983.

There have been calls for the development of a
general youth policy which would rationalise the
many forms of assistance[28] and the Hawke Government
in 1983 has established an office to co-ordinate
youth policy in what has become the Department of
Education and Youth Affairs. State education departments have contributed to recent reviews of programmes and policies and the meeting of state and
federal ministers for education in the Australian
Education Council has served as a vehicle for policy
development. There is not, however, anything like
the CTEC in the field of student financial
assistance. Its function of independent collection
and evaluation of evidence has been covered to a
limited extent through research projects contracted
by the government departments, and by their internal
processes, but policies in this area have not been
subject to the same degree of open and informed
debate as have those for funding of institutions
through the work of the Commission. Modifications
to TEAS and other schemes have been made as part of
the annual budget decisions apparently on the advice
of finance officers and on the basis of the personal
judgements of politicians without significant input
from professionals in the field. An increased
capacity for policy development and co-ordination
within the Commonwealth Department of Education and
Youth Affairs might be hoped for, but the remaining

division of functions between departments and
between the Commonwealth and the states make
significant achievement doubtful.

THE FUTURE

Emerging policy problems in the Australia education
system include questions of equity at a number of
points and difficulties related to the future of
the Australian economy. Involved in both is a
debate about the kind of society that it is desirable
for Australia to become. Education policy formation
always has some symbolic value, whether or not it
functions as an effective means of social change and
control. There may be less faith in intervention
through education than there was ten or fifteen
years ago. Nevertheless, advantages are seen to be
conferred on individuals, especially through higher
education in professional courses, and attendance
at the better non-government schools, especially for
secondary education. In so far as general education
is perceived to be a consumer good, questions of its
distribution and the balance between private and
public costs arise in that area also. Thus,
attention is directed to the level of participation
in post-compulsory education and to the breadth of
its social base as well as to problems in meeting
the educational needs of disadvantaged groups and
to the type of curriculum appropriate to the
society we envisage for the future. Although for a
decade, the 'state aid' controversy has been
largely defused with substantial Commonwealth grants
made on a needs basis, there is evidence that it
will reappear as a substantial issue of policy
debate, both nationally and at state level. With
increased pressure on education budgets, supporters
of state schools are beginning to question the
extent of grants made to non-government schools,
especially the more wealthy schools, and to advocate
greater accountability for such grants. Associated
with this is the pressure from Catholic and other
non-government school interests to establish new
schools, which in turn qualify for recurrent and
capital grants. The problems of youth in a post-
industrial society, if that is to be, and the
changing roles and statuses of women add further
points of tension.
    Australia has much in common with economically
less developed countries. We have already pointed
to the fact that solvency in international trade

depends largely on the scale of agricultural
products and minerals. About one-third of the
population consists of recent immigrants and their
families who are making a new start in what is for
them a new nation. At the same time, Australia
suffers the same kind of problems in secondary
industry as the older industrialised countries in
the period of economic recession which has developed
in the past decade and deepened recently. Foreign
corporate ownership and lack of local investment in
research and development have raised the question of
whether Australia will be able to participate in new
technological developments sufficiently to benefit
as much as other advanced economies. Some fear has
developed that it is not in the interests of
corporate decision-makers for a large proportion of
the Australian population to be well educated,
either in advanced technology or generally. It does
not require very many people with university degrees
to run a quarry and a farm. The type of education
to be offered and who is to benefit are closely
related to such questions concerning priorities in
national economic development. An interesting side
light on this problem, which might well indicate the
shape of the future, is the keen interest of
immigrants from non-English speaking backgrounds in
higher education and their early achievement of
equality with and perhaps superiority over the older
Anglo-Saxon population in rates of participation.
     'Multi-cultural education' has become something
of a catch cry. The teaching of community languages
of the immigrants groups and aboriginal people has
attracted special funding. The teaching of English
as a second language has similarly been a matter of
widespread interest. Something more than lip
service is given to a policy of guarding and
developing the cultural diversity which the varied
composition of the people demands. There is
certainly less official pressure to assimilate and
conform to a dominant culture than was the case in
the United States during its period of adjustment
to large-scale immigration from Europe, and something more of the tolerance of differences which has
been evident in America in recent years. Many
vexed questions remain, however, and there is little
clear-headed thinking on what it means to speak of
a multi-cultural society. Whatever it is found to
imply will have significant effects in education
policy.
     Rates of participation in post-compulsory
education in Australia are regarded as being low in

comparison with other OECD countries. This is partly due to problems of definition. When senior secondary education is taken together with parallel streams in TAFE, the proportion of 17 year olds retained in formal education is not especially low. What stands out, however, is that about half of those continuing to study are doing so on a part-time basis. Unemployment among the young became a serious problem in recent years so that it no longer seems possible for 60 per cent of the 15 to 19 year old group to be in the workforce. More full-time study in TAFE and in higher education is likely to be encouraged and new types of combination of work and study will be sought. Such changes have significant implications for policies on student financial assistance and for the structure of senior secondary education in relation to technical and further education.

The problem-solving capacity of the system is reasonably adequate in respect of those problems which can be dealt with by the Commonwealth Tertiary Education Commission and the Commonwealth Schools Commission, to the extent that they are allowed to act, or the newly revised mechanisms in the education departments of the states, provided that they can handle issues of local autonomy. Those which fall within the responsibility of the Common-wealth Department of Education and Youth Affairs and which relate to broader issues of social policy will require some new mechanisms for policy develop-ment and evaluation.

NOTES

1.   On the role of the Commonwealth Government in Australian education, see G. Harman and D. Smart (eds), *Federal Intervention in Australian Education: Past, Present and Future* (Georgian House, Melbourne, 1982); I.K.F. Birch and D. Smart (eds), *The Common-wealth Government and Education 1964-1974: Political Initiatives and Development* (Drummond, Melbourne, 1977); and D. Smart, *Federal Aid to Australian Schools* (University of Queensland Press, St Lucia, 1979).

2.   I.K.F. Birch, *Constitutional Responsibility for Education in Australia* (Australian National University Press, Canberra, 1975).

3.   Useful introductions to the Australian school systems are provided in P.H. Partridge, *Society, Schools and Progress in Australia* (Pergamon,

Oxford, 1968); L.E. Foster, *Australian Education: A Sociological Perspective* (Prentice-Hall of Australia, Sydney, 1981); and *Major Trends and Developments in Australian Education* (Australian Government Publishing Service, Canberra, 1981).

4. On the history of public and private education, see A. Barcan, *A History of Australian Education* (Oxford University Press, Melbourne, 1980); and J. Cleverley, *Half a Million Children: Studies of Non-Government Education in Australia* (Longman Cheshire, Melbourne, 1978).

5. For a more detailed treatment of tertiary education, see B. Williams, *Systems of Higher Education: Australia* (International Council for Educational Development, New York, 1978); G.S. Harman *et al.* (eds), *Academia Becalmed: Australian Tertiary Education in the Aftermath of Expansion* (Australian National University, Canberra, 1980); T. Hore, R.D. Linke and L. West (eds), *The Future of Higher Education in Australia* (Macmillan, Melbourne, 1978); and *Education, Training and Employment: Report of the Committee of Inquiry into Education and Training* (Australian Government Publishing Service, Canberra, 1979).

6. G. Blainey, *The Tyranny of Distance* (Sun Books, Melbourne, 1966).

7. *Yearbook Australia 1977-1978* (Australia Bureau of Statistics, Canberra, 1978), p.121.

8. *The Supply and Demand for Teachers in Australian Primary and Secondary Schools 1978-1985* (Australian Government Publishing Service, Canberra, 1978); and *The Changing Patterns of School Enrolment and their Implications for Education Policy and Management: Report to the Australian Education Council prepared by the Centre of Policy Studies, Monash University* (Australian Government Publishing Service, Canberra, 1981).

9. *Tertiary Education Commission: Report for 1982-84 Triennium, Volume 1* (Australian Government Publishing Service, Canberra, 1981).

10. P. Samuel in *The Bulletin* (15 May 1976).

11. *Learning and Earning: A study of education and employment opportunities for young people* (Australian Government Publishing Service, Canberra, 1982 - 2 volumes).

12. D.S. Anderson and D.G. Beswick, *Secondary School Student Survey in Secondary Education for Canberra*, Report of the Working Party on College Proposals for the Australian Capital Territory, Canberra (Australian Government Publishing Service, 1973), pp.126-179.

13.   D.S. Anderson and D.G. Beswick, 'Adolescents and School Reform', *Evaluation in Education: An International Review Series*, *3*, 1 (1979) (Pergamon Press), pp.1-92.

14.   D.S. Anderson, M. Saltet and A. Vervoorn, *Schools to Grow In: An Evaluation of Secondary Colleges* (ANU Press, Canberra, 1980).

15.   D. Smart, 'The Pattern of Post-War Federal Intervention in Education' in Harman and Smart, *Federal Intervention in Australian Education*, p.22.

16.   M.W. Hennessy, 'Pressures from Church and Independent School Agencies on Central Governments in England and Australia, 1951-1978', Ph.D. thesis (University of Western Australia, 1982), p.113.

17.   B. Wood, 'Pressures, Priorities and Politics: A Study of Certain Conditions and Responses in the ACT Government Schooling System, 1974-1983', M.Ed. field study (Canberra College of Advanced Education, 1983), p.8.

18.   *Schools in Australia: Report of the Interim Committee for the Australian Schools Commission* (Australian Government Publishing Service, Canberra, 1983).

19.   A.J. Hunt, 'The Government Thrusts Towards Change', unpublished paper (1983), p.2.

20.   *White Paper on Strategies and Structures for Education in Victorian Government Schools* (Government Printer, Melbourne, 1980).

21.   *The Victorian Education Department: The Rationale and Definition of the Proposed Organisation Structure* (PA Australia, Melbourne, 1981 - 2 volumes).

22.   For detail on schools councils, see *School Councils: Ministerial Paper Number 4* (Government Printer, Melbourne, 1983).

23.   Wood, M.Ed. field study, pp.16-17.

24.   *Education, Training and Employment*.

25.   G. Harman, 'The Razor Gang Decisions, the Guidelines to the Commissions, and Commonwealth Education Policy', *Vestes: The Australian Universities' Review*, *24*, 2 (1981).

26.   *Tertiary Education Commission: Report for the 1982-84 Triennium*, pp.138-165.

27.   D. Beswick *et al.*, *Evaluation of the Tertiary Education Assistance Scheme: An Investigation and Review of Policy on Student Financial Assistance* (Australian Government Publishing Service, Canberra, 1983).

28.   L.W. Shears and J.K. Matthews, *Youth Policies* (Office of the Co-ordinator General of Education, Melbourne, 1983).

Four

FRANCE

J.R. Hough

It can confidently be asserted that none of the
other countries included in the present volume, nor
indeed any other developed country in the world, has
such a centralised, controlled, and, in at least
some senses, bureaucratic system of education as has
France. The minutiae of the directions issued by
the Ministry of Education in Paris are baffling to
many foreign observers of the French scene even
though, as we shall see, it can be argued that this
centralised control not only has relaxed somewhat in
recent years but also is variable in its application
across the country: in far-flung schools sufficiently far removed from the rue de Grenelle, teachers
are liable to rely as much on their own good sense
as the precise wording of Ministry directives.
Nevertheless, the fact that the Haby reform
programme, to be dealt with at some length below,
gave rise in its first two years to eleven
Ministerial decrees, nineteen *arrêtés* and twenty
circulars[1] may be cited as an example of the
persisting centralised control of the French
educational system. Such a situation has obviously
not arisen overnight and can only be understood by
reference to its long history and special national
circumstances. This chapter will therefore give a
brief review of the historical background before
turning to concentrate on the more recent period.

HISTORICAL BACKGROUND

Official interest in and embryonic control of
education in France may be said to have commenced
with Napoleon Bonaparte and perhaps to date from
1808 when Louis de Fontanes, although not a member
of the government of the day, was given the

courtesy title of *Minister of National Education*[2].
(It might, indeed, be argued that official control
over education had been initiated over forty years
earlier since the official expulsion of the Jesuits
from France in 1762 was directly related to the
pattern of schools they were developing.) By 1828
de Fontanes' successor held official sway as a
member of the government, very much earlier than
similar developments occurred in other comparable
countries.

Napoleon Bonaparte saw great value in education,
partly for the promotion of patriotic and nationalistic sentiments, and he set in train the creation
of a national system of education, the relics of
which are still clearly visible today. He created
the *lycée,* France's famed academically-orientated
secondary school, which successfully withstood all
attempts at reform for over 150 years. France was
divided into *académies*, regions based on universities
and administered by Rectors with wide powers to
control all educational developments in their areas;
the baccalaureate was introduced as a demanding
school-leaving examination at age 18 giving
automatic right to entry to the newly-created
universities, a status which, in spite of many
attempts at reform, it has always retained.

Further significant periods of educational
development followed under Guizot, from 1833, and
Falloux, from 1850, but it was under Jules Ferry,
from 1870, that there took place the long phase of
integrated development of a national education
system that lasted for some thirty years. By 1900
the claim was that all children could receive at
least a basic education at their local primary
school. By the turn of the century, however,
education had also become a prime focus of
political conflict with a number of different and
competing factions seeking to put over their own
sectional interests[3], and with the disputes centred
on what may be called the religious question in
education. Such has, as we shall see, remained the
broad scenario ever since: various aspects of the
involvement of the Roman Catholic Church in
education continue to arouse more passion than any
other issue. Ferry's achievements in extending
free, compulsory, elementary education to virtually
all children, providing for a more modest growth of
secondary and higher education, expanding the
teacher training institutions or *écoles normales*,
and obtaining a greatly increased share of the
national budget for the purposes of education are

incontestable. What was, and is, more controversial
was his emphasis on the development of education
freed, as he saw it, from the tentacles of the
Church. Thus, progressively, all teaching of
religion was forbidden in state schools, no
ecclesiastics were allowed to teach in state schools,
members of religious orders were forbidden to teach
even in Catholic schools and, with the separation of
Church and State in 1905, the new Minister of
Education, Combes, began to close schools run by
religious orders[4] (*laicité* being one of his key
principles).

Education continued to grow, albeit rather
slowly, throughout the periods before and after the
First World War. The ending of fees in *lycées* in
1933 and the raising of the school-leaving age to
14 in 1936 were notable landmarks but from 1940
onwards education may be said to have taken several
steps backwards as it was used by the Vichy régime
to further their pro-Nazi policies, including
specific anti-semitic measures. One of the less
publicised achievements of the provisional government headed by General Charles de Gaulle was the
elaboration in 1944 of the Algiers Plan, a blueprint
for free, compulsory, secondary education for all
children up to age 15, including an initial
secondary phase of two years of *orientation*.
In view of what was to come later when de Gaulle was
President of the French Republic, this is not without interest. A series of reform plans were drawn
up by successive Ministers of Education including
Langevin-Wallon (1947), Depreux (1948), Delbos
(1949), Marie (1953), Berthoin (1955) and Belleres
(1956) but none of these was ever implemented or
was seriously likely to be. The reasons for this
state of affairs lay partly with the chaotic
political situation in France, with a series of
weak coalition governments unable to gain effective
control of the National Assembly, partly with other
aspects of the post-war reconstruction of France
having to take greater priority, and partly with the
nature of the reforms, the central element in which
was always the extension of secondary education to
all pupils. Prior to the return to power of
de Gaulle in 1958, therefore, it might be thought
that little changed; in fact, however, the
educational system mushroomed over these years, and
simultaneously greatly increased its share in
national budget expenditure, due to the post-war
rise in the birth rate combined with increasing
social demand for an improved, and extended,

education.
    With the return to power of General de Gaulle
in 1958, Berthoin, the architect of the still-born
reforms of 1955, returned to the Ministry of
Education and initiated a series of measures that
were to change the face of the French educational
system and were the first successfully-implemented
reforms for over twenty years.

THE NATIONAL CONTEXT OF EDUCATION

It can scarcely be doubted that education is, almost
continuously, at the heart of national and
political debate in France. Few, if any, other
areas of the life of the country were liable to
arouse such passions or to be seen by Frenchmen as
so crucial to their cultural and historical
heritage. This sense of culture and history is, in
fact, exceptionally strong in France for reasons
which we cannot explore here but which must surely
be related to the country's somewhat chequered (in
terms of peace, war and survival) past. At least
since the days of Napoleon the education system has
been seen as an instrument for fostering patriotic
and national sentiment and a whole series of
proposals for curriculum reform foundered on this
stumbling-block. At the same time education has
been primarily concerned with the pupils'
intellectual development, to the neglect of
character training, of the affective domain or of
the pupils' need for self-expression. The emphasis
has been on 'instruction' rather than on education
in the rounder sense of the term and even until
the late 1970s the Ministry's official inspectors
were called 'Inspectors-General of Public
Instruction' (now 'Inspectors-General of National
Education'). Indeed, as we shall see, one of the
recurring themes in connection with any attempts at
educational reform in France has been the
suggestion that too much knowledge was being
crammed into pupils.

THE EDUCATIONAL SYSTEM

Education is compulsory for children of ages 6 to
16; apart from a very small minority who are
educated at home, children receive their education
at either state schools or private schools, the
great majority of the latter being religious

foundations of the Roman Catholic Church. As
Table 4.1 shows, some 86 per cent of pre-primary,
85 per cent of primary and 79 per cent of secondary
pupils are in state schools, percentages which have
not varied significantly for some years. Private,
fee-paying, schools are therefore relatively
important in France - numerically about four times
more so than in the United Kingdom, for example -
even though they receive scant mention in a number
of major studies of the French educational system.
In state schools the teaching of religion is not
provided by the state as part of the normal time-
table taught to all children (the principle of
laicité) but it may be provided, for children of
families who so desire, at specified times by
priests or other religious representatives.
　　Table 4.1 shows the great importance attached
to nursery schools and the high take-up for higher
education, each of which will need to be considered
below. It might be inferred that the table,
comprising data supplied by the French government,
also says something about official attitudes
towards post-school further, vocational and
technical education since these receive no mention
at all: in fact, however, as we shall see, such an
inference would be misleading in that such forms of
education have received greater emphasis, and have
been developed to a much greater extent, than in
many other comparable countries including the UK.
　　The administration of the national system of
education is controlled centrally by the *Ministry of
Education* in Paris to a degree unthinkable in most
other countries. The Ministry employs directly the
800,000-odd teachers and ancillary workers,
prescribes or approves detailed curricula, teaching
methods and text books. It prescribes specific
duties for headteachers, deputy heads and holders
of other positions of responsibility, e.g. the
deputy head (*censeur*) is responsible for detailed
timetabling, substitution of teachers in case of
illness, the day-to-day running of the school,
discipline and punishment, checking premises for
damages and for library and school resources[5].
Some 50 per cent of all France's Civil Servants are
employed by the Ministry of Education which is also,
in most years, the country's largest building
contractor. Headteachers have no say in appointments of staff to their schools and have to spend
much time filling in the detailed and centralised
forms required by the Ministry of Education. On
appointment headteachers undergo a compulsory three-

Table 4.1:   Schools and Pupils in France (1981)

	State schools	Private schools
Number of schools		
Nursery, infant and junior	61,793	7,046
First and second cycle secondary	7,461	3,927
Number of pupils in full-time education		
Pre-primary level	2,070,060	313,386
Primary level	3,940,782	668,660
Secondary (first and second cycle)	3,983,623	1,030,043
Special schools	233,296	8,728
Higher education		
Universities		
(foreign students = 13%)	853,532	14,146*
Preparatory studies for *Grandes Ecoles*	33,531	3,545
Grandes Ecoles	96,726	–
Total of full-time pupils and students	13,506,226	

*Figure for 1979/80, which included 2,932 foreign students.

*Source: France in Figures, French Embassy, London,
1982.*

months training period, much of it devoted to
becoming familiar with the Ministry's requirements.
Even though some alleviation of this pattern of
centralised control has taken place in recent years
the overall picture is still one of quite remarkable
contrasts with the régimes in other countries.   It
is also not irrelevant that Ministers of Education
have typically remained in office for quite short
periods - two years would be considered a long
stay - even during the stable governments which
have characterised the Fifth Republic since 1958;
a consequence must be that greater power devolves
on the civil servants in the Ministry who
necessarily provide the continuity for the running
of the system.   Small wonder then that teachers in
the more remote parts of France view with some
suspicion the 'faceless bureaucrats' of the rue
de Grenelle.
          For most day-to-day purposes, however, schools
and teachers are liable to be more conscious of the
role of their local *Recteur* than of the civil
servants in Paris: since the days of Napoleon,

France has been divided, for the purposes of
administering the education system, into *académies*
or large sectors: there are currently 25 of these
so that each covers the areas of three or four
départments. Approximately, therefore, each such
académie is some four times as large, geographically
and numerically, as the area of a Local Education
Authority in the UK. There is, however, no
equivalence between the two: the French *académie* is
headed by a *Recteur* who is directly answerable to
the Ministry of Education and not to the local
Prefect or departmental administrations. The
Recteur receives regular annual reports on each
teacher and is responsible for the general
surveillance of schools in his district, for the
appointment, promotion and transfer of teaching
staff, and, with the aid of his *inspecteurs
d'académie*, for regular inspection of schools (in
accordance with a cumbersome procedure which,
fortunately, has gradually lessened in effect). He
is the Chancellor of local universities albeit now
with rather limited powers. It remains true that
any member of the educational service will do well
to keep on the right side of his or her local
Recteur. Indeed, in a number of respects the
relative powers of the *Recteur* have tended to
increase over the last twenty years as successive
Ministers of Education have sought, as part of a
trend towards decentralisation, to devolve on them
various functions previously exercised directly by
the Ministry[6]. Some indication of the continuing
power and importance of the position of *Recteur* came
in 1975 when Monsieur Haby, one of their number, was
appointed Minister of Education even though he was
not a member of the government and had not been
elected to the National Assembly. In view of the
nature of the reforms that he was to promulgate, it
is difficult to imagine him as the repressive
bureaucrat often deemed to be the typical holder of
the office of *Recteur*.

Pre-School Education
Children below the age of 6 are catered for in
France in the *école maternelle*, a quite remarkable
institution originally established, primarily in
Paris, over one hundred years ago. No other
country in the world provides so fully and
completely for children of this age range: there
are some difficulties in making such a categorical
statement since the available statistics permitting

international comparability are not easy to
reconcile, particularly in connection with the varying age-groups included. Nevertheless by 1979-1980
97.3 per cent of 3-to-6 year olds in France were
attending the *écoles maternelles*[7]: the Netherlands'
figure of 98.0 per cent related solely to 4-to-5
year olds. Belgium's figure of 96.2 per cent, for
3-to-6 year olds, reversed an earlier finding[8] that
her provision was more complete than that of France.
By 1980-81 official statistics[9] issued by the
Ministry of National Education showed that effectively 100 per cent of four and five year olds
attended *écoles maternelles*, as did some 90 per cent
of three year olds and 36 per cent of two year olds
(the latter two figures having risen in a decade
from around 66 per cent and 20 per cent respectively). There could hardly be a greater contrast than
with the situation in the UK where only 36 per cent
of pre-school children (3-to-5 year olds), fewer
than in any other comparable country[10], attended
nursery schools and where for two year olds to do so
was (and still is) frequently illegal under local
authority bye-laws.

Numbers of children are, of course, not everything and surprisingly France spends on early child-
hood education less, as a proportion of the national
educational budget, than many other countries in
Europe (6.3 per cent, compared with Ireland's 9.2
per cent, Netherlands' 8.7 per cent, or Belgium's
6.4 per cent, the UK's figure being 0.5 per cent).
As was shown in Table 4.1, of those children
attending nursery classes, over 86 per cent are in
institutions provided by the state; the great
majority, in both the public and private sectors,
are in the separate and distinctive *écoles
maternelles* but there are also in both sectors a
significant number of *classes maternelles* (nursery
classes) in ordinary primary schools, particularly
in rural areas. Private institutions had larger
class or group sizes until the mid-1970s but
subsequently these fell more rapidly than those in
the public sector to achieve parity on average
although still with a much larger degree of
dispersion around the mean[11].

A recent policy statement issued by the
Ministry of National Education after the coming to
power of the socialist government gives a clear
indication of France's objectives and priorities
relating to pre-primary provision[12]. This period
is seen as largely conditioning the whole of the
child's subsequent school career; nursery school

provision is but one aspect of the network of
agencies relating to the young child, pre-eminent
among which must be the family. The development of
parental involvement and participation in education
are therefore seen as crucial for the achievement of
an integrated policy. Current nursery school policy
is based on the view that in the past there has been
an over-emphasis on play and free expression and
that the top class especially should resemble more
closely the situation to which the child will have
to become accustomed in his or her primary school.
A further extension of the nursery school network
will have the aim at making attendance possible for
all children over the age of two and to introduce
greater flexibility in hours of opening and in
administrative arrangements. Simultaneously the
average size of classes or groups will be reduced
from the present 29 plus to 25. This still seems a
high figure for children of that age: and the high
child-adult ratio is one of the two aspects of pre-
school education admitted by the French authorities
to be controversial and open to criticism, the
other being the division into classes by age[13].

Primary Schools
The same policy statement referred to immediately
above also included references to primary schools,
which were seen as having become too rigid, with
their teaching methods too highly structured.
Although the transition from pre-primary to primary
schools had to be eased by the changes in nursery
classes already cited, the first years of primary
schooling, also, needed to be adapted, towards
'fostering the child's curiosity, imagination and
desire to create things'.
    An earlier, independent, report on the French
education system, prepared by an international team
of examiners appointed by OECD[14] concluded that the
influence of the subsequent stages of schooling was
so great that it 'introduces an atmosphere of
competitiveness and selectivity from the very
beginning of the primary school years which results
in a high rate of failure and grade-repeating'.
There can be little doubt that primary schooling was
formerly an arduous experience for the young French
child with a highly structured day, formally taught
lessons, single-sex classes, high standards of
achievement expected, and school continuing all day
on Saturdays. All religious teaching was forbidden
within the normal time-table of 'this most

Republican of institutions'[15]. Although major
reform was delayed for many years, some not-
insignificant changes did take place piecemeal: by
1970 the setting of homework and the use of corporal
punishment had each been forbidden, the single-sex
school relaxed in practice, Saturday afternoon
schooling had ceased, and the number of lessons per
week (still rigidly controlled by the Ministry) had
been reduced from 30 to 27. In the early 1970s even
the teaching of French was reformed somewhat, to
give more scope for spontaneity and free expression.

The emphasis remained, however, strongly on
providing an intellectual formation, to the
deliberate neglect of the affective and expressive
domains. The children in primary schools spent much
of their time being drilled in the 3Rs, begun in the
nursery school years, and prepared for the selective
examinations taken at age 11 that would decide the
future path of their education and would largely
predetermine their subsequent careers. Only when
those examinations were eventually removed were
primary schools released from an apparent straitjacket and given some freedom to innovate and to
vary their teaching approach. Following the Haby
reforms of 1975, to be considered below, considerable change was introduced although still within the
context of central Ministerial prescription. Thus
an official French government policy statement
issued in 1980 could say, in sharp contrast to the
earlier approach,

> the curriculum includes subjects relating to
> the child's environment - nature, space, time,
> society - and self-expression through manual
> activities and art (seven hours a week
> altogether), and five hours of physical
> education including both individual and team
> sports[16].

One problem has been cited by most commentators
as applying throughout the years of schooling in
France but as being particularly important in
primary schools, namely *grade-repeating*.
Traditionally, children failing to achieve the
rigorous prescribed standards by the end of each
year have not been permitted to progress to the next
class with their contemporaries and have had to
repeat the entire year, therefore being older and
usually larger and more mature than their new classmates. One child in three had to repeat the first
grade of primary school and many children had to

repeat grades in later years. Grades lost were
rarely caught up subsequently and as many as one
child in four ended up two grades behind their age
contemporaries[17]. Such 'failures' came largely from
disadvantaged families: of all the children of
personnel de service, one in three fell behind[18].
The extent of such grade-repeating at the present
time is not clear: the official rhetoric is that the
1975 reforms have 'made it unnecessary'[19] by
providing extra teaching in small groups throughout
the year for those pupils in need of additional
assistance, particularly in mathematics and French,
together with earlier diagnosis of children with
special learning difficulties. Save in exceptional
circumstances the teacher must fit such additional
tuition into the framework of her normal working
day[20]. It seems clear, however, that grade-
repeating does still take place: one report
concluded that it had shown a marked increase so
that by 1979-80 'no fewer than 40 per cent of the
pupils in the top class of the primary school were
at least one year older than the expected age'[21].

The original reform proposals put forward by
M. Haby in 1975 included (i) the lowering of the
age of compulsory schooling to five, (ii) varying
the age of transfer from nursery to primary school
between 5 and 7 according to the stage of development of the individual child, and (iii) ending
grade-repeating; (i) was not implemented, (ii) has
had rather little impact and (iii) has happened in
principle but not in practice, at least not
universally. Haby also raised the question of the
competitive pressures on children depicted by one
writer in the following terms:

> Success and failure are judged by a child's
> ability to absorb facts at an intellectual
> level and not by the level of his affective
> development or range of skills. In Primary
> school the demands of scholastic language
> at a level of cognitive and verbal develop-
> ment are beyond many children's reach and
> the volume of material which a child is
> required to master is criticised as being
> too great[22].

In the post-Haby period there does seem to have been
some lessening of this pressure, doubtless
influenced by the postponement of the differentiation between children to the later secondary
years.

Secondary Education

When General de Gaulle returned to power as
President of the fifth French Republic he initiated
a long series of reforms which were to alter the
character of secondary education in France, embodying broadly the same principles as had been
expressed in his Algiers Plan of 1944. The stiff
entrance examination to the *lycée*, the approximate
equivalent of the UK's 'eleven plus', was abolished
and all children were to progress at around age
eleven to a common two-year *first cycle* of secondary
schooling labelled 'the observation phase'.
Definitive judgements on children were postponed to
around age $13^{2\ 3}$ and, with the school-leaving age
raised to 16 (from 1967), for the first time a
meaningful and coherent programme of secondary
education was provided for all pupils.

At around age 11 all pupils would enter the
collège d'enseignement secondaire (CES) - college
of secondary education - for a four-year course.
This was essentially a comprehensive school but with
a fairly rigid system of three separate streams or
'tracks', respectively for the academically high
achievers who would formerly have gone to the *lycée*,
for those children somewhat less gifted but still
deemed to require an essentially academic
curriculum, and for those, some 25 per cent of the
total, who had fallen behind and for whom a more
practical education was seen as appropriate.
Although theoretically movement of children from
one track to another could take place easily since
they were all within the same institution, in
practice such transfers were never very frequent
and were more likely to happen in a downward
direction. For their *second cycle*, at age 15-plus
the high achievers would progress to the reformed
lycée, now more akin to a sixth-form college in the
UK, and thence to the *baccalauréat*, success in which
conveyed, still, automatic right of entry to higher
education, whilst other pupils transferred to a
collège d'enseignement technique (CET) for a course
of essentially pre-vocational and vocational training.

The CES sought to combine the social aim of
equalising educational opportunity with the
educational aim of raising standards of achievement
but it was increasingly criticised for being
excessively rigid in the operation of its tracking
system, so that essentially children had once again
been sorted and selected by age 11 and the previous
close correlation of educational success with socio-

France

economic background continued unhindered. Such
criticisms formed the background to the major reforms
proposed by the new Minister, Monsieur Haby, in 1974
and enacted in 1975. Much the major change, and the
one that aroused strong views for and against, was
that in the first secondary cycle, to take place in
the institution to be known simply as the *collège*,
tracking or streaming would be abolished and all
pupils would be taught in mixed ability classes.
For the first two years, or *observation cycle*, pupils
would follow a common curriculum, with additional
supportive teaching provided for slow-learning pupils.
From the commencement of the *orientation cycle* in the
third year some degree of specialisation takes place
in that the common core course covered only twenty-
four and a half hours per week and for the remaining
two or three hours the pupils chose from Latin,
Greek, a second modern language, or technology, none
of which were included in the common core. At the
end of the four-year course pupils could be awarded
the *Brevet d'Etudes du Premier Cycle*, later re-named
Brevet des Collèges. Only after age 15 was there to
be differentiation of pupils, with the term *lycée*
now used to embrace different types of institutions,
the *lycée d'enseignement général* (LEG) preparing for
the *Baccalauréat*, the *lycée technique* preparing for
the *Baccalauréat de technicien* and the *lycée
d'enseignement professionnel* (LEP) preparing for
the *Brevet d'études professionnelles* (BEP) after two
years or the *Certificat d'aptitude professionnelle*
(CAP) after three years. The full *lycée* course
takes three years and over 90 per cent of pupils now
remain at school after age 16 and over 73 per cent
after age 17 (comparable figures for the UK are 62
per cent and 32 per cent)[24].

The *Baccalauréat* itself, still the most
prestigious of the various certificates attainable
at about age 18 and still conferring automatic right
of entry to higher education, has been made much
more flexible in that it can now be taken in any one
of the five different *series*, or subject specialisms,
and, for example, the philosophy-arts series comprises seven separate options; non-specialist or
'general knowledge' studies are continued within all
five series and will take up between one-third and
one-half of the student's time-table[25].

The Haby reforms had a considerable impact on
the school curriculum, perhaps most noticeably at
the lower secondary level: history and geography,
formerly distinct subjects, were combined with
'economics and civil instruction' in a new integrated

course, physics was introduced for the first time
and increased importance was attached to craftwork
and technology; by no means all teachers were happy
with these changes[26].

Much the greatest problem in connection with
the Haby reforms related to the introduction of
mixed ability teaching in a context in which grade-
repetition was still common. French secondary
classes are numbered backwards with the first
secondary year, intended for pupils aged 11, called
the *sixième*, down to the *première* for age 16-plus
and the *terminal* for 17-plus: the prevalence of
grade-repetition, however, is shown in the Ministry's
statistics for 1980-81: some 30 per cent of 12-year-
olds were still in the *sixième*, as were some 13 per
cent of 13-year-olds (an increase over the figure
for ten years previously) and about one per cent of
14-15-year-olds, together with about four per cent
of advanced ten-year-olds. Formerly such age mixing
was masked by the universal streaming, so that, for
example, an advanced 10-year-old and a slow-learning
pupil of 14 or 15 would never be together in the same
class; now they may and, given that the ages in
question are those of puberty and rapid physical
development, this has given rise to considerable
concern as to possibly disturbing psychological and
emotional effects. In this respect, therefore it
is important to understand that the French and
English concepts of 'mixed ability' are not the
same[27]. Mixed ability grouping tends to arouse
strong views for and against and it is not
surprising that in the particular French situation
these should be even more acute than elsewhere. The
Haby reforms were based on the educational principle
that each pupil should move up through the grades at
his or her own pace but this inevitably exacerbated
the problem outlined above. Clearly the additional,
supportive, teaching prescribed proved inadequate to
remedy this state of affairs, which is hardly
surprising when it is recalled that subject-teachers
were allocated only one hour per week for all extra
classes.

Only from the third secondary years is there
some departure from the concept of mixed ability
grouping, partly because of the introduction of the
options mentioned above and partly because the less
academic pupils may leave the *collège* to enter the
LEP and follow more directly vocational courses
embodying work experience. At the start of the
1979-80 academic year nearly one-third of pupils did
so, on a national average[28].

Standards expected of pupils in France remain very high. Of the 234,500 entering for the main *Baccalauréat* in 1979 only 154,400 (66 per cent) passed and approximately similar success rates applied in all the other main examinations, falling to only 56 per cent in the case of the CAP[29].

Other aspects of the Haby reforms were less controversial: sizes of classes in secondary schools were to be reduced and the allocation of time-table hours re-arranged. In addition to the extra supportive teaching for weaker pupils mentioned above, depth or enrichment classes could be provided for the more advanced pupils in French, mathematics and the first foreign language (usually English), but all within the available time of only one hour per week.

THE POST-HABY PERIOD

The *Haby Law* represented a very considerable watering-down of the original reform proposals: the latter's 147 pages had been reduced to a mere two with many of the more controversial points omitted. Indeed, by the early part of 1975 the hostility of the teachers' unions was so great that it seemed probable that the reforms would be shelved[30]. The law was, however, enacted in mid-1975, to be implemented progressively from the beginning of the 1977-78 academic year.

From 1977 onwards progress was mixed and implementation of the new measures was by no means uniform across France. The intense opposition of many teachers and their unions, which had taken M. Haby by surprise, could not be expected to abate overnight, particularly in a national mood that was generally unfavourable: even the *lycée* students in Paris came out against the reform with strikes and demonstrations[31]. Even within a system under which centralised control of virtually all aspects of schooling remained firmly entrenched in the Ministry of National Education, individual schools and teachers could still find room for manoeuvre, so that it was possible to refer to:

the many discrepancies that exist between, on the one hand, idealistic planning of school organisation and curricula and, on the other hand, actual practice when one comes down to schools and personalities in different parts of France[32].

Some reforms never really happened, notably the
additional *enrichment* teaching for brighter pupils,
the one hour per week available being used almost
solely for remedial work with slow-learning pupils[33].
This was, perhaps, hardly surprising.

Of rather greater significance were the gradual
series of measures the combined effect of which was
to lessen the impact of the principles embodied in
the Haby Law. Thus by June 1978, less than one full
academic year after the commencement of the 'mixed
ability' approach, the Ministry issued a circular
permitting the formation of separate remedial
classes for the teaching of French in the first and
second years of secondary education. By the
summer of 1979 further circulars had extended this
principle 'in circumstances where the need could be
clearly justified, provided always that there was no
return to the former rigid *banding* system'[34]. By
the third year of secondary school with the introduction of the option subjects and with less academic
pupils being guided away from the *collège*, possibly
in increasing numbers, to complete their education
elsewhere, the 'problem' (if that is what it was –
certainly that was how many French teachers saw it)
of mixed ability teaching was substantially
diminished. For the lower-ability pupils very
little had changed, many of them departing from the
education system proper at about age 14 to continue
training, in various forms, elsewhere.

Significant changes were planned to take place
within the curricula of the principal school subjects aiming at such objectives as 'to create a more
personalised form of education within a school which
seeks to have an increased awareness of the world
beyond the school walls'[35]. Such wording is in
sharp contrast to the rigidity which was previously
characteristic of much of secondary schooling in
France. Thus, within the teaching of French, reforms
initiated in the early 1970s were to be continued
and extended, to counter 'the excessive dogmatism
and the accumulation of theoretical concepts in the
study of French'[36]. Greater attention was to be
paid, within the study of the language, to
'psychological factors in human development, to personal motivation, to the needs of oral and written
communication in meeting the demands of modern
civilization'[37]. Oral communication, previously
allegedly neglected at the expense of the written
word, was in future to receive greater emphasis.
That the more traditional aspects of French
language teaching were not being completely neglected

and that the Ministry's control of the minutiae of
the curriculum was not intended to diminish, were
clearly shown by the circular of July 1975 giving an
official list of the grammatical terms to be taught.
Rather similarly in the mathematics syllabus
emphasis was to be placed on the acquisition of
skills useful for the solution of practical problems
and to aid studies in other subjects such as the
physical sciences. Again, the Ministry specified
precise topics to be mastered at each level - by the
end of the first year, for example, these should
include 'the addition and subtraction of decimals to
more than one place, the use of drawing instruments,
the vocabulary of plane geometry, practice in the
use of formulae for common areas'[38]. Likewise in
the teaching of modern languages there was emphasis
on a more individualised and less mechanical
approach and on modern usage and applications,
including in the mass media. Some 80 per cent of
pupils now choose English as their first foreign
language and some 13 per cent choose German. The
far-reaching changes in the teaching of Social
Studies, and the problems to which these have given
rise, have already been mentioned above. In both
years three and four a significant topic is the
development of the EEC.
To what extent all of the above alterations to
syllabuses have given rise to meaningful changes in
the actual teaching taking place in schools it is
difficult to say and rather little specific
information has yet appeared. Notoriously,
proposals for curriculum development and modernisation lead, after the expenditure of much money,
paper, time and effort, to very little real change
at 'the chalkface'[39], and it must at least be
suspected that this may be the case in France.
Even though the Ministry apparently specifies
precisely what is to be taught and when, clearly
considerable freedom still remains for the
individual teacher to interpret such prescriptions
as he or she wishes - as, for example, when the
Social Studies syllabus for the third year specifies
'Western civilisation from the sixteenth to the end
of the nineteenth centuries'! Indeed, the Ministry
now clearly envisages that the teacher will select
among alternatives - e.g. 'at least one regional
subject in each continent' (second year) or 'one
region of France' (third year). This is evidently
a departure from the previous all-embracing or
'encyclopaedic' approach[40].
The 'progressive' implementation of the Haby

reform plans envisaged substantial change in the later secondary years with the theme of delaying for as long as possible any choice which commits the pupils' future[41]. Thus, the first year in the *lycée* was to be treated as an introductory common core. Similarly the *Baccalauréat* was to have been divided into two stages, the first in basic subjects after the first secondary cycle and the second in optional specialised subjects two years later[42]. Such proposals were never implemented even though an official survey commissioned by the Minister of Education showed that there would be overwhelming public support for further change[43]. By 1981 one commentator could write, 'the reform can now be considered as complete'[44].

A principal reason for the postponement or cancellation of further reforms was the extreme difficulty encountered in implementing the measures already promulgated. A candid report on the progress of the reform to date, published by the Ministry of Education in 1979, found that only 25 per cent of pupils in the first two years of secondary education could be described as fully unstreamed and that 'truly comprehensive teaching was so rare as to be practically exceptional'; this situation resulted from a compound of grade-repetition and pupils' subject choices and separate 'vocational' courses from the third year onwards[45], quite apart from the increased incidence of the more privileged families opting, in increasing numbers, to send their children to private schools.

As indicated above, the ability of the teachers' unions to oppose and frustrate educational reforms has been, and remains, considerable and should not be under-estimated.

VOCATIONAL EDUCATION AND TRAINING

France has a complex and wide-ranging system of vocational education and training, intended largely for those pupils, perhaps one-third of the total, who are less successful with the academically-oriented courses of the lower secondary years. Many of those pupils have had to repeat at least one year of schooling before they reach the end of the second year of the secondary school. Some will then leave the *collège* to enter a *lycée d'enseignement professionnel* (technical school) where the course will combine continued general education with practical experience of industry; some pupils divide

their time between the *collège* and pre-apprentice-
ship training with industrial firms, normally leading to a full apprenticeship at age 16; others will
remain full-time students in the *collège* but will
follow courses with a strong practical or vocational
orientation. From any of these avenues the more
successful students can progress to the *Lycée
Technique* which can open up the doors to higher
education. In official Ministry reports rather
little is said about this complex system even though
it caters for large numbers of students and is much
admired by observers from other European countries
often lacking such detailed provision[46]. The
various examination qualifications (and the problems
of their high failure rates) taken after such
courses have already been mentioned.

This system of vocational preparation has
existed for many years and was not affected by the
Haby reforms. Although the system is remarkably
comprehensive in scope and provides sound technical
and practical training, it has recently been argued
that it has become an unattractive 'ghetto', not
highly valued by prospective employers or by
society at large and from which it is difficult for
the students to escape to return to the general
education stream, if they so wish[47]. At the time of
writing, further reforms relating to this sector are
under consideration by the socialist government, a
major objective being to re-integrate such pupils
within the main stream of education.

THE SOCIALIST GOVERNMENT AND EDUCATION

Before it came to power in the government headed by
President Mitterrand in May 1981, the socialist
party had already enunciated at some length its
proposals for major reform of the French educational
system at all levels. Inequality in society was
seen as stemming from and rooted in the country's
educational system with its perceived emphases on
selection of the most able, concentration of
resources on the most favoured pupils, alienation
of many pupils from less privileged backgrounds,
discrimination against girls and imparting of
patriotic, nationalistic and right-wing attitudes.
In the pursuit of such general objectives the party
would, once in power, provide creches for children
from three months old, end any formal teaching in
nursery schools, create one unified body of teachers
in place of the present stratified hierarchy, and

stress democracy and participation in the school
curriculum. The state would even support religious
education provided *outside* schools, e.g. by the
churches, in view of its contribution towards moral
values and social stability. All of this was set
forth in quite uncompromising terms. What was much
less clear, however, was the party's attitude
towards private schools, largely run by the Roman
Catholic Church: on ideological grounds these should
all be abolished but at the level of practical
politics this might not be feasible or acceptable
in the foreseeable future. Those private schools
receiving funds from the state would probably see
these progressively curtailed and would be invited
to join the state system. Other, more truly
independent, schools would largely be left alone at
least for an interim period[48].

Once in office the socialist government, or
more strictly the socialist-communist coalition, was
not slow to turn its attention to education. A
universal objective of the new government over the
whole field of public policy was the decentralisation of power, the curbing of the monolithic and
increasing control of the government bureaucracy in
Paris over almost every aspect of the life of the
country. The new Minister of National Education,
Alain Savary, indicated that the Ministry would
continue to lay down broad principles relating to
the whole field of education and would continue to
have direct responsibility for higher education and
especially for the universities but would devolve to
the level of the region or *académie* much of the
responsibility for the administration of primary and
secondary education[49]. Some indication of the
increased importance attached to the *académie* may be
gained from the fact that by April 1983 only four of
the country's 27 *Recteurs* had kept their jobs since
the socialist government had come to power.

During its first twelve months in office the
new régime was responsible for issuing 16 major
documents relating to educational policy. Teachers
saw their salaries and employment conditions
improved and over 28,000 new jobs created, additional bodies were set up to provide for the increased
participation in education of parents and local
communities, a plan was drawn up for the renewal of
technical education and the universities were asked
to consider how access to higher education could be
democratised. Two separate commissions were set up
to consider the reform of the *collège* and the *lycée*
respectively[50]. Perhaps the major reform to appear

during the period, however, was the creation of
Zones d'éducation et d'action prioritaires, soon
shortened in popular usage to *Zones prioritaires*
(Priority Zones): areas of the country identified as
being in need of particular assistance in view of
their disadvantaged social conditions and their poor
record of educational achievement. The priority
zone policy was specified to have the twin aims of
lessening educational inequalities and increasing
social justice. Although details of the location of
the zones and their boundaries have not yet been
published, the Ministry envisaged that these would
include both depressed inner city areas, particularly in the north-west part of France, and underdeveloped rural areas, perhaps especially in the
west and south-west of the country[51].

By September 1982 one aspect of the decentralisation of decision-making had come to an end: before
the start of the previous academic year local
authorities throughout France had been given freedom
to determine the dates of their school terms. In a
France accustomed to centuries of bureaucratic
centralisation the opposition to the ensuing
variations in dates was so great that by the start
of the 1982-83 academic year the concession was
withdrawn and once again the Ministry announced the
dates on a national basis[52]. In other respects the
principle of decentralisation has not greatly
affected the education system. From 1985 the
construction and capital financing of colleges and
of *lycées* are to devolve on *départements* and *régions*
respectively and gradually colleges are to be given
greater control over their own internal functioning.

Despite the various proposals and the volume of
paper issued, by the close of 1982 not a great deal
had changed: one review described the achievements
as 'modest'[53]. Major changes do appear probable
over many aspects of education but at the time of
writing it is not clear how far-reaching these will
be: since there are inevitably large time lags
involved in introducing major educational changes
(partly due to the attitude of the teachers' unions),
the outcome may well depend on whether the socialist
government is returned to power at the next general
election. Battle-lines are currently being drawn
over the vexed question of private schools with
strong pressures being exerted on the government
from both sides and with the Minister apparently
seeking to achieve some degree of compromise[54],
whilst still achieving some form of bridging of the
divide between the state and private sectors.

HIGHER EDUCATION

Higher education in France is described[55] as having
three main characteristics:

  (i)   the predominance of state institutions,
         financed by the state and alone entitled
         to award state diplomas
  (ii)   the fact that instruction in the majority
         of state institutions is nearly or
         completely free, and
  (iii) the existence of *grandes écoles* awarding
         state-recognised diplomas or qualifi-
         cations, access to whose courses is by
         competitive examination.

    The *Baccalauréat* confers automatic right of
entry to the country's universities; hence the
chronic overcrowding in the latter's first-year
courses. A rigorous examination at the end of the
first year will eliminate some 40 per cent of the
students and what is sometimes seen as the course
proper can then commence in the second year. This
wasteful and anachronistic system has defied many
attempts at reform over a long period of years.
Unsuccessful students may go to a variety of
colleges at sub-university level, offering mainly
vocationally- and technically-oriented courses.
The most able students, however, will aim to go not
to a university but to one of the 250 or so highly
competitive *grandes écoles*, for which a 2- or 3-year
period of *preparation* may be needed after taking the
Baccalauréat. Success in one of the *grandes écoles*
will mean that the student is virtually assured of
a high-flying career in almost any avenue he (or
increasingly she) chooses, save only that certain
specialisms such as law and medicine are effectively
confined to the universities.
    When the Law of Orientation of Higher Education
was introduced in 1968 it brought the first major
reforms to the rather fossilised university world
in France for many years. The universities themselves were given greater autonomy and within each
university considerable autonomy was further
devolved on *unités d'enseignement et de recherche*
(UER) - teaching and research units - in which for
the first time academic staff could largely
determine their own teaching and research.
The attempt was made to steer such units towards
'pluridisciplinarity' in courses with a view to
breaking down the strongly entrenched barriers

between academic subjects, each of which had tended
to remain within its own watertight compartment;
this attempt met with strong resistance but
gradually had a measure of success. Universities
were given greater freedom to manage their own
finances and regulate their own internal discipline
and for the first time students could hold political
meetings but still only the State could award
degrees. The mammoth University of Paris was
broken down into 13 separate universities each of
which could not exceed a maximum of 20,000 students.
By the same reform a measure of de Gaulle's much-
favoured concept of 'participation' was introduced
in universities, some years before it spread
throughout many other aspects of French life, so
that one writer was led to refer to it as 'an
anomaly in modern French society'[56]. The new
position was created of Secretary of State for the
Universities, reporting direct to the Prime Minister.
    Doubtless such reforms would in any event have
happened in France sooner or later but their advent
was undoubtedly hastened and facilitated by the
social unrest of May 1968 which began when the
students at Nanterre University threw the Minister
of Education into the new swimming pool which he had
just opened. The ensuing revolts largely focussed
on the bleak, poorly-equipped university campuses,
catering for very large numbers of students (on
average much larger than their UK counterparts).
The students' feelings of alienation from what they
saw as over-authoritarian and often absent
professors had been increasingly exacerbated by the
mushrooming of higher education, which had seen the
numbers of students double within the preceding four
years. As seen by the students the universities had
largely failed to modernise their courses or to
relate these to the needs of industry or technology.
The same writer quoted above was led to comment,
'France had developed no counterpart to the red-
brick universities of northern (*sic*) England'.
    The local *Recteur d'Académie* is the Chancellor
of each university and sits on its Council, where he
represents the Ministry of Education. He has the
right to suspend the carrying into effect of Council
decisions pending a ruling from the Minister,
although this power is not often invoked. Even
after 1968 'many topics on which decisions are taken
by British University Councils and Senates are not
open for discussion in France'[57] since they are
decided upon nationally by the Ministry in Paris.
    The 76 universities between them have some

796,000 students, in contrast to the 250 or so *grandes écoles* with some 100,000. The elitist traditions of the latter have successfully resisted change and indeed the whole of higher education in France remains, as before, heavily over-represent-ative of the children of the middle- and elite-classes[58]. Further changes have, however, continued since 1968, perhaps most notably, but rather little noticed, in connection with admissions to universities and similar institutions: 'a policy of selection is slowly being introduced into the university sector'[59]. Not only did certain disciplines come to require *Baccalauréat* success in their specific subjects as a condition for accept-ance, but also selection took place prior to entry to the newer University Institutes of Technology. Only for courses in the humanities and social sciences did entry remain completely open[60].

During the Giscard years the government gradually sought to re-assert central control over the universities, particularly during the régime of the autocratic Madame Saunier-Seité, Minister of Higher Education from December 1975, whose policy was to 'ignore any need to be based on consensus within the University'[61]. Both before and during her reign there was 'a significant reassertion of central government planning of the curriculum'[62], including the validation of all graduate courses: such validation was seen by the government in terms of economic planning and the national need and it was estimated that in 1980 only 50 per cent of submissions in arts subjects were accepted.

The socialists have long been committed to a thorough overhaul of the whole of higher education, with the prime aim of ending the distinctions between the different categories of institutions and of achieving more integrated institutions in which students of different calibre and on different courses will mix freely; their courses, too, will be redesigned to reflect more closely the needs of the world of work[63]. What is not clear at present is the probable effect on the universities' autonomy. The socialist government is committed to opening up access to higher education to mature students, industrial workers, and increased numbers from the working-class, which will require a major overhaul of the present admissions policy. Perhaps the greatest changes may occur in the privileged and essentially upper-middle-class world of the *grandes écoles*, which has long been anathema to socialist thinkers but the value of which is recognised by

the more realistic members of the socialist
government.

SOME CONCLUSIONS

Whichever aspect of the French education system is
considered, examples abound of the all-embracing
control of the system exercised by the Ministry of
Education. This is the single most important
characteristic of educational policy in France and
at the same time the major way in which French
educational policy differs from that in many other
countries. Even before the advent to power of the
socialist government it could be argued that such
centralisation of control was gradually declining
for the various reasons considered above, including
the question of curriculum reform. Once significant
option choices have been made available to pupils
and significant areas of discretion opened to
teachers the apparent uniformity of the national
system was liable to decline.
    Paradoxically the Haby reforms accelerated this
process: though they set out to reduce inequalities
and bring greater uniformity via the introduction of
mixed-ability teaching in secondary schools throughout France, they also extended the options and areas
of discretion referred to above. And since it
proved virtually impossible to introduce mixed-
ability teaching in the fullest sense it is not
clear whether educational inequality was significantly reduced. After May 1981 the pronouncements
of the socialist government pointed towards major
developments in educational policy, but after they
had had nearly two years in power rather little
seemed to have changed. By early 1983 the
privileged routes through the French education
system, including the *lycées*, the private sector,
and the *grandes écoles*, were still unscathed. By
April 1983 a report could cite as the major
educational policy problems:

> a comprehensive reform that has not
> fulfilled high hopes; a private sector
> considered to be divisive; a large
> minority of immigrant pupils, with
> language and employment problems; and
> inevitably, growing youth unemployment[64].

    Such a list suggests that France's basic
problems are much the same as those found in other

developed countries, even though the same report
could also refer to 'the bewildering contrast
between our decentralized system and the highly
centralized French model'.

The reference above to a process of diminution
of the centralised power of the Ministry should not
therefore be exaggerated. When the Ministry could
devolve on local authorities the power to vary dates
of school terms and then just as easily take this
power back again a year later, cynics could say
that it was still clear that virtually every aspect
of educational policy continued to be determined
within the vast bureaucracy in the rue de Grenelle.

NOTES

For helpful comments on an earlier draft of this
chapter I am grateful to Monsieur T. Malan of the
Ministry of National Education, Paris, Miss V.
Dundas-Grant of the University of Keele and
Dr J. Frears of Loughborough University.

1. M. Vaughan, 'French Post-Primary Education:
What is Left of the Haby Reform', *Comparative
Education*, *17*, 1 (March 1981), p.9.
2. J-L. Boursin, *L'Administration de
l'Education Nationale* (PUF, Paris, 1981), p.7.
3. W.D. Halls, *Education, Culture and Politics
in Modern France* (Pergammon, Oxford, 1976), p.7.
4. *Ibid.*, p.9.
5. *Ibid.*, p.55.
6. Boursin, *L'Administration de l'Education
Nationale*, p.55.
7. W. Van der Eyken, *The Education of Three-
to-Eight Year Olds in Europe in the Eighties*, Report
commissioned by Council of Europe for Standing
Conference of European Ministers of Education
(NFER-Nelson, 1982).
8. A.F.B. Roberts, 'Pressures on French Pre-
school Education', *Comparative Education*, *13*, 3
(October 1977).
9. Ministère de l'Education Nationale,
'Scolarisation par age en 1980-81', *Note
d'Information* No.82-29 (23 August 1982).
10. Van der Eyken, *The Education of Three-to-
Eight Year Olds in Europe in the Eighties*.
11. Ministère de l'Education Nationale,
'Repartition en 1981-82 des classes et des divisions,
Note d'Information No.82-28 (16 August 1982).
12. Reproduced in part in Van der Eyken, *The

Education of Three-to-Eight Year Olds in Europe in the Eighties.
13. Roberts, *Pressures on French Preschool Education.*
14. OECD, *Reviews of National Policies for Education: France* (OECD, Paris, 1971), p.52.
15. Halls, *Education, Culture and Politics in Modern France.*
16. Organization of Nursery, Primary and Secondary Education in France, *Note d'Information* No.19/80 (French Embassy, London, 1980).
17. OECD, *Reviews of National Policies for Education: France.*
18. Roberts, *Pressures on French Preschool Education.*
19. Organization of Nursery, Primary and Secondary Education in France.
20. L. Elvin, *The Educational Systems in the European Community: A Guide* (NFER-Nelson, 1981).
21. Statistics from Ministère de l'Education, *Note d'Information* No.80-10 (10 March 1980), quoted in V. Dundas-Grant, 'The Education of the Adolescent: Recent Developments in Secondary Education in France, *Comparative Education, 18,* 1 (1982).
22. D.A. Groarke, 'The 1975 Haby Reform Project in France - the Background to the Political and Pedagogical Debate', *Gazette,* No.21 (Summer 1977) (University of Manchester, School of Education).
23. Halls, *Education, Culture and Politics in Modern France.*
24. Both French and UK statistics quoted in 'Scolarisation par age en 1980-81', *Note d'Information* No.82-29 (23 August 1982) (Ministère de l'Education Nationale).
25. Organization of Nursery, Primary and Secondary Education in France.
26. Dundas-Grant, 'The Education of the Adolescent: Recent Developments in Secondary Education in France'.
27. *Ibid.*
28. *Ibid.*
29. Organization of Nursery, Primary and Secondary Education in France.
30. Groarke, 'The 1975 Haby Reform Project in France - the Background to the Political and Pedagogical Debate'.
31. *Ibid.*
32. Dundas-Grant, 'The Education of the Adolescent: Recent Developments in Secondary Education in France'.
33. *Ibid.*

34. Ministry of Education, *Annual Report 1980*, quoted in Dundas-Grant, 'The Education of the Adolescent: Recent Developments in Secondary Education in France'.

35. J. Poujol, 'The Lower Secondary School in France: A Note on the Haby Reforms', *Compare*, *10*, 2 (1980).

36. *Ibid*.

37. *Ibid*.

38. *Ibid*.

39. P. Robinson, *Perspectives on the Sociology of Education* (Routledge & Kegan Paul, 1978).

40. Poujol, 'The Lower Secondary School in France: A Note on the Haby Reforms'.

41. Vaughan, 'French Post-Primary Education: What is Left of the Haby Reform'.

42. J. Jessel, 'Haby Plans Quietly Put Aside', *The Times Educational Supplement* (14 December 1979).

43. J. Jessel, 'Minister Ignores Wide Support for Baccalaureat Reform', *The Times Educational Supplement* (22 February 1980).

44. Vaughan, 'French Post-Primary Education: What is Left of the Haby Reform'.

45. Jessel, 'Haby Plans Quietly Put Aside'.

46. Dundas-Grant, 'The Education of the Adolescent: Recent Developments in Secondary Education in France'.

47. M. Tournier, 'Towards a Transformation of the French Educational System in the 1980's?', *Comparative Education*, *16*, 3 (October 1980).

48. *Libérer l'Ecole: Plan Socialiste pour l'Education Nationale*, presented by L. Mexendeau and R. Quilliot (with Preface by F. Mitterrand) (Flammarion, Paris, 1978).

49. 'Pour une école une et diverse', *L'Education*, No.472/3 (3 December 1981).

50. 'Un An d'Action', *Cahiers de l'Education Nationale*, No.5 (May 1982) (Ministère de l'Education Nationale).

51. 'Les Zones Prioritaires', *Cahiers de l'Education Nationale*, No.1 (January 1982) (Ministère de l'Education Nationale).

52. 'Les Engagements pris seront tenus', *Cahiers de l'Education Nationale*, No.7 (September 1982) (Ministère de l'Education Nationale).

53. 'La Rentrée 82', *L'Education*, No.1 (new series) (16 September 1982).

54. C. Hargrove, 'France Faces Risk of New War in Education', *The Times* (2 February 1982).

55. UNESCO, *World Guide to Higher Education* (UNESCO, 1982).

56.   Halls, *Education, Culture and Politics in Modern France*.

57.   T.A. Owen, 'The Université after 1968: as seen from Britain', *Compare*, *8*, 2 (1978).

58.   B. Millot, 'Social Differentiation and Higher Education: the French Case', *Comparative Education Review*, *25*, Part 3 (October 1981).

59.   S. Jenkinson and G. Neave, 'Universities under Giscard', *The Times Higher Educational Supplement* (10 April 1981).

60.   Millot, 'Social Differentiation and Higher Education: the French Case'.

61.   G. Neave, 'Start of the Giscard Era Means an End of the Siege' (*sic*: presumably mis-print for 'End of the Giscard Era Means Start of the Siege'), *The Times Higher Educational Supplement* (26 June 1981).

62.   Jenkinson and Neave, 'Universities under Giscard'.

63.   G. Neave, 'Socialists Leave Their Mark', *The Times Higher Educational Supplement* (19 November 1982).

64.   B. Passmore, 'The Lyons Lesson', *The Times Educational Supplement* (15 April 1983).

Five

JAPAN

Shogo Ichikawa

HISTORICAL BACKGROUND

<u>Formation of the Modern Educational System</u>
So far the Japanese educational system has twice
undergone a drastic change. The first reformation,
accompanying the *Meiji Restoration* (1868) replaced
the conventional system with a modern school system.
On that occasion, the legacy of the preceding
society was very useful in performing the task so
rapidly, as Japan had already achieved a high level
of culture and education in the late part of the *Edo
Era* (1603-1868)[1]. It enjoyed 45 per cent male and
15 per cent female literacy in the 1860s, which
easily stood comparison with those in European
countries and the United States[2].

The new *Meiji* government was aware of the
urgent need for modernisation, and in pursuit of it,
it determined to establish a system of national
education. Accordingly, in 1872, only a few years
after the Restoration, it promptly launched its plan
based on the model of the modern school systems in
advanced countries. In spite of some deterrents,
its task was steadily carried out and by the turn of
the century it had eventually erected a new school
system whose pinnacle was the imperial universities
and which included six-year free and compulsory
education.

In other words, although Japan was a late
comer in social modernisation, it did not fall
behind on the establishment of a modern school
system. With an old tradition of valueing education
and favouring learning, Japanese people had been
ready to accept schooling. The participation rate
in compulsory education was 48.9 per cent in 1890,
and 81.5 per cent in 1900, and it continued
increasing until it achieved near-complete attendance,

97.8 per cent, in 1910.

Japanese formal education thus developed rapidly, but the national economy in those days remained at the underdeveloped stage. With due regard to this, Japanese school education could be considered to have reached abnormal maturity, which had been brought about as a result of the government's and people's serious and sustained effort to make a huge investment in education. In fact, Japan kept on allotting a much larger portion of national income and government revenue for education than Western counterparts till the middle of the twentieth century[3].

Besides, it is worth noting here that Japan was quick in introducing a single-track system on the model of the United States when multi-track systems still lingered on in Europe[4], and that the great expense for improvement in compulsory education, which was given a priority, occupied the bulk of the public education expenditure. These facts were the main causes underlying the Japanese egalitarian approach to education.

Post-war Reconstruction

The educational system founded in the *Meiji Era* developed with only minor modifications and lasted for about seven decades, maintaining its original framework, until defeat in the Second World War compelled Japan to effect another radical alteration during the United States Occupation (September 1945 - April 1952). The core principles of initial Occupation policy were demilitarisation and democratisation. Educational reform which was carried out under the guidance and supervision of the Occupation Force served to abolish war-time ultra-nationalism and militarism and to erect a new structure of education based on democracy. This latter change implied an ironic contradiction because, aimed at democratic education, it was enforced as one of the dictatorial occupation policies. Nevertheless, it must be noted that the Japanese side also fundamentally approved the necessity of the reform and complied with the directions[5]. Consequently, the reform made rapid progress and had almost been completed by the end of the Occupation.

This new system, however, as transplanted from the mother country, the United States, without careful research or a sufficient knowledge of Japan, turned out to have a few unsuitable elements to the

Japanese situation. At the same time, because the
General Headquarters carried out their plan
compulsorily, determined to accomplish it within the
Occupation period, leaving the ruin and destitution
by the war out of consideration, much still remained
to be re-examined. Therefore, for several years
after Japan had regained political independence, the
main tasks before the government were to adjust the
post-war reformation to the domestic circumstances
and to improve learning conditions which had been
left behind in the sudden change in the educational
system.

Although measures to re-adjust the policies
under the Occupation were condemned as a 'reverse'
course policy by the leftists, actually it did not
mean to reproduce the pre-war education structure,
but, in appreciation of the outcomes of the post-war
reform, to rectify some misfits with the following
intentions[6]:

(1) To accept the political system and
educational goals based on democracy,
individualism and liberty, but at the
same time, to have a pupil recognise
himself fully as a Japanese citizen and
to place a special emphasis on moral
education.

(2) To develop pupils' scholastic ability
in the key subjects - mathematics and
Japanese - by adding sequence and
logical consistency to the empirical
core curriculum.

(3) To keep up the new 6-3-3-4 system, but
allow for some differentiation or
specialisation in secondary and higher
education.

(4) To maintain the local autonomy and the
independence of educational administration
ad hoc from administration *ad omni*, but
on the other hand, to promote co-operation
between the central government and local
governments and to secure harmony
between educational administration and
administration in other fields.

It should be noted that, on one side the
Japanese government re-examined the various reforms
that had been enacted during the Occupation, while
on the other side it took active steps in equipping
and staffing schools so as to put the new system
into perfect working order[7]. The fact that the

national economy made a remarkable recovery encouraged the government to proceed to improve educational facilities, augment school staff and reduce class sizes. Subsequently, various government funding systems were established and in sequence the standard size of school, class and regular staff came to be fixed.

The White Paper on Economy published in 1956 reported that the Japanese economy had already regained the pre-war level and declared that the period of post-war sufferings was over. By 1958 the educational reform and its re-adjustment had also almost finished. During the 1960s a rapid economic and social development occurred, with a corresponding expansion in educational opportunity, urged by the population explosion after the war. Following this, the 1970s were spent seeking any possible means to bridge the human gap brought by the high economic and educational growth.

EDUCATIONAL POLICY: AT PRIMARY AND SECONDARY SCHOOL LEVEL

Educational policy at primary and secondary school level has borne two main aims - to extend educational opportunity and to improve educational quality.

Education Explosion

The former aim includes measures which were taken to cope with the population explosion after the Second World War. The birth rate rose sharply in the second half of the 1940s. The number of births increased from about 1,576,000 in 1945 by 70 per cent to about 2,718,000 in 1947. Consequently, how to provide these children with places at school became a serious problem. This so-called 'baby boom' generation was to enter primary schools in 1954, lower secondary schools in 1960, upper secondary schools in 1963 and universities in 1966. In sequence, places at each school level needed expansion. In 1960 when this bulge left primary schools, the task of expanding the intake capacity of lower and upper secondary schools and universities still remained to be done. The government spent all the 1960s on this task.

A rise in the percentage of pupils continuing through upper secondary and higher education placed a premium on this demand. The new 6-3-3-4 system

established in the late 1940s gave people much
easier access to higher levels of education than the
old system, and an economic revival in the late
1950s followed by a period of high economic growth
in the 1960s and the first half of the 1970s, made
educational opportunity which had been institution-
ally offered, feasible. Innovation in scientific
technology, rapid economic growth, a rise in family
income and the up-grading of living standards were
factors which introduced the education explosion in
terms of manpower and social demands.

Accordingly, the applicants for admission to
upper secondary schools increased rapidly. For the
purpose of ensuring educational opportunity, the
government worked out measures to cope with the baby
boom bulge and implemented a scheme for expanding
upper secondary education in January 1962.
Consequently, its enrolment ratio amounted to 82 per
cent in 1970, which was 10 per cent higher than the
initial estimate. By the end of the 1970s, teen-
agers' three-year upper secondary education had
become almost universal and almost all applicants
had come to be able to find places within upper
secondary schools.

As regards pre-school education, the enrolment
rate of kindergartens doubled for a decade in the
1960s and covered half of the children. The government ten-year plan designed in September 1971 to
promote kindergarten education favoured their
attendance, and in the late 1970s two-thirds of
children came to receive kindergarten education
prior to compulsory education. Since then,
including day nurseries under the jurisdiction of
the Ministry of Public Welfare, pre-school
education has been extended to over 90 per cent of
five-year-old children and shows a tendency towards
universalisation.

Promoting Equal Educational Opportunity
Meanwhile, policies to offer educational
opportunity to working youth and the physically
and mentally handicapped were effectively executed
and their attendance became easier during the 1960s
and 1970s. The numbers of students began declining
in the part-time and correspondence courses of the
upper secondary schools, and also in compulsory
schools for the blind and deaf, but these decreases
were due to the rise in income standard and the
decrease in the number of children at school age.
As the government made efforts to improve the

learning conditions of schools for the mentally
handicapped and special classes for the handicapped
in primary and secondary schools, the majority of
them came to participate in schooling and finally
in 1979 their compulsory attendance became
institutionalised.

Nevertheless, in order to accomplish
educational equality for children in need, it was
still necessary to enable them to enjoy educational
opportunity which was offered to them. Public
support was furnished to relieve children from their
economic, regional or physical difficulties. This
meant giving financial aid to pupils whose family
income was far below the average, who lived in
isolated areas or who were mentally or physically
disabled. By means of covering their expenses for
school attendance, the government intended to
substantially equalise educational opportunity.

Improvement in Educational Quality
The question of improvement of educational quality
has been dealt with in both the provision of
resources and the actual teaching in the schools and
colleges. The former includes class size, the fixed
number of teachers, facilities and finances, while
the latter covers curricula, course of study,
methods of instruction and standards of achievement.

As an illustration of the improvements
relating to the former, since 1958 four five-year
plans for improving class size and the number of
staff at compulsory education level have been
carried out, and at present, a twelve-year plan
(1980-1991), the fifth stage of improvement, is in
practice. Through the implementation of these
plans, maximal class size has decreased steadily
from 50 to 45, and then to 40. What is more, one-
teacher schools and classes composed of mixed grade
pupils were abolished, and non-teaching staff
members, such as nurse-teachers, clerical workers,
school meal personnel and janitors have been
increased. Upper secondary schools have also
passed three stages of the timetabled improvement
since 1961 and they are now under the fourth plan
(1980-1991). Owing to these plans, average class
size has become smaller and the student/teacher
ratio has been declining through these two decades.

With regard to the actual teaching, every ten
years the Ministry has revised the official courses
of study which are the guideline for curricula in
primary and secondary schools, enabling them to

respond to changes in the times. In the late 1950s the first revision was made with the intention of examining the post-war education which had commenced under the United States Occupation. The second revision in 1968-70, since technology and economy had made great strides in the 1960s, aimed chiefly at providing up-to-date material for education, that is, more advanced study of mathematics, science and other school subjects.

These repetitions of curriculum reform might in part account for Japanese pupils' high marks in the *International Survey on Educational Achievement* conducted by IEA, but there proved to be some defects as the 1970s passed. The lessons were too advanced for ordinary pupils to take, which produced a high rate of underachievers. Furthermore, teachers were under pressure to teach the packed curricula and had no time to spare for the character formation and personality development of pupils. In order to remedy these faults, the Ministry submitted the official course of study to its third revision in 1977-78 and a new curriculum has been put into effect in the 1980s.

The main points of its proposals are as follows:

(1) The necessity to emphasise moral education, physical education and working experience, which will contribute toward the well-balanced development of brain, heart and body.
(2) The instruction is to suit a learner's ability and aptitude and encourage him/her to develop individuality and creativity.
(3) So as to achieve the above-mentioned goals, lessons are to be consistent throughout primary, lower secondary and upper secondary schools, and contents of the subjects and class hours to be reduced.
(4) A school and teaching staff is to be allowed more latitude concerning the curricula and timetables, and the spirit of initiative and intelligent adaptation to local environment and the capacities and needs of pupils is to be encouraged[8].

Nevertheless, it is the school teachers' efficiency and devotion that counts for enrichment in

education, and without their contribution the outcome would be doubtful. The Japan Teachers' Union
(JTU), however, has kept rejecting the Ministry's
ideas of internal improvement, though they have
raised no objection to external improvement.
Therefore, most of the policies on internal improvement have been blocked and sometimes have fallen
through.

Teacher Policies

In these circumstances, some measures have had to be
taken to better the quality of the staff and to
persuade them to co-operate with the authorities.
    First of all, it was considered important to
create a disciplined and ordered environment in
schools, and practically to clarify the scope of
the managerial staff members' responsibility and
authority, and accord them the treatment due to
their positions. This was why principals came to be
given 12-14 per cent extra pay in 1958, and vice-
principals 10-12 per cent in 1960, for their
administrative duties. A few years afterwards, in
May 1965, they were prohibited from joining the
union of ordinary teachers on account of their
supervising positions. Moreover, in June 1974, the
position of a vice-principal was prescribed clearly
in the law as a managerial officer, which was
followed by raising the salary grades for them and
principals. Subsequently, in December 1975, head
teachers of the grades and departments were
instituted, and they came to obtain extra monthly
pay two years later.
    The second step was the betterment of working
conditions of ordinary teachers at national and
public schools. Though they had been paid on even
terms with other civil servants, the problem was
that their salaries, which had been fixed according
to the average sum paid at private enterprises, were
lower than those of workers in the employ of large
enterprises. Comparing with other civil servants,
school teachers' initial salaries were reasonable,
but the maximum salaries they could reach were
lower. In addition, although those in charge of
the handicapped, industrial education, part-time and
correspondence courses, or those working for schools
in isolated areas had had extra pay, ordinary
teachers had not been paid extra for overtime on the
ground that overtime was not properly quantified.
    Owing to the unattractive salary, the teaching
profession no longer appealed to university

graduates, especially to male graduates, since the
rapid economic growth enlarged the labour market for
them. In this embarrassing situation, the government allowed school teachers to have a 4 per cent
rise in May 1971 in compensation for overtime, and
subsequently in February 1974 decided to attract
capable and well-qualified people by increasing
their salary by about 30 per cent between 1972 and
1978.

Lastly, as the third step, the authorities have
promoted in-service training of teachers. Since the
war they had been occupied in filling vacant
positions or offering complementary courses to non-
qualified teachers, and until 1960 they had not been
able to afford in-service training for teachers.
The Ministry launched long-term workshops for training principals and vice-principals and those who
finished these workshops became eligible to be
members of a teachers' study tour abroad programme.
It also opened up a National Education Centre which
has lodging facilities, educational equipment and
professional staff.

Furthermore, the Ministry gave grants to
prefectures so that they could set up since 1960
scientific education centres and since 1965 teacher
training centres, and so that they could carry out
various programmes for training recruits or veteran
teachers. In addition, for the purpose of stimu-
lating teachers' voluntary study, it has given grants
to educational study groups organised by school
teachers since 1960. In the 1970s and later, efforts
have been made to enrich and systematise the in-
service training programmes at prefectural level.

EDUCATIONAL POLICY: HIGHER AND FURTHER EDUCATION

Japanese policy goals related to higher education
naturally include both expansion of educational
opportunities and improvement in educational
quality, but policy measures in the latter tend to
have centred rather more on its system or structure
than on curricula or teaching methods, unlike at
primary or secondary education level.

Expansion of Higher Education
For fifteen years between 1960 and 1975 the number
of higher education institutions almost doubled from
525 to 1,007, and the number of students tripled
from about 710,000 to 2,107,000. This enormous

increase seems to have been due to the following four causes.

Firstly, since 1957 the government had proceeded with their plan to create places for students in science and technology in order to meet the manpower shortage arising from the technical innovations in industry. Also, since 1970, places were made for medical students as a response to the rising demand for medical treatment following the introduction of the national health insurance scheme.

Secondly, in 1963 the Ministry framed a policy of expanding university enrolments for fear that competition in entrance examination would be intensified during the second half of the 1960s when the bulge of 'baby boom' reached the age of higher education. The plan, aimed at keeping the admission rate at more than 60 per cent of the candidates, was put into action in 1965, and in addition it determined to ignore the private sector's extra admission beyond its capacity. Consequently, in the latter half of the 1960s while the so-called student entry quota (i.e. the number of first-year students allowed by the Ministry) increased by 100,000, the number of actual students jumped by 180,000. So more than 60 per cent of the applicants were provided places within higher education institutions and, moreover, in the 1970s when the bulge of students had left, the rate of admission exceeded 70 per cent.

Thirdly, the rise in living standards which had been realised by the rapid economic growth, stimulated people's desire to enjoy higher education in combination with the academic bent and inclination for a degree inherent in Japanese people. Thanks to the above-mentioned expansion measures, higher education became more accessible and this fact attracted more school-leavers. The number of applicants for universities and junior colleges only occupied 26 per cent of the upper secondary school-leavers in 1960, but in 1975 the figure rose to 47 per cent, and the percentage of the cohort of eighteen-year-olds attending higher education institutions shot up from 10 per cent in 1960 to 39 per cent in 1976.

Lastly, as the Ministry depended on the private sector for the expansion, it virtually abdicated its responsibility for examining university charter applications, and dropped its prior requirements that universities should consult with the Minister when they sought to increase the student quota, or

to create new departments. That was why
universities and junior colleges were founded with
a rush and accordingly the number of departments
almost doubled in fifteen years[9]. Furthermore
the private institutions, whose diluted standards
were condoned by the Ministry, exceeded their quota
by 60 or 70 per cent.

Differentiation among Institutions

The spread of higher education did not simply mean
the increase in student places but it reshuffled the
structure of higher education. It led to diversification of the higher education system unified by
the occupation policy, and resulted in establishment
of short-cycle higher education and sharing the
function among universities.

There had been some specialised schools before
the war which had produced middle-level managers and
technicians and the backbone of society. When these
schools had been promoted to universities by the
post-war reform they lost their original function,
but the demand for this function remained as great
as before. Therefore, making a precedent of these
specialised schools, the government erected a system
of five-year technical colleges in 1962, and subsequently changed the two-year junior colleges from
temporary to permanent status as formal educational
institutions in 1964. The technical colleges offer
technical education for lower secondary school-
leavers, and the junior colleges post-secondary,
practical or vocational education.

Both types of institution have developed by
leaps and bounds in the intervening years because
the technical colleges have satisfied the demands
for middle-level technicians in the industrial
field, and junior colleges have met parents' wishes
to give their daughters some higher education. In
1975 there came to be 65 technical colleges with
enrolments of about 48,000 students and 513 junior
colleges which about 354,000 students were attending.
Though both types are qualified to be called
institutions of higher education, striking contrasts
exist between them; as many as 434 junior colleges
are private and 91 per cent of the students are
female, while 54 technical colleges are national
and 99 per cent male.

Meanwhile, the government adopted a policy to
have the national sector and the private sector play
different roles and, moreover to differentiate the
national universities into two categories. As the

comparison between junior colleges and technical colleges illustrates, the Ministry attempted to make up the manpower shortage mostly by graduates from the national sector on one hand, and to rely on the private sector for the social demand for higher education on the other hand. As a result, during the fifteen years between 1960 and 1975 when only nine national universities were established, the number of private universities chartered amounted to 165, and the share of enrolment in private institutions to the overall enrolment increased from 64 per cent to 76 per cent.

In addition, since 1956, the government had drawn a line within national universities, based on the structure of pre-war higher education, that is, a course system was applied to newly promoted universities, which had previously been specialised schools or higher schools under the pre-war system, whereas the former seven imperial universities and some others established before the war were allowed to hold the traditional chair system. Such discriminations proceeded during the 1960s and the latter were also favourable in such areas as research funds and salary scales of the faculty. These prestigious universities were defined as institutions which offered postgraduate courses for a doctor's degree, had research institutes attached and had the function of both teaching and research, while the remainder which did not offer doctoral courses, except medical departments, were to focus on the role of teaching[10].

Student Unrest and University Reform

Japanese higher education thus achieved a remarkable expansion with some differentiation through the 1960s, but its quality was not successfully improved. This was because, for one reason, higher education had been financially neglected; 73 per cent of the government expenditure for education had been allocated to primary and secondary education and only 12 per cent to higher education. For another thing, the government did not have so much authority to lead the reform of higher education, and its attempt to innovate in universities was blocked because of their academic freedom, or the autonomy of private institutions, and ended in failure.

In this tantalising situation a change occurred during the 1970s. It started with enormous campus protests which had been prevalent among universities in the second half of the 1960s. A total of 67

universities in 1968, and 127 in 1969 had been the
scene of students' rebellions. They had barricaded
the university buildings or occupied the campus.
Riots were put down by the police and eventually
when, according to the *University Control Law*
promulgated in August 1969, the government expressed
their readiness to use their influence directly upon
the management of individual universities, the
protests began to subside and did not last another
six months.
    However, these campus protests made people feel
uneasy and convinced them that it was high time to
reconsider higher education comprehensively.
Supported by the wave of public opinion and by its
extended authority in university administration, the
Ministry finally changed its policy from quantitative
expansion to qualitative enrichment in line with
comprehensive plan. Under its long-term plan for
the 1970s, which was made separately for the first
term (1976-1980) in March 1976 and for the second
term (1981-86) in December 1979, the following
measures were advocated.

Planning in Higher Education

The questions of government funding to the private
sector and a ban on further expansion were considered
first. The private sector which had enlarged its
share during the period of *laissez-faire* policy,
had been resigned to a much more unfavourable
educational environment than the national sector.
In addition, campus protests in the late 1960s
prevented them from raising student fees, and one
after another they fell into financial difficulties.
In these circumstances, the government inaugurated
the *Foundation for Promotion of Private Schools* in
May 1970 through which it began to grant subsidies
to private institutions. Subsequently, enacting the
Private School Promotion and Assistance Law in July
1975, it developed a programme to make public funds
available to cover up to 50 per cent of their
operating expenses, and changed its policy for
restraints on new universities or junior colleges[11].
As a result, the grant in 1981 became 38 times as
much as that in 1969 and its share in the national
budget for education rose from 1.3 per cent to 8.5
per cent, whereas the proportion of all university
students attending private sector institutions
decreased by about 2 per cent.
    The second point at issue was the equalisation
of higher education opportunities among regions. In

order to avoid further imbalance, the government
suggested that the universities and junior colleges
situated close together in large cities should move
their campuses to provincial areas, and at the same
time, restraints were planned to control the development of new institutions in metropolitan areas.
Accordingly, the percentage of student enrolment in
inner-city Tokyo and the ten second largest cities
lessened from 61 per cent to 51 per cent between
1973 and 1980.

The third point related to the internal reform
of higher education institutions. The Ministry
inspired universities, national or private, to
tackle problems related to the structure of departments, curricula, course fulfilment and teaching
methods and also encouraged them by relaxing legal
restrictions including the criteria for establishing
a university.

Another challenge was the creation of several
experimental institutions. One of these was *Tsukuba
University* created in 1973 as a model institution
with reformed internal organisation. Several
national universities, being expected to keep in
close touch with society, were established in
various locations. These included two universities
of science and technology, three universities of
education, a university of library science and a
university of physical education. Moreover, a long-
considered plan for the University of the Air was
officially approved in July 1981 and it is scheduled
to open in April 1985[12].

The last point was the introduction of a system
of vocational schools which are immediately relevant
to employment. In 1981, five years after it had
been formalised, about 473,000 students were
participating in 2,945 vocational schools. This
type of further education has been mainly in the
private sector. In 1981, 87 per cent of these
schools and 92 per cent of the students were in the
private sector, as most of them had been converted
from the cream of miscellaneous schools. Three-
quarters of the students are taking specialised
courses for upper secondary school-leavers.
Therefore, there seem to be good prospects for
their development as institutions offering short-
cycle post-secondary education[13].

IMPLICATIONS/INTERACTIONS FOR THE ECONOMY AND
SOCIETY

High Economic Growth and Increase in Educational Outlay

During the 1960s and 1970s Japanese educational
policy was supported by contemporaneous high
economic and social development and in return it was
designed to serve the new needs of the age.

As has already been mentioned, for twenty years
between 1960 and 1980 Japanese education expanded so
rapidly that, taking the 1960 figures as a base for
comparison, enrolment in 1980 increased to 3.2 times
in kindergartens, 1.4 times in upper secondary
schools, 3.1 times in higher education institutions
and 25.7 times in the schools for the handicapped.
The increase is not so noticeable in the growth rate
in the total number of educational institutions
(8 per cent) and in the total enrolment for all
levels of education (12 per cent), but these small
figures are attributed to the shrinking in compulsory
education.

In connection with this expansion, the total
education expenditure (net total of public expenditure on education and expenses on private schools)
increased to 22.2 times in nominal terms and 10.9
times in real terms the expenditure of twenty years
before. It was the steady development of the
national economy during the same period that enabled
the government to be lavish with expenditure. In
fact, because of the mushroom growth in GNP which
became 14.8 times in nominal terms and 7.3 times in
real terms, the increase in the ratio of the total
education expenditure to the national income was no
more than 51 per cent between 1960 and 1980.
Especially in the 1960s when Japan had enjoyed more
than 10 per cent annual economic growth, the
increasing expense for education had not been an
intolerable burden on the nation[14].

Manpower Planning for Economic Growth

Meanwhile, one of the most prominent efforts to meet
the demands of the business and industrial world was
a plan to make good the manpower shortage mainly in
scientific and technological fields. As soon as the
Occupation had ended and the economic revival had
begun in the 1950s, major organisations of the
economic community such as the *Federation of
Economic Organisations*, the *Japan Federation of
Employers' Associations*, the *Japan Committee for*

Economic Development, and the *Japan Chamber of
Commerce and Industry*, had been calling loudly for
the government to increase university enrolment in
science and technology, to establish five-year
technical colleges, to provide in-service training
for engineers and to have greater collaboration
between education and industry. In response to
their earnest demands, the government took active
steps promptly to satisfy the manpower shortage in
a series of their economic programmes.

Firstly, under the new long-term economic plan
which started in 1957, the government faced a task
of creating 8,000 new places for an annual intake to
science and technology, and by 1960 it had nearly
accomplished this. Secondly, in 1960, with
reference to the economic plan aimed at doubling
the national income over the next decade in which
the shortage of scientists and engineers was
estimated at 170,000, the Ministry issued a seven-
year plan for adding 16,000 places in yearly
admission to these fields. This plan was
subsequently replaced by a four-year plan for
20,000 more places, and this was virtually realised
within three years. At the same time, as it decided
to expand by 85,000 places the annual intake to
technical courses in upper secondary schools, this
necessitated the urgent supply of technical teachers.
As a result, temporary three-year training institutes
for engineering teachers were opened and affiliated
with nine major national universities. For the
following seven years 800 students per year obtained
admission to these institutes[15].

Through this expansion of students' places, the
government had been giving priority to the
specialities in electronics, nuclear energy, and
information processing, because the technical
innovations in industry and the changed industrial
structure caused a big demand for experts in these
areas. Moreover, as already referred to in the
previous section, since technical colleges were
established in 1962, they have been producing
middle-level technicians ranked between technologist
or engineers with degrees, and mechanics without any
higher education.

The government's manpower policy altered a
great deal after 1970. For one thing, there
occurred a change in the situation of the work-force
in industries. The demand for scientists and
engineers had been almost satisfied in quantity and
slackened in accordance with the statistical
evidence that the percentage of students in those

fields to the total university students, which had been only 15 per cent in 1955, then amounted to 24 per cent. Of course, as the fact that postgraduate students specialising in technology increased by more than 50 per cent shows, technical innovations created a new demand for high quality manpower, but this was by no means large in scale.

For another thing, since the spread of higher education resulted in wide variation in capabilities among students, the industrial world came to expect formal education to play a role of screening students rather than of specialist training. It turned out to be common among companies to employ people with great potential first and afterwards equip them to have specific knowledge or technical skill under the in-service training.

Meeting Demands for Social Welfare

Furthermore, as some societal problems caused by rapid economic growth were emerging, people sought for an improvement in the quality of living and also improved social welfare, and consequently workers in these areas became much sought after. Especially, in conjunction with the introduction of the national health insurance system in 1961, an explosive demand developed for medical treatment and accordingly the government had to offer enough training opportunities for the medical and para-medical profession. Under the slogan 'one university of medicine within one prefecture', a considerable number of medical schools were successfully established as national or private universities and colleges. In 1969, 45 institutions had taken about 4,000 new students in their medical departments, but in 1981, when no prefecture lacked a medical school, places for new medical students doubled to about 8,000 in 79 universities or colleges throughout Japan. In addition, schools of dentistry, junior colleges of para-medical professions and vocational schools for nurses were steadily expanded and improved.

Subsequently the number of training courses for teachers of kindergartens, day nurseries and primary schools, and social workers represented a remarkable increase within departments of education or welfare in junior colleges and universities, as well as in vocational schools. In order to carry on the compulsory education of handicapped children, as mentioned in the section on educational policy at primary and secondary school level, courses for teachers in charge of them were also added one after another in teacher training schools in national universities. Moreover, the government provisionally set up nine national training institutes for nursing teachers during the second half of the 1960s, which lasted until 1979 when the shortage had been met.

Recently, Japanese society has entered upon a new phase, suffering from traffic congestion, air pollution and destruction of natural environment and being involved in drastic urbanisation and internationalisation. In order to produce people to handle these serious problems, departments of new disciplines such as town planning, traffic engineering, environmental engineering, social engineering and international relations have come into existence within higher education.

Implicit Policy to Meet Social Demand

Although the government thus answered the demands of the industrial world, most of the concern for manpower planning arose only in such professional fields as science, technology or engineering, teaching and medicine which occupy only a small part of the labour force. Therefore, educational policy has been not so much influenced by manpower demand as by the people's clamour for education, or in other words, by social demand. How to respond politically to this growing social demand has been a more serious policy issue for the government.

Of course, the government did not adopt the same action with regard to social demand as to manpower demand. It took the initiative in having the public sector supply manpower while it relied on the private sector to create more places within educational institutions except ones for compulsory education. The difference, as pointed out in the section on educational policy for higher and further education, is typically shown between technical colleges, most of which are public sector, and junior colleges which are mostly private. As for universities, the two sectors also hold various fields of study in entirely different proportions. A comparison shows that 74 per cent of undergraduate students in national universities specialise in science, technology, medical sciences, agriculture and education, while in private universities 69 per cent of students enrol in humanities, social studies and other fields. Furthermore, 66 per cent of postgraduate students are registered in the public sector and, on the other hand, private kindergartens have 74 per cent of the total enrolled.

Therefore there is little doubt that the government has been content to observe the private sector serving people's needs for education at the same time as it set forth manpower planning as one of the specific policy goals in its educational project. However, it is also important to note that the former task, as its goal has been implicit, has not fully been appreciated, though the success in the latter with an explicit goal was liable to attract considerable attention. In fact, social demand has been regarded as a matter of no small concern in educational policy lest the competition in entrance examination should become so severe as to bring about social unrest.

Therefore, the education explosion, one of the most distinctive phenomena of the 1960s and 1970s, was primarily due to the surprising growth of social demand stemming from the sharp rise in income levels brought about by high economic growth. The Ministry might have thought that production of qualified people afforded ample excuse for spending a large share of public funding on education. Nevertheless, in the sense that it whipped up social interest in education, the policy to meet manpower shortages surely played an important part in the education explosion.

Consequences of Educational Expansion

The popularisation of higher education, the universalisation of upper secondary education and the spread of pre-primary education have wrought amazing changes in school education. Although there has been no fundamental alteration in the school system since its overhaul reform in the late 1940s, the realities of education were revolutionalised through the period of expansion between 1960 and 1980. Before 1960, as one out of ten people had received higher education, universities had maintained their position on the educational ladder for the élite. The enrolment rate in upper secondary schools had been no higher than 50 per cent and they had retained the pattern handed down from the middle schools under the pre-war system that had been producing the backbone of the society. Only about a quarter of the children had attended kindergartens and most of them came from the urban middle class.

However, for the last twenty years these educational institutions have been losing their long-held positions or traditional ethos of the students. Contemporary universities and upper secondary schools

no longer display a characteristically superior
culture, and the student culture has been taken over
by the general youth culture. A great many school-
leavers without academic bent or any purpose in mind
have rushed into university, and, consequently,
complaints are often heard that universities have
turned into leisure centres. In upper secondary
schools, the majority of the students have
difficulty in keeping up with their lessons, so
virtual drop-outs are growing in significant
numbers.

Contrary to expectations, the expansion of
educational opportunities has entailed greater
differences between schools, and hence competition
for admission to reputable schools has even been
intensified. Moreover, in a society where the idea
of keeping up with the Joneses has been prevailing,
people have felt themselves forced to attend upper
secondary schools, kindergartens and universities.
Then, reluctant attendants have increased, and at
the same time the burden of education cost has begun
to affect the household economy.

As examination pressures have increased, a
so-called 'examination industry' which includes
coaching schools, crammers, and private tutors has
been booming[16]. Some private secondary schools have
won fame as effective cramming schools. As a
consequence, children whose parents can afford extra
expense to spend on this additional education have
come to gain an advantage in the competition. In
spite of the fact that governments have aimed at
equality of educational opportunity through their
policies of expanding student places and of removing
differences among public upper secondary schools, or
have introduced extreme egalitarianism in the public
compulsory schools, these efforts ironically have
intensified competition in entrance examinations,
put schools into a hierarchical system and invited
virtual inequality of educational opportunity, after
all[17].

POLITICAL STRUCTURE AND POLITICAL FORCES

Policymaking through Political Party Conflicts
Through the 1960s and 1970s the *Liberal Democratic
Party* (LDP), a conservative political camp, held the
reins of government in Japan. The *Japan Socialist
Party* (JSP) was once in office for less than one
year and a half between May 1947 and October 1948,
but no other party on the left has ever come into

power since the Second World War. Especially since
November 1955 when the LDP was formed from a merger
of the existing conservative parties, it has always
been in office. Therefore, post-war Japan has never
seen a change of régime bring about a drastic
alteration in national educational policy.

Of course, it has been influenced by changes in
the socio-economic situation and has shown some
variation in its nuances on several occasions of a
government re-shuffle or the selection of a new
Minister of Education, as stated previously. Nevertheless, since a single party has long held the
dominant position, educational administration in
Japan has operated fundamentally along the same
lines, and has had more continuity and consistency
than those in other advanced countries.

Under these political circumstances, the government party and the Ministry form educational policies
after mutual consultations. For the drawing up of
bills, the members of the Education Committee and the
Educational Investigation Committee of the LDP, most
of whom are former Ministers or Vice-Ministers, and
higher officials in the Ministry are responsible.
As the conservative government has lasted for many
years, the relationship between these two groups
seems to have become closer and the Party has been
able to claim a voice more often than before.

The *Diet*, where the ruling party holds the
majority, would be more precisely defined as a policy
enacting body than as a policymaking body. The
Opposition took the initiative in enacting the *Law
Guaranteeing the Hiring of Substitute Teachers for
Women Teachers Absent for Childbirth* (1955) and some
others but such cases are extremely unusual, mainly
because a law is not passed in the *Diet* unless it
has approval of the party in power which compose the
majority. On these occasions the conservative camp
would impose the condition that the party out of
power should grant a concession on the detailed
provisions in a proposed bill or it should agree to
pass another important bill.

Therefore, in most cases, a striking aspect of
the Opposition's influence has been their negative,
rather than positive, quality directed against
governmental policies; for instance, having a bill
fail by delaying tactics. In fact, they succeeded
in rejecting the university administration bill, the
textbook bill and a considerable number of other
bills. Over educational policies the JSP and the
Japan Communist Party (JCP) have some influence
because they are inseparably linked with the *Japan*

Teachers' Union, while the *Democratic Socialist Party* (DSP) and the *Clean Government Party* (CGP), which are middle-of-the-road, are not so influential. The first two opposition parties have been openly in conflict with the LDP concerning every significant educational policy.

These two camps hold completely different ideologies and the political situation in Japan is coming to have an air of bipolarity. The government or the LDP intends to maintain liberalism and the market economy and to reinforce national defence under the US-Japan Security Treaty, whereas its opponents advocate socialism and a planned economy, and aim at the ending of the treaty and disarmed neutrality or even friendship with communist countries.

Main Issues of Political Conflict
Thus two political forces, for and against the present régime, represent two extremes of opinion. Above all, an issue of education which might lay the foundation for a personal viewpoint will cause a sharp disagreement or a heated controversy between them, as they know that their future positions depend on people's attitudes towards the politics. Accordingly, so far, whenever the occasion has arisen, they have come into conflict. The points of issue have been, in a word, 'Who should decide what and whom to teach?'

Their opinions basically agree about the extent school enrolment should be increased or opportunities should be expanded, although, comparatively, the conservative camp is in favour of equity according to students' capabilities while the JSP and JCP believe in ensuring a place for every applicant. The reason why no severe confrontation has occurred about this point could be that the question is not one of quality but quantity, or that egalitarianism is deeply rooted in the Japanese.

However, on another point, the content of education, there has been a hot dispute between the LDP and the left-wing parties. The former values equipping children with national pride as a Japanese and developing a sense of responsibility as a member of society and stresses the need for vocational education, while the latter intends to use school education for inspiring class consciousness and fostering a strong sense of the rights for pupils and emphasises the importance of general education.

Their views also differ on the question of who

should play a leading part in policymaking. The
majority party attempts to give more authority to
the central government for maintaining national
integration, improving educational standards and
ensuring educational opportunity. Its opponents
insist on local autonomy as a precaution against
statism, adjustment of education according to
locality and people's participation in administration.
Furthermore, the former claims that, following the
purpose of legislation in the *Diet* which represents
the consensus of the people throughout the country,
administrative bodies should be responsible for
internal matters of education as well as external
ones, while the latter argues that neither the
legislative nor administrative body should interfere
in 'interna' and demands academic freedom of teachers
and their right to participate in policymaking on
the ground of professional autonomy of teachers.

For all that, either of their arguments is
adopted chiefly from expediency in a position of
permanent government or permanent opposition and,
unlike the controversy concerning the content of
education, their opinions do not have a substantial
difference. Therefore, they might be interchanged
if their positions were reversed.

Forces Blocking the Policy of the Ruling Party

Apart from irreconcilable conflicts with the JSP and
JCP, the fact that the LDP has kept holding the
reins of government for over a quarter of a century
naturally suggests smoothness in carrying out its
intentions. However, they have not always been
accomplished for the following reasons.

Firstly, the Japanese have a custom of valuing
unanimous approval above majority decisions, and
that has restricted the activities of lawmaking by
the principle of the majority rule. With the long-
cherished idea that significant decisionmaking must
be done with unified consent, if the government
party pushed its policy through to a decision by the
force of numbers, it would be regarded as 'the
tyranny of the majority' and encounter public
criticism. In order to escape this, the party has
to make a compromise on some details of the bill so
that it can reach an agreement with at least some of
the non-governmental parties, or to give its approval
to a bill supported by the Opposition. Therefore,
though dominant in the *Diet*, the LDP cannot help
hesitating to form a policy which is likely to
stiffen the resistance of its opponent, and even if

it dared to present a bill for such a policy, it would usually reach no decision.

Secondly, owing to local autonomy, educational policies employed by the central government are sometimes blocked at local level. A prefectural board of education which is responsible for primary and secondary education, fearing that disorder might arise in schools resulting from struggles of teachers' unions, tries to reach an agreement by conceding some of its demands. A head of the local government who is elected by direct vote of the inhabitants uses his influence to effect a compromise between them. In addition, during the late 1960s and 1970s, renovative local governments where left-wing renovative forces took control were set up one after another. As a result, government policies were often rejected or crippled by them.

The Struggle of the Teachers' Union

Thirdly, the government policy towards education and teachers has not been able to avoid strenuous opposition by anti-government organisations of school teachers. Above all, the Japan Teachers' Union (JTU), the second largest trade union in Japan, has 680,000 members and its membership fee totalled the sum of 46,600 million yen in the 1981 fiscal year. Since 39 per cent of all school personnel, 52 per cent of those in public primary and secondary schools, and as many as 65 per cent of non-managerial teaching staff are members of it, it wields a vast influence over educational activities within schools. The members are split into two camps: about two-thirds are the mainstream in favour of the JSP and the other third anti-mainstream are on the side of the JCP. Both of them are firmly entrenched within the left-wing parties, and so the Union has waged fierce struggles against a whole series of major government policies. Accordingly, only a few of the intentions of the national or local administrative bodies have extended to schools or classrooms.

Furthermore, the pressure of public opinion is not negligible. The JTU which is not thoroughly satisifed with the frail support by the minority parties and the small number of renovative local governments, has been working hand in hand with the mass media and intellectuals in various mass movements, and in nation-wide campaigns in strategies for confronting the government[18]. The *General Council of Japanese Trade Unions*, the largest union collective in Japan and the national centre for left-

wing unions, which comprises mainly those
representing government employees, is backing the
JTU without reservation. Moreover, some of the
Japanese journalists and intellectuals feel antagonism for the government and are apt to take pro-Union
attitudes.

The Union has also been making the best use of
the judiciary or international organisations in order
to obstruct the free action of the government. It
has fought for academic freedom and fundamental
labour rights of teachers in the courts, and lodged
claims for them before the ILO. Thus its efforts to
stir public anti-government spirit by asking various
fields for co-operation have effectively induced the
government to reconsider its educational policies
and to make some concessions.

Lastly, workers in schools retain an autonomous
posture, which prevents national or local educational
policies from meeting with success in schools.
Teaching staff with beliefs in their honorable
profession accept no outside interference in
educational activities within schools and, at the
same time, they are inclined to think that the entire
staff should participate in decisionmaking in running
the school. Accordingly, most of the decisions at
staff meetings are virtually final even in primary
and secondary schools whose principals are invested
with full authority for management, as well as in
universities whose faculties are admitted to autonomy
under legislation. Therefore, the intentions of
the administrative authorities are not fulfilled in
some schools where the Teachers' Union is influential.

In such bitter rivalry between the two
political powers, the government or the LDP has
never succeeded in coming to an agreement with the
JTU or the Opposition on the aims and content of
education, and on the due process of policymaking.
It has naturally shrunk from employing a policy which
is expected to meet with firm resistance from the
Opposition, and the policies applied daringly have
rarely made satisfactory progress[19]. These circumstances have caused great delay in improvement in
the quality of education. However, both camps have
held the same view in regard to the increase in
quantity of education and expansion of educational
opportunity. To put it more correctly, all they
could do for the patronage of the public who have
voting rights was to compete in efforts at expansion.
As a result, with no firm principle in policymaking,
educational opportunities have kept increasing.

NATIONAL/LOCAL DICHOTOMIES AND FOREIGN INFLUENCE

Japanese education is administered at both national and local level. The duty of the Ministry of Education, Science and Culture, which is the national organ for education, includes framing fundamental policy, prescribing the standards for schools and offering financial aids, technical guidance and advice to the local governments and private higher education institutions. Each local government has a major responsibility for managing education except higher education. Prefectural boards of education play a central role in the operation of public schools, and social and pre-school education are conducted by municipal boards of education. In addition, private primary and secondary schools are under the jurisdiction of a prefectural governor, and local universities and junior colleges are maintained and supervised by a head of the government: a prefectural governor or a mayor[20].

Causes of Variation among Districts

As national, prefectural and municipal educational agencies are in principle independent of each other, educational policy carried out by the local government does not always concur with that by another, and sometimes differs considerably from the guidelines issued by the Ministry. One of the reasons for their disagreement is the fact that each district has had to deal with quite different administrative tasks; for example, measures taken in metropolitian areas naturally have formed some striking contrasts to those in more sparsely populated districts.

Firstly, in provincial towns one of their important policy tasks is typically to invite a university to set up its campus in their towns, while in metropolitan areas the authorities are examining the possibility of the dispersion of the university campuses to the provinces. That is because most of higher education institutions, especially private ones, are situated in metropolitan areas, and this has caused differentials in enrolments between the students' districts of origin.

Secondly, when the scheme for increase in upper secondary education was implemented, newly-established schools in metropolitan areas offered more academic courses and the private sector played an important role, but in provincial areas most of the new schools were public and some of them

offered vocational courses. This stemmed from
unequal opportunities for employment and differences
in economic and cultural development. Moreover, at
present, a serious policy task of expanding upper
secondary education is again emerging in metropolitan areas as the second generation of the so-called
'baby boom' will be in their middle teens in a
couple of years, while in the provinces, excessive
capacity of some school premises is at issue.

Another reason lies in the fact that
educational policy depends on whether the
conservative or renovative party is dominant at the
local government level and whether a teachers' union
is influential in the prefecture. A local government controlled by the renovationist camp is quite
reluctant to co-operate with the Ministry, and some
of the plans made at national level have only been
implemented after being crippled or after several
delays. Policies such as introducing 'teachers'
efficiency rating system' and authorising the
position of the head teacher are good examples. On
the other hand, renovative local governments sometimes implement their own peculiar policies. The
most typical one is the scheme 'one district - one
upper secondary school system and no entrance
examination' by Kyoto Prefectural Government which
is labelled 'the Western Ministry of Education' as
a supposed match for the Ministry in Tokyo[21].

Fundamental Uniformity of Local Policies
Although some variations are found, major
discrepancies are confined to a few measures or in
specific local governments, and the national policy
basically has influence over all the local governments. Therefore, the quality and method of
education, not to mention the system, are almost the
same throughout the country in spite of the legal
system which charges local governments with
educational administration. This uniformity seems
to have been brought about by the following
circumstances.

For one thing, an American occupation policy of
decentralisation did not work successfully enough to
sweep away the traditional Japanese trend towards
centralisation; the central government still maintain a supervisory attitude towards the local
governments which, on the other side of the coin,
have not yet sloughed off dependence upon the
support of the central government.

For another thing, educational finance has been

more centralised since after the war, contrary to
decentralisation of educational governance, in order
to promote the educational equality which was
another principle of the post-war educational
policy. As a result, the local governments are
required to fulfil the standards set by the central
body in order that they obtain annual national
grants.

Thirdly, the keen competition for admission to
reputable universities or for posts within leading
firms has brought social pressure. Inhabitants
desire to receive education in accord with the
national standard lest their localism should put
them at a disadvantage when they participate in
this national competition.

Fourthly, egalitarianism is deeply rooted in
the Japanese people[22]. There seems to be no
apparent reason for this. The Japanese, whose
nation is composed of a single race with a common
language, and has a history covering a period of
more than twenty centuries, have always been
remarkably homogeneous. In addition, their native
preference for egalitarianism as a result of being
an agricultural people might have been intensified
during the occupation days when they were well
exposed to American egalitarian ideology.

Sensitivity to Overseas Trends

As stated above, Japanese educational policy could
be characterised by its small variation among
districts and uniformity throughout the nation, but
at the same time it has been particularly eager to
learn from international trends and is exceptionally
sensitive to influences from overseas, especially
from advanced countries. Its island situation has
always made the people of Japan feel nervous about
political isolation and for the last hundred years
as a late comer to modernisation they have been
eager to catch up with the European countries and
the United States.

In the distant past Japan learnt a great deal
from Chinese education and the pre-war school
system was established on the basis of those in
Europe or America (see the section on Historical
Background above). Furthermore, even at a time of
extreme nationalism during the war we can perceive
some influence from Nazi Germany upon Japanese
educational policy. In addition, the United States
Occupation Force compelled the Japanese government
to reform the educational system by transplanting an

American domestic system. Although it can be readily understood that as a defeated nation Japan had no alternative, no one would deny her extraordinary obedience in following almost all the advice, compared with West Germany under similar circumstances, who complied with only a few of the Occupation requests for educational reform.

Since the 1960s Japanese educational policy has never come under any foreign control, but it still has been subject to influence from overseas, especially of theoretical study or policy measures in major advanced countries. To give an example, the *Law for the Organisation and Management of Local Educational Administration* (1956) was modelled on the British Education Act of 1944 in empowering the Minister of Education to approve a superintendent appointed by the prefectural board of education to request surveys and reports carried out by the local governments as part of the fulfilment of their duties, though this law replaced the *Board of Education Law* (1948), promulgated during the occupation period, on the ground that it needed adjusting to the domestic condition.

Another example would be the curriculum reform during the second half of the 1960s, which is referred to in the section on educational policy at primary and secondary school level. This reform is interpreted as the Japanese 'post-sputnik' move, because it followed after the curriculum improvement movement such as the PSSC textbook in the United States.

In addition, after the end of the 1950s, scientific and technological education attained greater importance and manpower planning and educational investment theory came into fashion in Europe. This information stimulated Japan to launch manpower training schemes in the field of science and technology.

Influences from International Organisations
Lastly, such international organisations as UNESCO, ILO and OECD had a considerable influence in Japanese educational policy throughout the last two decades. The ratification of ILO's '*Convention 87 concerning Freedom of Association and Protection of the Right to Organise*' and its accompanying '*Report of the Fact-finding and Conciliation Commission on Freedom of Association concerning Persons Employed in the Public Sector in Japan*' brought a notable change in Japanese teacher policy by means of the

amendment of Local Public Service Law in 1965.
UNESCO's *Recommendation Concerning the Status of
Teachers* (1966) also gave rise to much controversy
on whether school teachers are professionals and
whether a teacher's organisation should act as
professional organisation or trade union.

Furthermore, the *Review of National Policies
for Japan* (1971) published by OECD and the results
of IEA international tests of achievement aroused
public attention. The recent report on *Lifelong
Education* (1981) submitted by the Central Council
for Education, the supreme advisory organ to the
Ministry, was also made in the light of the
activities of UNESCO or OECD and followed the international trend[23]. Japanese educational policy has
thus been exposed to influence from overseas as a
result of imported publications, participation in
international conferences and researches, and
scholars studying abroad.

It is possible to argue that in all nations
foreign influence has naturally become stronger since
the end of the war and that Japan is not an
exception. Undoubtedly, every country sometimes
learns from educational policy in other countries
and takes advice from international organisations in
an attempt to develop her educational system.
However, I wonder if there is any other country
whose government is so continuously concerned as is
Japan's about whether she is keeping track of the
international trend, whether she has not fallen
behind the other developed countries, or whether her
educational outcomes have reached international
standards.

THE CONTRACTION OF THE SYSTEM AND FUTURE PROSPECTS

Through the 1960s and 1970s the main task allotted
in educational policy was to expand school
education. It was favoured with: (1) an increase in
the school age population and in the rate of school
leavers going on to higher levels of education,
(2) rises in the government tax revenue and in
family income which had been brought about by the
rapid economic growth, and (3) public reliance on
school education and expectation of its effects
upon social status. However, these three factors
which contributed to the education explosion have
quickly been vanishing since the late 1970s.

Dealing with School Population and Financial Stringency

Firstly, the school age population has already begun declining. The number of children enrolled has been on the decrease in kindergartens since 1979 and in primary schools since 1981. This wave of decline will extend to the lower secondary school level by 1987, the upper secondary school level in 1990 and higher education in 1993. As the birth rate has taken a sharp downward turn recently, Japan is most unlikely to regain an increase in school age population in the foreseeable future.

In addition, the rate of attendance among school aged children, which was steadily increasing, has shown little growth since the middle 1970s. The enrolment rates in kindergartens and day nurseries, which exceeded 90 per cent, and in upper secondary schools, which amounted to 94 per cent, are barely maintained at the same level, and especially the latter has begun falling in metropolitan areas. That might mean that demand has been satiated for these levels of education. Moreover, the ratio of applicants for universities and junior colleges from the upper secondary school-leavers significantly decreased from 47 per cent to 45 per cent between 1975 and 1981.

Secondly, Japan has been losing the economic basis for steady growth in education. With the oil crisis at the end of 1973, the situation of the national economy turned from rapid growth to slow growth. The average annual economic growth in real terms was kept at 9.1 per cent for fifteen years between 1959 and 1973 but suddenly lowered to 4.0 per cent between 1974 and 1980. Accordingly, the ratio of government educational expenditure to national income jumped from 4.7 per cent in 1970 to 7.2 per cent in 1980; the ratio of total educational outlay (including expenditure on private institutions) to national income increased from 5.8 per cent to 8.6 per cent during the same period.

Thus the reason why educational expenditure has become a greater burden does not lie in its own rapid increase but in the slower growth of the national economy. Owing to the economic recession, although the percentage of taxation to the national income rose drastically from 18 per cent to 25 per cent between 1975 and 1982, taxation has not been bringing adequate revenue to the government and the deficit has been accumulating. Therefore, the present financial difficulty permits of no real increase in the budget expenditure of the government, but instead needs a reduction. As for the local governments, the statistics clearly show that they suffered from little growth in the second half of the 1970s, though their financial conditions in the 1980s have not yet become known.

Quite apart from the only moderate increase in total government budget expenditure, education's share has also been reduced. Expenditure on education occupied 12.7 per cent of the total government expenditure in 1975, but this fell to 9.0 per cent in 1983, and the ratio of educational expenditure to total local government expenditure decreased from 27.8 per cent in 1975 to 26.4 per cent in 1980. The combined figures are 22.3 per cent in 1975 and 19.7 per cent in 1980.

Decreasing Demand for Schooling

Thirdly, school education has been losing its socio-economic effectiveness and has invited criticism. Under the post-war educational reform the period of compulsory education was extended and during the years of high economic growth a large number of places were created within post-compulsory schools. Hence, while people have been offered generous learning opportunities, as more people have higher levels of education, the chance of obtaining positions suitable to their educational background has been more limited, and the rate of return from educational investment has decreased. For instance, the private rate of return to male white-collar workers with university education was about 9 per cent in the first half of the 1960s, but in the late 1970s it lowered to approximately 6 per cent.

Besides, students who lack in ability and will to learn have been on the increase; secondary schools have come to produce a considerable number of repeaters, drop-outs and fall-behinds and incur juvenile delinquency and school violence, and universities are said by their critics to have turned into leisure centres. As these phemonena are frequently observed, the climate of opinion has turned against further expansion of school education, and this is one of the causes leading to the reduction in the budget for education.

The economic recession and increase in tax burden have begun to affect family income, so its disposable income does not show any increase in real terms. Meanwhile, tuition and initiation fees have risen every year and expenditure on education is growing to become a strain on the household budget.

Thus the rate of school-leavers who go on to higher
levels of education remains stationary mainly
because of the heavy costs of and little perceived
benefit from education.

Nevertheless, the Japanese educational system
has not yet reached a stage of constriction. For
the total number of schools, students and teachers
and the sum of educational expenditure are still
slightly on the increase and such radical reductions
as some advanced countries have undergone have never
been put through. This, however, is only due to the
fact that Japan will lose its adolescent population
ten years later than those countries and that the
national economy is still achieving a growth rate of
some 4 per cent.

Considering the above-mentioned disappearance
of the factors conducive to educational growth,
shrinkage in the total size of the system is quite
within the bounds of possibility, and in any case
it is clear that there is little prospect of
further expansion of educational opportunities. In
this sense, the government is under pressure to
replace their policy of expansion of educational
opportunities with a policy of improvement in
educational quality. Of course, this change has
been recognised as a necessity for the past ten
years. In 1971 the *Central Council for Education*
pointed this out clearly in its report and called
for a so-called third educational reform. However,
only a few of its suggestions have been acted upon
and the main things have been left undone.

Difficulties of the Third Reform
At present Japan is faced with the more urgent
necessity of an educational reform, but it has as
many difficulties to smooth away in carrying it out
as she had ten years ago. The difficulties lie in
the fact that this educational reform is proposed
under a situation entirely different from the past
two reforms.

(a) The earliest reform following the *Meiji
Restoration* in 1868 was accomplished in the process
of modernisation and establishment of diplomatic
relation with foreign countries under the influence
of the great western powers, and the second reform
was also effected under the military occupation
after the defeat in the war in 1945 through the
process of disarmament and democratisation.
Accordingly, under heavy outside pressure, the
execution of reforms was taken seriously as

imperative and the results were considered as liable
to sway the destiny of the nation. However, people
do not bear a feeling of national crisis in their
mind today as they did in those days. They sometimes
feel a malaise about the future of Japan in international society where all nations share a common
fate, but this uneasiness has not forced them to
determine to put through an immediate reform and
recover the critical situation.
   (b)   Both of the first and second reforms
could be regarded as one of the steps in radical
political change including establishment of the
constitutions. However, for the time being the
third educational reform has little possibility of
accompanying such a political revolution. The
matters which the government has to treat as urgent
are contraction in administration and reduction of
the accumulated financial deficit. This kind of
reform in financial structure and administration
might stall the plan for an educational reform by
stemming active progress in educational policy, but
is unlikely to prompt it.
   (c)   The first reform was made by the *Meiji*
despotic government prior to the establishment of
the *Meiji Constitution* and the post-war reform was
backed up by the occupation force which was beyond
the control of the New Constitution. Nowadays
Japan has no absolute ruler and instead the government is required to follow democratic procedures for
formulating and implementing any policy. Now
people do not share their sense of values, and a
clash of interests sometimes happens among organisations which are linked to influential pressure
groups.   Therefore, it would be extremely difficult
to find a consensus among people concerned.
   (d)   Japan modelled its modern educational
system on those in advanced western countries during
the time of the earliest reform and effected the
second one by copying after the precedent in the
United States.   Then the government could set it as
a national goal to catch up with those counterparts
and so stimulated people.   However, nowadays when
Japan seems to have achieved this goal, learning
from the situations in other developed countries
does not supply a suitable goal.   Furthermore, now,
for the first time, society is making a demand upon
the government for reform, in the form of criticism
of school education.   Hence, the government has to
devise such a design on its own.
   (e)   In carrying out the previous reforms, the
former at the take-off period of modernisation and

the latter in the complete destitution just after
the end of the war, the government suffered from a
shortage of financial resources. Facing a third
reform, Japan is under favourable financial
conditions as compared with those days. On the
other hand, strong demands for other administrative
tasks such as social welfare would not yield a
priority to education, and people are offering
stubborn resistance to increasing burdens. That
means Japan has only limited financial resources
available for the reform.

Such deterrents might not warrant any sanguine
expectations regarding the prompt and heroic
achievement of a third reform. It could be
considered more appropriate to aim at more gradual
progress toward the reform under a long-term
perspective.

NOTES

1. R.P. Dore, *Education in Tokugawa Japan*
(University of California Press, Berkeley, 1965),
p.291.
2. H. Passin, 'Japan' in J.S. Coleman (ed.),
Education and Political Development (Princeton
University Press, Princeton, 1965), p.276.
3. M.C. Kaser, 'Education and Economic
Process: Experience in Industrialized Market
Economies' in E.A.G. Robinson and J.E. Vaizey (eds),
The Economics of Education (Macmillan, London, 1966),
pp.119-120.
4. R.P. Dore, *The Diploma Disease* (University
of California Press, Berkeley and Los Angeles,
1975), p.39.
5. R.S. Anderson, *Education in Japan*
(US Department of Health, Education and Welfare,
Washington DC, 1975), p.86.
6. M. Aso and I. Amano, *Education and Japan's
Modernization* (Ministry of Foreign Affairs, Japan,
Tokyo, 1972), pp.70-75.
7. Ministry of Education, Science and Culture,
Japan, *Japan's Modern Educational System* (Government Printing Office, Tokyo, 1980), p.266.
8. Ministry of Education, Science and Culture,
Japan, *Educational Standards in Japan* (Government
Printing Office, Tokyo, 1975), pp.81-90.
9. S. Ichikawa, 'Statistical Significance and
Characteristics of Private Institutions' in
K. Narita (ed.), *Systems of Higher Education: Japan*
(International Council for Educational Development,

New York, 1978), pp.30-33.
    10.   T.J. Pempel, *Patterns of Japanese Policy-making: Experiences from Higher Education* (Westview Press, Boulder, 1978), pp.171-72.
    11.   S. Ichikawa, 'Finance of Higher Education' in W.K. Cummings, I. Amano and K. Kitamura (eds), *Changes in the Japanese University: A Comparative Perspective* (Praeger, New York, 1979), pp.59-60.
    12.   T.J. Pempel, *Policy and Politics in Japan: Creative Conservatism* (Temple University Press, Philadelphia, 1982), p.185.
    13.   S. Ichikawa, 'Povratno obrazovanje u Japanu' in N.N. Šoljan (ed.), *Povratno Obrazovanje i Promjene u Politici i Sistemu Obrazovanja* (Zavod za Pedagogiju Filozofskog Fakulteta Sveučilišta, Zagreb, 1981), p.242.
    14.   Ministry of Education, Science and Culture, Japan, *Statistical Abstract of Education, Science and Culture* (Government Printing Office, Tokyo, 1981), pp.30-33 and 160-63.
    15.   T.J. Pempel, 'Patterns of Policymaking: Higher Education' in T.J. Pempel (ed.), *Policymaking in Contemporary Japan* (Cornell University Press, Ithaca and London, 1977), p.293.
    16.   T.P. Rohlen, 'The *Juku* Phenomenon: An Exploratory Essay', *Journal of Japanese Studies*, vol.6, no.2 (1980), p.213.
    17.   T.P. Rohlen, 'Is Japanese Education Becoming Less Egalitarian?: Notes on High School Stratification and Reform', *Journal of Japanese Studies*, vol.3, no.1 (1977), p.68.
    18.   B.C. Duke, *Japan's Militant Teachers* (University Press of Hawaii, Honolulu, 1973), p.189.
    19.   D.R. Thurston, *Teachers and Politics in Japan* (Princeton University Press, Princeton, 1973), p.263.
    20.   Ministry of Education, Science and Culture, Japan, *Education in Japan* (Gyosei Publishers, Tokyo, 1982), pp.32-35.
    21.   W.K. Cummings, *Education and Equality in Japan* (Princeton University Press, Princeton, 1980), p.63.
    22.   N. Glazer, 'Social and Cultural Factors in Japanese Economic Growth' in H. Patrick and H. Rosovsky (eds), *Asia's New Giant* (Brookings Institution, Washington DC, 1976), p.837.
    23.   K. Moro-oka, *Recurrent Education: Japan* (OECD, Paris, 1976), p.7.

Six

SWEDEN

Sixten Marklund

In this article the concept educational policy refers primarily to the content of extensive political decisions, expressed by the Swedish Parliament (*Riksdag*) and Government in laws, statutes, budget decisions and corresponding kinds of guiding material. Yet policy is not restricted to the documents given but includes also execution, administration and interpretation of policies in a national perspective, i.e. not only the goals and the aims of educational policy but also their practical implication, primarily in structural changes of educational institutions, designed to give increased possibilities to achieve these goals and aims. The policy is therefore analysed and described as a series of reforms of the educational framework.

The year 1950 is here a critical turning-point. From that year Sweden introduced an educational policy of a type which gradually, although in a decisive way broke new ground. From that time it is hardly possible to talk of separate policies for primary, secondary and tertiary education, nor even for academic, vocational and general education. A policy of 'comprehensivisation' was started and developed all through the system of schools and higher institutions, which in spite of its different implications at different levels had a common denominator, the democratisation of education.

HISTORICAL AND POLITICAL BACKGROUND

In the mid-1940s Sweden still had a school system that by European standards was fairly old-fashioned and not particularly extensive. The compulsory elementary school covered only six or seven years of

schooling. After it came various types of lower
secondary schools, attended by fewer than one-fourth
of all elementary school leavers. Only about ten
per cent of all elementary school students completed
a secondary education. Technical and vocational
training were correspondingly limited in scale.
Fewer than five per cent of each annual cohort
attended universities and professional colleges.
This was the system from which the current structure
has developed over the space of three decades.

The most important aspect of this reform was
the introduction of the new nine-year compulsory
comprehensive school. This started in 1950,
following a decision by the *Riksdag*. It ran in two
phases, an experimental phase during the period
1950-1962 and an implementation phase 1962-1972.
During these two phases the old primary school and
the various types of lower secondary schools were
replaced by the new and unified system. This reform
provided the foundation for subsequent change in
upper secondary education, vocational education,
higher education and adult education.

Practically nothing remains today of the school
system Sweden had before 1950; in terms of both
school structure and content of education, the
changes have been almost total. It is true that
teaching-learning processes have changed less, but
even in this respect the school of today is very
different from the school of 1950. Some of the more
important development trends since 1950 have been:

(1) the extension of compulsory schooling to
     16 years of age;
(2) the postponement of the organisational
     diversification of students in different
     fields of study;
(3) an increase in students in post-compulsory
     schooling;
(4) a move towards comprehensivisation and
     integration of upper-secondary, tertiary
     (university) and adult education; and
(5) decentralisation in decision-making and
     responsibility for the schools.

A circumstance of considerable significance in
connection with reform activities in recent years
has been Sweden's political stability. The dominant
political party has been the Social Democrats.
Between 1932 and 1976, i.e. for 44 years, they were
in power practically without interruption, including brief periods in coalition with other parties.

Figure 6.1: School Structure in Sweden in 1980

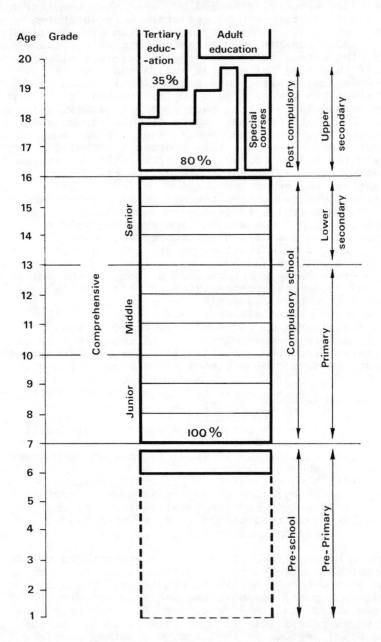

But for most of this time they ruled through a one-party Government, and for long periods they had the support of a majority in the *Riksdag*. By and large, the same political party situation has prevailed in the decision-making bodies of local government, which have come to operate most of the school system. Political stability has had its parallel in a comparatively conflict-free labour market. By means of their strong organisations and smoothly functioning negotiating system, labour and management in industry and in the rest of the labour market have generally reached mutually acceptable solutions. This has applied both to blue-collar and white-collar employees. Strikes and other industrial actions have occurred relatively infrequently; unemployment has also been low.

An additional factor of importance has been the growth of material prosperity in Sweden during the same period. Industrialisation and efficiency measures on the labour market, not least in agriculture, have contributed to a noticeable rise in standards of living as a whole. Using a conventional yardstick such as the Gross National Product (GNP) per capita, Sweden has climbed to the top level among industrialised countries. If material prosperity has facilitated educational reforms, the same can be said of social welfare standards. By means of social welfare activities, there has been an effort to give everyone a share of social welfare, broadly defined. Unemployment insurance, basic old-age and supplementary income-related pensions, public health and medical care, child allowances and housing allowances are important examples of this. The reform of the educational system all the way from the pre-school level to the higher education level has been part of this welfare programme. It includes such social benefits to students as free schooling and higher education, school health and dental care programmes, free school meals and transportation, free teaching materials, study grants and interest-free study loans. These benefits are provided to everyone.

Educational reforms have been regarded as both a necessary prerequisite and as a consequence of rising standards in general: a growing number of people have demanded an increasingly long education. At the same time, it has become more and more difficult than before to move directly from compulsory school on to the labour market and young people often have no alternative to continuing their studies. A problem which has thus become

increasingly topical in recent years is how to
co-ordinate education and gainful employment in a
way which is meaningful both for young people, for
industry and for the labour market as a whole.

It has sometimes been claimed that reforms in
Sweden, including educational reforms, have been
possible or in any event easier because Sweden is a
homogeneous country: no real conflicts due to
differences in race, religion and language have been
thought to exist here. A global comparision
undoubtedly provides some support for this viewpoint
but conflicts of this type have not been entirely
lacking. Due not least to large-scale immigration
from other countries in the past twenty years, the
multiplicity of opinions and value systems has also
clearly increased: of Sweden's inhabitants one in
eight is now an immigrant or child of an immigrant.
The homogeneity which may once have existed has thus
become much less marked.

THE REFORM OF THE SCHOOL SYSTEM

In the basic reform decision by the *Riksdag* in 1950,
the system of education was seen as a unity: the
policy was wide-ranging in that it aimed at
solutions not only to immediate problems but also to
a continuous renewal according to future needs. An
immediate need was to raise the general standard of
education. Another was to replace the clearly
dualistic school system with a more unified one, to
'democratise' education as a whole. Quite
naturally, opinions on how to change and improve the
schools and the higher education system have varied
in Sweden just as in other countries. During the
1940s, when people began to question the traditional
school system, views in Sweden were divided, too
and these issues were examined by two major
government-appointed commissions. The first of
these more or less arrived at the conclusion that
the schools could be reformed through improvement
and organisational co-ordination of the existing
types of schools but the second commission wanted to
go further and recommended replacing the prevailing
system of parallel schools with a comprehensive
school for pupils up to age 16: the Social
Democratic Government presented the issue to the
Riksdag in 1950.

The *Riksdag* decided unanimously to extend the
compulsory school-leaving age to 16. One question
caused much dissent, namely whether the many

different kinds of lower secondary schools should be
kept or replaced by one school. The conservative
party wanted to keep the old types of *realskola* as
parallel forms to an extended elementary school. In
this they were supported by the secondary academic
teachers. The *Riksdag* ended up with a compromise,
saying that there should be a ten-year period of
experiments all over the country to ascertain whether
it was 'suitable' to have the 'parallel school
system' or to introduce a unified school.

Experiments were started under the auspices of
the *National Board of Education* (an independent
central authority corresponding to the administrative branch of the school ministry in most other
countries). They grew rapidly and embraced ten
years later nearly half of the nation. Comparisons
of the 'old' and the 'new' school showed that
students achieved more in the old parallel school
system than in the new comprehensive school but the
comparability was strongly reduced since the new
schools generally had lower standards of teachers
and student ability. This led for some years to a
kind of streaming of the new schools for the last
three years of schooling. This 'restored' the
achievements of students in 'positively
differentiated' classes but again gave generally
unacceptable results in the 'negatively
differentiated' classes. After a broad evaluation
of results of varying kinds (including cognitive and
non-cognitive results and organisational and
financial problems) by a state school commission
during 1957-1961, the *Riksdag* in 1962 decided to
follow the first proposals put forward by the Social
Democrat Government in 1950, saying that the
parallel school system should be gradually replaced
by comprehensive schools over the period 1962-1972.
The conservative party and the secondary academic
teachers' union wanted such comprehensive schools to
be organised into different streams for students in
grades 7-9 and the system introduced was a compromise with electives in grades 7-8 and different
lines in the final grade.*

After this reform, the *Riksdag* decided upon
corresponding changes for upper secondary schools
including vocational training (1964 and 1968), adult
education (1967), universities and colleges (1969
and 1975) and finally also pre-school education

*Editor's note: the numbering of grades rises from grade 1 for
approximately 7-year-olds to grade 10 for approximately 16-
year olds.

Figure 6.2: The Development of the 9-year Comprehensive School

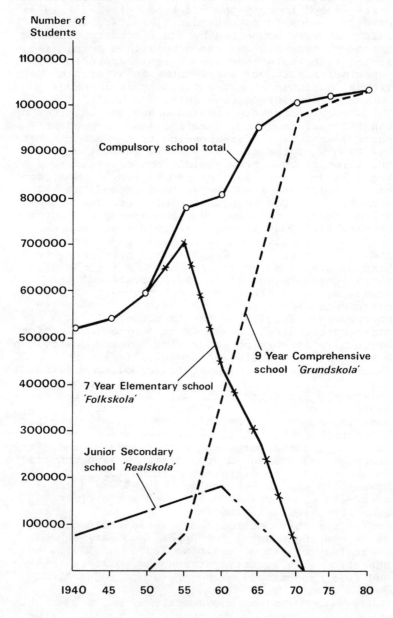

(1973). (The pre-school institutions are administered by the social welfare authorities, not by the school authorities, and will not be discussed here.) This was the so-called *rolling reform*, a strategy of change which in some respects still continues.

DIFFERENTIATION - A DIFFICULT POLICY ISSUE

The most widely discussed issue throughout the experimental period in the 1950s was the question of when and how students in the compulsory school should be divided up into different study programmes, i.e. tracking or streaming. There were two traditional viewpoints on this: one was that at an early stage, and no later than age 12-13, students should be divided up into so-called theoretical and practical orientations. The other viewpoint was that such tracking should take place as late as possible, preferably not until after compulsory schooling, i.e. at age 16. The issue was closely intertwined with that of free choice: should students and their parents be allowed to choose freely, or should the school and its teachers be able to create special requirements for certain choices and thereby them-selves carry out the distribution of students into various study programmes? As in the 1950 parlia-mentary set of principles, the 1962 decision was that students should have free choice.

The issue of tracking was also closely connected with the question of how to assign marks to students for their performance in their studies. Should any marks be given at all in the compulsory school and, if so, should marks be based on a fixed scale of achievement ('absolute marks') or on a ranking scale ('relative marks')? The curricular guidelines published in 1962, 1969 and 1980 have resulted in an abolition of marks at primary levels. But in grades 7-9 (age 13-16) of the compulsory school, i.e. at lower secondary level, marks are still used. Final marks are also crucial to students who have chosen a study line at upper secondary school where in certain types of specialisation the number of places is smaller than the number of applicants and a selection is therefore necessary. There is a five-point scale of marks, on which 1 is lowest and 5 is highest on a relative basis for the country as a whole and to help arrive at norms for assigning marks, nationally standardised tests are given in Swedish, foreign languages and mathematics in the comprehensive school. At the upper secondary level, standardised tests are administered at all schools throughout the country in a number of additional theoretical skill subjects. These tests are compulsory only in the upper secondary school. Public debate on differentiation (tracking, ability grouping, etc.) has fluctuated ever since 1950, sometimes lively and sometimes subdued, but it has never died out completely. Since 1976 in particular, it has gained new life in connection with the recommendations of a government-appointed commission on the internal work of the schools, and the revisions of the comprehensive school curriculum these recommendations required. Another important factor was the transfer of power from the Social Democrats to a coalition Government of non-socialist parties in that same year. Public debate has, among other things, come to deal with the question of whether the school system created in Sweden by the educational reforms of recent decades is capable of benefiting and helping so-called gifted students.

EQUALITY OF OPPORTUNITY

Nowadays the goal of social equality is mentioned in practically all school laws and school codes throughout the world. But it is implemented in many different ways. An important aspect of social equality in education is whether various social classes have access to education and the decision to introduce the nine-year compulsory school throughout the country increased this access in stages. By 1972, the nine-year compulsory school had been completely implemented and the different types of previously existing schools at lower secondary level had been abolished.

A first and significant step in the efforts to create social equality had thus been taken and everyone had access to a universal system of compulsory schooling to age 16. In corresponding fashion but somewhat later in time, access to post-compulsory education increased. As the compulsory comprehensive school grew, recruitment to secondary schooling expanded. The existing areas of specialisation in the secondary school - in classics and in natural sciences - were supplemented by a 'general area' in 1954. In the early 1960s, these three areas were co-ordinated with the formerly independent technical secondary schools and commercial secondary schools into a new upper

secondary school. At the same time, two-year
continuation schools with technical, economic, and
social study programmes were established as a form
of continuing education following the new compulsory
comprehensive school. By 1970, recruitment to the
existing upper secondary school (*gymnasium*) system
had risen to about 30 per cent of all young people
of the appropriate age. At the same time, nearly 20
per cent attended the new two-year continuation
schools. This meant that about half of all young
people had access to upper secondary studies.

Parallel with this, municipal vocational schools
were expanded during the decade 1955-1965.
Eventually 30-35 per cent of the appropriate age
bracket attended these schools. Beginning in 1971,
a continuing series of reforms co-ordinated the
various study programmes within the *gymnasium*, the
continuation schools and most of the municipal
vocational schools into a new type of 'integrated'
upper secondary school. This school was designed to
follow the nine-year compulsory comprehensive school.
It includes a total of 22 areas of specialisation
and a large number of special courses. The number
of students who begin their studies in this
integrated upper secondary school each year is now
about 90 per cent of all 16-year-olds completing
comprehensive school the same year. (Of these 84
per cent follow the 22 specialisms and 6 per cent
the special courses.) But the percentage who go
straight from comprehensive schools to upper
secondary schools is lower, and it varies greatly
from one municipal district to another. In 1968,
the *Riksdag* decided that all comprehensive school
'graduates' should have access to continuing
education. This aim has been achieved, in that
nowadays the upper secondary schools can provide
places to everyone who applies to them. But about
one-third of these applicants are not admitted into
the specialism of their first choice, but have to
accept their second or subsequent choice.

Access to education is an important aspect of
social equality. But it is not enough that
educational opportunities exist. They should also
be within reach of the individual. Sweden has
always had problems with uneven distribution of
population, long travel distances and the need for
boarding arrangements even in compulsory schools.
The new nine-year compulsory comprehensive school
came to include the lower secondary school level,
previously known as the *realskola*, in which the
teachers specialise in different subjects. At this

level each school needs a certain minimum number of
students and classes. This may require concentrating students in a limited number of schools, thereby
making long journeys necessary even for students in
compulsory schools.

It is characteristic of Sweden that students in
grades 1-9 form one unit, the compulsory comprehensive school, separate from the subsequent non-
compulsory upper secondary school for grades 10 and
up. Lower and upper secondary education, which
previously were often provided together, have been
split up by the comprehensive school reform. The
country is divided into comprehensive school
districts and upper secondary school regions and
there is thus always a particular comprehensive
school and a particular upper secondary school for
each student. In thinly populated areas, it is
common for both comprehensive school students and
upper secondary school students to have to travel up
to one hour from home but there are also boarding
arrangements for rural students, especially those in
upper secondary school.

Each individual secondary school region cannot
normally offer all study specialisms. The secondary
school regions thus collaborate in creating larger
regions for specialisms which attract only small
numbers of students. The practical availability of
schooling therefore varies. One part of the
efforts to achieve social equality has been to
provide comprehensive school students with free
travel either on ordinary public transportation
systems or on special school vehicles (and, where
appropriate, also free board and lodging).
Secondary school students who need transportation or
board and lodging receive, regardless of the
economic status of their families, special grants in
addition to the general study allowance paid to
everyone.

CHOICE OF SPECIALISATION BY STUDENTS

One of the objectives specified in the 1950
parliamentary decision on the future development of
the schools, and one that has often been repeated
since then in school legislation and official
curricula, was that the choice of study programme
should be a free one. The intention is thus that
each student and his or her parents should choose a
study programme from among those provided in the
schools operated by the public authorities and a

Figure 6.3: The Development of the Integrated
Upper-secondary School

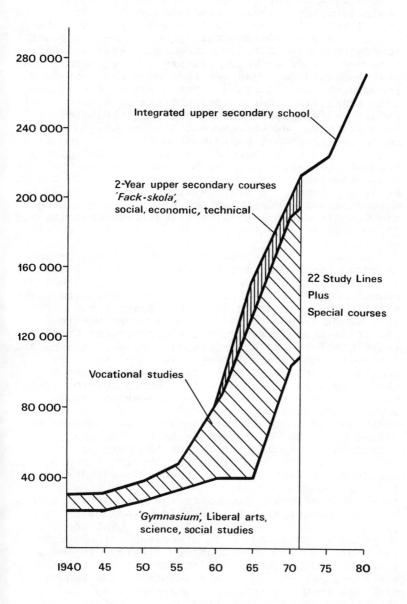

student should not be ordered by teachers or the principal to take a particular programme or subject. Free choice of studies became one of the cornerstones of the 1962 Education Act and the practical implementation of this principle has had far-reaching consequences for the structure and function of the schools and the educational system. One important consequence was that the concepts of Pass and Fail were removed from the compulsory school system. The system should be organised in such a way that it encourages the all-round development of the individual: in other words, the aim of studies should be formulated on the basis of the needs of each student. Another aspect of free choice is that repeating of grades has almost entirely disappeared from the schools: there are a few instances of students repeating a year, but as a rule only at the student's own request in connection with a change of study programme. A prerequisite for free choice is more adequate educational and vocational guidance in the schools and expanded practical work training and vocational orientation periods outside the school as well.

Sweden is not alone in lengthening the period of compulsory schooling to age 16 since this has been done in most industrialised countries since the Second World War. Nor is Sweden unique in its efforts to incorporate lower secondary school into its school system. But Sweden is among the few countries that have consistently postponed tracking (streaming) of secondary school pupils into separate categories until after they have completed compulsory school, i.e. at age 16, as decided by the *Riksdag* in 1968. A certain amount of room for elective subjects is given to students from age 13 beyond those subjects common to all of them and in addition, from age 13, students may choose between easier or harder course alternatives in foreign languages and mathematics. But the main principle is that until the end of their compulsory schooling, students are kept together in undifferentiated classes, and that regardless of their choice of electives and course types in the compulsory school, they can choose either theoretical (academic) or practical study lines in their subsequent non-compulsory schooling. The experience of the first few years of free choice after 1962 was, in some respects, surprising: in planning, it was assumed that about one-third of the comprehensive school students in grade 9 would choose 9g, i.e. the theoretically oriented, pre-upper secondary

programme in the final year but it soon turned out
that the number of students in 9g exceeded this
proportion. (The g stood for '*pre-gymnasium*'.)
After only a few years, half of all students were
choosing this programme and by 1967 three out of
four students chose academic specialisations. In
other words, 9g was flooded with students while some
of the other programmes were chosen by so few
students that they could not be organised. The
shift toward theoretical - or academic - alternatives
appears to have been due to a desire by students
finishing compulsory school to leave open all the
alternative choices for subsequent studies in upper
secondary school.

Obviously it was difficult to satisfy the
students' free choice in grades 7-9 while at the
same time dividing up students into various study
programmes in their subsequent schooling in
accordance with other, more general, principles.
In 1968, the *Riksdag* accepted the consequences of
this trend (as mentioned above) by abolishing the
tracking system in grade 9 as well and thus in the
compulsory school as a whole. Instead, it was made
possible for students in grade 7 to begin a second
foreign language (German or French) in addition to
English or alternatively technology, economics or
art but the novelty was mainly in the fact that
these four alternatives became essentially equivalent
in value for purposes of admission to subsequent
non-compulsory schooling. There was no longer any
9g which was 'better' than other programmes. This
meant that the nine-year compulsory comprehensive
school had become entirely untracked, which was
regarded as a victory for efforts at achieving
social equality but it also meant that, more than
previously, tracking and individualisation problems
were moved from the administrative level to the
internal, pedagogical level.

Measures to support and encourage individualised learning have been undertaken: some of these
have assumed the form of resources for internal
differentiation, e.g. alternative courses in
mathematics and foreign languages in grades 7-9,
which can be regarded as the last remaining relics
of the previous system of differentiated schools.
The main advantage of alternative courses is that as
a rule they mean fewer students per teacher in these
subjects but their weakness is in the fact that with
only two courses to choose from, it is by no means
possible to satisfy the full range of needs for
individualisation of learning in these subjects.

In addition, it has become clear that social class factors enter into the choice of alternative since among students with equally good aptitude for mathematics and foreign languages, those from working-class homes tend to choose the easier alternative while their classmates from more favoured backgrounds choose the difficult one.

Another resource aimed at individualisation is special education. It was established during the 1950s mainly in the form of remedial and school-readiness classes but special education within the framework of the comprehensive school was further developed and differentiated during the 1960s. More types of special classes were created, for example reading classes, observation classes and classes for the physically handicapped, visually impaired and hard-of-hearing whilst the expansion of special education in recent years has also assumed the form of limited remedial instruction for individual students who otherwise remain with their regular class. An effort has been made in recent years to bridge the gap between special education and ordinary instruction: in practice this means that the schools have attempted to provide individualisation within the regular class instead of differentiation by dividing up students in various groups. This has given Sweden a low student/teacher ratio (14:1 in grades 1-9 and 12:1 in grades 10-12) and hence also an expensive school system.

EQUALITY BETWEEN THE SEXES AND FREEDOM OF CHOICE

Efforts to achieve equality between the sexes are a good example of how, in redistribution policy, we must expect confrontations between deeply rooted values and traditions within the family and society as to what kinds of social equality and equal opportunity we can and should aim for. Among the first measures the educational system has consistently tried to enforce is opening all types of education to both sexes and seeking recruitment of both male and female teachers and other officials in the schools. Special girls' schools existed until the end of the 1960s and were finally abolished when the comprehensive school was introduced. All classes are now co-educational. Another step has been to provide the schools with a selection of subjects and courses without regard to sex: in the compulsory school, boys and girls study the same subjects, boys and girls receive instruction in wood and metal crafts as well as textile crafts and boys have the same home economics courses as girls.

In practice, efforts to achieve equality are often in conflict with free choice. Most of the subjects taught in the comprehensive school are compulsory, but in grades 7-9 students may choose electives for 15-20 per cent of their time and boys and girls often make different choices: boys tend to choose technology, while girls are more inclined to choose art and economics. The same is true of choosing study specialisms in the upper secondary school after age 16: girls are in majority in nursing, domestic science, and clothing manufacturing, while boys are correspondingly over-represented in motor engineering, electro-technicals, and workshops. Experience tells us that equality between the sexes in these study lines cannot be reconciled with freedom of choice. Proposals have recently been made to introduce sex quotas. Under such a system, students from the minority sex (e.g. boys in the nursing line) would receive priority over students from the majority sex in admissions to studies regardless of other qualifications such as gradepoint averages or relevant experience. Within the higher education system, a kind of sex quota is already being used in certain cases: in choosing students for training as pre-school teachers and class teachers, male applicants are accepted in proportion to their share of total applicants, regardless of whether their formal qualifications are lower than those of female applicants, and the same is true for training of nurses.

ADULT EDUCATION

Adult education has a long tradition in Sweden. The first folk high schools came into existence as early as 1868 and adult education associations affiliated with special-interest, trade union or political organisations emerged around the turn of the century. It was, however, during the 1960s that adult education became a major factor in Swedish educational policy, for a number of reasons. The almost explosive growth of the regular school system resulted in a generation gap - the adult population who carried the main economic burden for the country had not received anywhere near the educational benefits now available to young people: as late as 1970, nearly two-thirds of the 30-35 age bracket had only seven years of elementary schooling plus whatever vocational training they had received. It was considered only fair to demand that the older generation, too, should be entitled to more education and adult studies came to be viewed as an essential asset to continued national development, not only in economic terms but also to provide deeper roots for democracy and cultural life.

There are 120 *folk high schools* for adult students. They are owned by county councils, popular movements, other organisations or special associations and their objective is to provide a general civic education, with the special aim of giving students an insight into their responsibilities as human beings and as members of the society. Each school designs its own programme, within the context of *folk high schools* trying to meet educational needs not fulfilled by the regular schools. In 1977, the *Riksdag* approved legislation on the general aims of folk high schools and the structure of increased state subsidies to them. This decision confirmed the local freedom of the schools in their programme making. Full time courses (minimum 34 weeks per year) are now taken by 16,000 adults. Shorter courses of 1-8 weeks are taken by nearly 200,000 adults per year.

There are about ten nationwide *adult education associations* which operate study circles entitled to state grants and which have links with various organisations and popular movements, e.g. blue-collar and white-collar trade union movements, political parties and churches. The associations collaborate with libraries, folk high schools and other cultural institutions. Their study circles include a broad range of subjects, the subjects available varying considerably from one association to another. The study circles are short, usually only 20 hours in evening time, but the number of participants is remarkable, in 1981 near 3 million. *Municipal adult education* aims at providing preparation for continuing studies or an occupation. About 30 per cent of the participants are taking comprehensive school courses, 40 per cent are in upper secondary courses, and 30 per cent are in special vocationally oriented courses. Municipal adult education is provided, in principle, within all of Sweden's municipal districts but regulations requiring a certain minimum number of participants per class result in a concentration of courses in larger population centres. In 1981 municipal adult education had 310,000 participants. *Labour market training* aims at providing vocational education to

people who are unemployed or in danger of losing
their jobs. It is sponsored by the *National Board
of Education* both at 54 training centres and within
the regular educational system. The main emphasis
within labour market training programmes is on
manufacturing occupations. Students in labour
market training programmes receive training
allowances: the number of trainees varies according
to the labour market but in recent years it has been
around 100,000.

One general objective in planning adult
education is to encourage people with little
schooling from their early years, or with special
educational needs, to take part in studies. Every
employee is legally entitled to take a leave of
absence from his or her job to pursue studies. A
person may then be eligible for a special adult
study grant.

SPECIAL TREATMENT IN EDUCATION

A clear shift in the meaning of the term equality
can be noted over the decades. During the 1940s and
1950s, it often meant equality in the sense of
expanded opportunities for everyone regardless of
social class, geographical origins or sex. Open up
educational opportunities for everyone, it was said,
and a levelling process will automatically take
place: longer schooling for everyone, postponement
of tracking into different study programmes,
expanded opportunities to attend post-compulsory
schools and democratisation (broadly defined) of
admissions to higher education were regarded as the
high road to achieving greater social equality.
This optimistic belief in 'equal opportunity' was
subsequently partially repudiated, and there has
been a shift in the definition of social equality
since the 1950s. Equality should not be limited to
equal opportunities to compete: special provisions
and compensatory measures for the disadvantaged are
a necessary part of a school for everyone. Only in
one respect does social equality aim at 'sameness'
among individuals: it tries to provide everyone with
the same general, fundamental civic skills, the
ability to function as active, contributing members
of society, a basic competence in communication,
speaking, reading, writing and mathematics, a basic
orientation in natural and social sciences and -
above all - a belief and confidence in their own
worth and their own opportunities to continue a

life-long learning process. Underlying this partial
change in views on social equality in Sweden is, not
least, experience from the immigration wave of
recent years. Of the country's 8.3 million
inhabitants, one million are now immigrants or
children of immigrants. Special educational
provisions are needed for them and for other
populations in need of support, such as physically
and mentally handicapped students, mentally retarded,
national minority groups, unemployed youth and
students living in isolated areas.

Table 6.1 indicates some of the more important
groups of this kind with some statistics for
1978/79 of number of students (column 2) and forms
of funding special provisions for them (columns 3-5).
The table also shows figures of the costs per
student (column 6). In order to facilitate
comparisions of these special provisions with
provisions for ordinary education, there are also
given corresponding figures for the compulsory
school and the upper secondary school. The largest
group with special provisions are students in
ordinary school who are subject to special education
(row 3): nearly one-fourth of the state grant to the
compulsory school goes to this special education,
the group consisting of slow learners, students with
reading and writing disorders, with socio-emotional
disturbances. This type of special education is
given entirely in ordinary schools, mostly also in
ordinary classes. Special costs exist for mentally
retarded (row 7) and physically handicapped (row 6);
nomad schools for some of the Laplanders (row 4) and
so-called approved schools (row 8) are other
examples of special provisions. As can be seen
from the table, the costs per student (column 6) are
much higher in these special schools than in the
ordinary schools, an exception being the Swedish
schools abroad (row 5) where, however, the figure
indicates only the state subsidiary to these schools
and not the total costs.

A recently created form of special provision is
the state grant for home language teaching of
immigrants (row 9), which seems to be a typical
Swedish provision. As far as international
statistics are available[1], no other country,
including countries with large immigrant populations
such as USA, Britain, France and West Germany, seem
to spend comparable sums for home language training
of immigrants. Other provisions for immigrants are
introductory courses, mainly during the summer
vacation, of young immigrants (row 10) and teaching

154

Table 6.1: Costs for Ordinary Schools and Special Educational Provisions for Special Populations in Sweden during the Fiscal Year 1978/79, costs in US$ (Exchange rate Sw.Kr. 100 = US$ 23). (... means that adequate statistics are missing.)

(1) Educational provisions	(2) Number of students	(3) Funded by State	(4) Munici-pality	(5) Total (in US$ m.)	(6) Cost per student (in US$)
Ordinary education:					
1. Compulsory school (grades 1-9)	1,038,000[2]	2,024.0	2,010.7	4,034.7	3,887
2. Upper secondary school (both general and vocational)	235,000	532.0	473.3	1,005.3	4,278
Special provisions:					
3. Special education in ordinary schools	232,000[3]	(460.0)[6]	...	...	...
4. Nomad schools[1]	190	2.1	–	2.1	11,822
5. Swedish schools abroad	1,100	2.3	–	2.3	1,909[7]
6. Schools for deaf and blind students[1]	830	21.4	–	21.4	25,208
7. Schools for mentally retarded[5]	14,600	63.7	79.0	142.7	...
8. Approved schools (earlier correction schools)[1]	530	34.8	–	34.8	6,657
9. Home language teaching for immigrants	25,000	30.7	30.4	61.1	2,438
10. Introductory courses for young immigrants	...	1.2	...	...	...
11. Auxiliary Swedish for immigrant students	30,000	23.0	22.7	45.7	1,523
12. Vocational courses for unemployed youth	12,000[4]	8.4	...	...	...
13. Economic study assistance in upper schools	...	127.0	–	127.0	...

Notes: (1) Including board and lodging. (2) Including students under special provisions No.3. (3) 14,000 of these in special remedial classes, remaining 218,000 in ordinary classes but with co-ordinated special instruction. (4) 3,000 'year places', which gives 12,000 places in 10-week courses. (5) Has 14,600 students in compulsory school ages, plus 11,500 adults in education programmes. (6) Included in costs for basic school (row 1). (7) Private schools with state subsidies.

Source: Survey by University of Stockholm.

of 'Swedish as a foreign language' to immigrants
(row 11). As can be seen in column 7 the costs per
student in these areas of special provision are
fairly high, considering that they have to be added
to the individual costs for ordinary teaching (rows
1 and 2). Another recent special provision relates
to short courses for unemployed youth under 19 years
of age (row 12), voluntary for the students and paid
for by the state and the municipality (from 19 years
they can get support through the general unemployment
support). The last provision in the table, economic
study assistance in upper secondary school (row 13),
aims at helping students in sparsely populated areas
for travelling and boarding in upper secondary
education. This is one of the largest special
provisions.

The total state school budget was 14.5 billion
Swedish Kronor (= US$ 3.4 billion) in the fiscal
year 1978/79. This includes a number of items not
listed in the table, such as central and regional
administration, in-service training of school
personnel, educational research and development,
building subsidies and adult education. The
proportions of this total school budget relating
specifically to special provisions, are seemingly
low. Yet the provision per single student is of a
relatively high level (column 6). In recent years
there has been growing clamour for increased local
influence over the school system: according to a law
passed by the *Riksdag* in 1976 greater freedom will
be allowed at the local level to shape the school
system within limits defined by central governmental
authorities. The task to uphold the principles of
equality, uniform schooling and equivalent standards
will from now on to a greater extent than before
depend on the local school board and school staff.

A typical feature of the Swedish school system
is the very inconspicuous part played by the *private*
schools. The Education Act of 1962 does not put any
obstacles in the way of private persons or groups
wishing to provide for their own education or that
of their children, but it does oblige municipal
authorities to ensure that all children of school
age can receive a compulsory nine-year education.
Little use is made of the liberty provided for the
establishment of private schools and private
instruction, even though schools of this kind
normally receive state grants on the same terms as
the public school system. The state grants, however,
cover only about half of the total expenditures. The
rest is paid by the local authorities, through local

income taxation, and these authorities - quite
naturally - are not eager to subsidise a system
parallel to their own. This is the main reason why
there are very few private schools in Sweden. About
98 per cent of all students are publicly educated.
It seems fair to say, moreover, that there are no
differences of status or standard between private
and public education.

HIGHER EDUCATION

As a consequence of the reforms of compulsory and
post-compulsory school education the *Riksdag* in 1963
and 1965 outlined new general directions of policy
relating to *Higher Education*. As previously, there
was to be a sector with a limited number of places
for applicants, plus a sector with an unlimited
number of places. The first category mainly
included clearly occupationally oriented study
programmes with relatively high costs per student
and with limited capacity at laboratories and in
educational traineeships. The open sector mainly
included study programmes without laboratory work or
traineeships and with less clear occupational ties.
This meant that there were unlimited admissions to
the university faculties of theology (which nonethe-
less had only a modest number of applications), law,
humanities, social sciences, and natural sciences
(in mathematics and other non-laboratory subjects).
As previously, a specific number of applicants were
to be admitted to the remaining four of the nine
faculties into which the universities had been
re-organised in 1964 - medicine, dentistry,
pharmacology, and technology.
      Planning was generally based on a major
expansion of these restricted-admissions faculties
to meet the country's need for doctors, engineers
and so on, and to achieve a certain balance within
higher education as a whole. The open sector was
designed to provide everyone formally qualified for
higher studies with an opportunity to pursue them,
while meeting the need for clergymen, lawyers,
teachers and similar professions. The expansion of
the restricted-admissions faculties did not, however,
suffice to create a balance in relation to the
wishes of applicants for study programmes and the
country's needs. There was an expansion in various
educational programmes whose admission rules and
other conditions turned them into alternatives to
university studies. They included training of

journalists, social workers, and teachers for
grades 1-6. These 'non-academic post-secondary'
programmes were available at institutions which in
many cases were granted the status of professional
colleges during the 1960s - schools of journalism,
schools of social work and public administration,
teacher-training colleges - without simultaneously
being provided with their own research structure,
except in a few cases. Furthermore, other
educational institutions which recruited people of
university age, such as schools for training nurses
and pre-school teachers, increased their intake
capacity, and the contents and lengths of their
programmes were adapted to new conditions and
demands. They were nevertheless mainly peripheral
to the deliberations on higher education which took
place in the 1950s and 1960s. Colleges in artistic
fields underwent a developmental process completely
independent of the mainstream of higher education
policy.

The three university faculties - humanities,
social sciences and mathematics/natural sciences -
which were the heirs of the old Liberal Arts Faculty
and are indeed nowadays collectively referred to as
liberal arts faculties, nevertheless expanded beyond
all expectations, especially the first two. In 1960,
they had altogether 15,000 students and by 1970 had
grown to more than 70,000. An automatic budgeting
system allotted teachers' salaries for undergraduate
instruction in proportion to the number of students.
Major efforts were undertaken to rent and build
classroom and research facilities and to expand
student housing run by the student unions. Nonethe-
less, in order to limit the growth in student
enrolments to some extent, initiatives were taken to
make higher studies more efficient and to streamline
course contents. An important prerequisite for this
work was that for many years, studies for the
Bachelor of Arts degree at the liberal arts
faculties were nominally supposed to require only
3-3½ years of full-time study. By means of a
parliamentary decision in 1969, studies at these
faculties were organised into well-defined
programmes. The purpose was to achieve greater
coherence and efficiency in undergraduate education
as a whole and to improve conditions for designing
the contents of study programmes in keeping with
national needs. Finally, the training of teachers
in specialised subjects for secondary schools was
reformed so that in addition to their undergraduate
studies at a university, student teachers underwent

a final practical-pedagogical year at a teacher-training college. A college of library sciences was established in 1972 with similar functions for those who aimed at library work.

University reform policies during the 1960s also included an appraisal of postgraduate education, which earlier was organised in two stages: the degree of *licenciat* and the doctoral degree. In 1969, the *Riksdag* decided that postgraduate studies should require 4 years beyond the undergraduate degree at each faculty and should lead without any intermediary stage directly to the doctorate.

HIGHER EDUCATION FOR NEW CATEGORIES OF STUDENTS

For a long time, university policy was based on the requirement of a *studentexamen*, a matriculation certificate, usually at the age of 19, based on tests taken upon completion of secondary studies, for admission to any of the faculties. These regulations were waived in the early 1950s, which made it possible also for certain other groups, in limited numbers, to begin university studies. At this time, access to the so-called free faculties was only ostensibly free since the volume of students at these faculties was in fact regulated by admissions to the then existing upper secondary school (*gymnasium*): in this way, about two-thirds of each age bracket were excluded from university studies in the mid-1960s.

A seed with great explosive power was sowed by the Government in 1965 when it appointed a commission to examine proposals for new rules on admission qualifications and selection of students for higher education. In 1972, when the *Riksdag* approved a decision in principle on the basis of the commission's proposals, the system of an 'integrated' upper secondary school had been implemented, with three-year and four-year study courses equivalent to the traditional *gymnasium* as well as two-year courses which in most cases were directly vocationally oriented. According to the decision of parliament, which after consideration by a further commission was eventually implemented in 1977 along with the remainder of the reform of higher education, each course of study in the upper secondary school (in some cases after supplementary studies in Swedish and English), as well as other studies with equivalent aims and lengths, was held to fulfil the general admission requirement for higher education.

Any person at least 25 years old and with at least
four years of occupational experience, regardless of
the level of schooling achieved, also fulfils the
general admission requirement. On top of this there
are special admission requirements - expressed as
knowledge equivalent to upper secondary school
courses in special subjects - for various programmes
and courses in the higher education system. The new
rules mean that, in principle, every adult is
formally entitled to begin higher studies, and the
expanded system of adult education provides genuine
opportunities for most people to acquire the
previous knowledge required for higher education.
The reform decision also includes the application of
new rules for selecting students for higher
education programmes with limited admissions, rules
which guarantee admission to applicant categories
with different backgrounds, in accordance with
proportional quotas: in addition to school marks,
working experience and other criteria also entitle
a person to qualification points.

The impact of the new admissions are now
becoming obvious. The behaviour patterns of those
applying to higher education adapt themselves to
the prevailing rule system. The median age of those
accepted into high-status study programmes, in
particular, has risen noticeably and student bodies
generally appear to have become more heterogeneous,
even if the reformers' dream of reaching entirely
new categories of students has not been realised to
the extent perhaps hoped for.

The new admission rules for higher education
can, to some extent, be said to be the result of
reform in the upper secondary school and in adult
education. The task assigned to the *1968
Educational Commission (U68)* - to make recommendations on the size, location and structure of post-
secondary education - may be regarded more generally
as a continuation of the intentions behind the
comprehensive school and upper secondary school
reforms of the 1950s and 1960s. (It was not the
student movements of 1968 which caused the U68
commission to begin its work, as is occasionally
claimed in public debate, although obviously these
events influenced both its working methods and the
direction of its proposals to some extent.) The
ideas found in the U68 commission's main report
(1973) have their origins rather in the debates of
the 1960s within the white-collar trade union
confederations. It was stressed in the Government's
instructions to the U68 commission that the

distinction between academic and non-academic post-
secondary education should no longer be applied.
There should be a common fundamental approach to the
activities and planning of the whole post-secondary
field - the higher education system - at the same
time as its various parts should, within this common
approach, preserve and develop their special
character. All undergraduate studies in the higher
education system should prepare a person for a
future occupation, even if this is not intended as
its only aim. All higher education should have
links with research, even if this cannot always take
place in traditional forms through local and
personal links. It is obvious that the intentions
of the reform implied different things for
programmes at the liberal arts faculties of the
universities and for strongly vocationally linked
programmes for training nurses, pre-school teachers,
musicians, and so on.

In 1975, the *Riksdag* approved the principles
behind the new higher education system. Within the
new structure, the faculties - bearers of the
academic nucleus of the previous post-secondary
system - lost their role in under-graduate education.
Instead, undergraduate studies are organised in
study programmes grouped into five vocational
training sectors (technical, administrative-economic-
social welfare, medical-paramedical, teaching, and
cultural-informational), as well as in single
courses.

The recommendations of the U68 commission also
included removing another dividing line which had
played a crucial part in previous higher education
policy - the one between programmes with restricted
admissions and those with open admissions. This
proposal was based on a common fundamental approach
in principle to all higher education: every part of
the system should be planned with reference both to
the educational needs of individuals and to
national needs for trained people. An important
prerequisite of the proposal to limit admissions to
all higher education was that the new rules on
eligibility for admission made it possible in
principle for every adult to apply for higher
education. Resources for higher education had to
be weighed against resources available for other
educational purposes, especially other study
programmes for adults. According to the 1975
decision the intake capacity of every study
programme should be determined not only by
utilising forecasts of the demand for people with

such training; the total capacity of the higher education system should, as far as possible, be based on the demands of individuals. In distributing resources to the various programmes, assessments of future national needs within different occupational categories - in themselves extremely difficult to make - were only one of many factors to be taken into account.

Efforts to create greater diversity in available undergraduate programmes had long been part of higher education policy. They became an even more important part of a policy which aims at reaching new categories of students. The demand for education, which after all determines the number of new students, aims at the courses and study programmes which actually exist and educational needs which are not met by any form of education remain latent. Due to a declining number of new students entering the liberal arts faculties in the early 1970s, the universities had taken initiatives to create new courses to reach new categories of students: centralised committee work led to the establishment of 'technical-vocational higher education' - courses of 1-1½ years duration, intended for skilled workers in the engineering and other industries. Since 1977 when the new organisational system was implemented and responsibility for courses was shifted to the individual institutions of higher education, a large number of new courses have been started, responding to a variety of needs. Development of the contents of study programmes and their structure has thus been a necessary complement to the new admission rules when it comes to reaching new categories of students.

A major issue in preparing the parliamentary decision of 1975 on the structure of higher education was whether open admissions should be retained within part of the system. The U68 commission's recommendations - which, of course, would have meant just the opposite - awakened opposition among students and within the Liberal and Conservative parties, which together with the Centre party formed a new Government in 1976: thus, in the first years of the new higher education system, open admission was granted to a small sector, including, for example, the economics programme. In 1979, however, the *Riksdag* decided that the same framework planning system is to be applied to the whole field of higher education, making it possible to limit the intake capacity of any free study programme or single course.

POLICY FOR SCHOOL-COMMUNITY RELATIONS

In many respects the introduction of the nine-year
comprehensive basic school and the integrated upper
secondary school on a national basis during the
1950s and 1960s had the effect of reinforcing the
position of school in the community: more and more
young people came to spend longer periods of their
lives in school. Efforts to give schools a
practical and communal orientation also led to the
introduction of new subjects such as civics,
technology, economics and domestic science, whilst
the older form of vocational training comprising
specialised apprenticeship training on an in-plant
basis was reduced or abolished. A wider scheme of
vocational education, with interchangeable practical
and theoretical components, was introduced in
schools and compulsory school was made to include
three weeks (subsequently increased to 6-10 weeks)
of practical vocational guidance in trade and
industry, etc., for all students. Facilities were
provided for a considerable prolongation of this
form of vocational guidance in the case of students
suffering from 'school fatigue' and special study
and vocational guidance teachers were appointed in
schools. These teachers also operated within the
Labour Market Administration to arrange vocational
practice opportunities for students from their
schools. Upper secondary schools now have special
*Study and Vocational Guidance Advisers (SYO
Advisers)* to whom students can turn for help and
advice.
      All of these innovations involving wider
contacts between school and the community were aimed
at making school more communally oriented and at
bringing the community into school life. In recent
years there have been signs of another, somewhat
contrary movement: efforts have been made to
re-acquaint students with practical work and to
give them more experience of the community at large
and other persons besides teachers have been given
the opportunity of teaching in schools. The police,
for example, have taken over the task of traffic
education in schools. It has also been said that
teachers should engage in other activities besides
teaching. Local projects whereby students have been
enabled in various ways to participate in work outside school have been organised in many places and

schools have been opened to pre-school children and adults, one such scheme being the serving of lunches to pensioners in school dining rooms.

One sign that students themselves wish to alternate between studies and practical work is to be seen in the big drop-out rate in upper secondary school. About one-fifth of all upper secondary students discontinue their studies for one or more years in favour of practical employment before subsequently returning to resume their studies. Generally speaking, however, experience within the Swedish school system suggests that the introduction of a regular scheme of recurrent education is more dependent on measures in industry and working life than on changes within school itself which are seen as presenting less of a problem.

This discussion and the local projects to which it has given rise cannot be gone into here. A short description will be given, however, of a scheme which has recently been launched by the *National Board of Education*, the *National Labour Market Board*, trade unions and employers' associations, and which is expected to yield more general solutions. Together these authorities and organisations set up a commission which in 1975 presented a report on co-operation between school and working life. On the basis of this report every municipality now has organised a *SSA committee* (SSA stands for *Samarbete Skola-Arbetsliv = Co-operation between School and Working Life*). It is up to these committees to help young people in accordance with local conditions and within the following sectors, having reference to the connection between education, working life and vocational training:

(a)   Mutual information between school and working life and within the education system itself.

(b)   The organisation, forms and content of study and vocational guidance.

(c)   The activities and organisation of the local vocational committees.

(d)   Education on work environment questions and labour market orientation.

(e)   The enumeration and presentation of school requirements in the way of contacts with working life and the ability of trade unions, firms, etc., to cater for those requirements.

(f)   Work allocation and co-ordination - chronologically and in other respects -

with regard to the procurement of work
places for working life orientation in
schools.
(g) Efforts on behalf of premature compulsory
school-leavers, regular compulsory school-
leavers, who do not go on to upper
secondary school or who fail to complete
the course of education/training they
commence in upper secondary after leaving
elementary school.
(h) Measures on behalf of handicapped students.
(i) Extension training facilities for school
personnel and representatives of working
life.
(j) The forms, content and methods of contacts
between school and working life and of the
evaluation of activities.

The members of each committee should be appointed by
the local education authority after nominations have
been received from central employers' associations
concluding collective agreements on behalf of
private employers and, where employee representatives are concerned, from local trade union
organisations, TCO (salaried employees) union
committee and SACO/SR (graduate employees)
associations. Both the public and private sectors
of working life are to be represented. Employers
and employees are to be equally represented. Each
SSA committee is also to include representatives of
the local Employment Service. The local education
authority is to be responsible for the activities of
the SSA committee and for the provision of
secretarial and other clerical facilities. Efforts
are to be made to achieve equal representation of
the sexes in the SSA committees. After two years
of experimental activities with SSA committees in a
restricted number of municipalities such committees
were established in all municipalities from 1977.
Their experiences seem to show that it is necessary,
by means of fairly intense house-to-house calls,
firstly to find the unemployed young persons and
secondly to convince employers to 'create' suitable
jobs for them.

IMPLICIT POLICIES AND DRIVING FORCES

The forces underlying the efforts to reform the
entire school system were of different kinds and
were anchored in different pressure groups. To

simplify the matter slightly, one can group these
forces under three different heads: socio-political
progressivism, pedagogic progressivism, and
administrative progressivism.

Socio-political progressivism, the stronger of
the three, existed above all in some of Sweden's
traditional 'Popular Movements'. The labour
movement, both blue-collar and white-collar, which
embraced the majority of workers and salaried staff
in industry and the administration, had long urged
in its programmes the need for better education for
all. The same was true in other Popular Movements,
including the temperance movement, the sporting and
athletic movement, the women's associations, the
consumer co-operative movement, and the 'Home and
School' movement. Many of these had their own
organisations for popular education, which arranged
courses in Folk High Schools, study circles, and
lectures. The largest was the *Workers' Educational
Association (ABF)*, which as early as 1950 had
around half a million members (the Swedish
population being about 7 million). The main aim of
socio-political progressivism was equality, i.e. to
open the paths to higher education to all, and to
offer everyone the same educational opportunities
regardless of socio-economic status and geographical
domicile: the new school was to be common to all.
And it would not involve - or not until as late as
possible - any division of students into what were
then regarded as better and less desirable paths of
study (known in Sweden at the time as 'theoretical'
and 'practical' studies).

This sort of socio-political progressivism had
long had its champions in Swedish politics, above
all in the *Liberal Party* but it was not until after
the Second World War that it acquired firm anchorage
in the Swedish debate on educational policy. It was
at this point that the *Social Democratic Party* took
it over, incorporating in its general welfare
programme the educational ideology that had
previously been urged mainly by the Popular
Movements. This, then, is an example - and one
among many - of how the Popular Movements have given
rise to political movements. The Social Democratic
Party, which was essentially a workers' party, was
in all essentials supported in its social political
educational progressivism by the Liberal Party
(whose programme had even previously included a
more uniform and improved basic education) and by
the *Agrarian Party*, subsequently renamed the *Centre
Party*, which was concerned above all to see better

education for the rural population.

The aim of socio-political educational progressivism was thus educational equality for different socio-economic groups in the community, which also implied equality of educational opportunities between urban and rural areas. From the very beginning, but ever more clearly over the years, there was also a demand for educational equality between men and women. This socio-political progressivism acquired its focal point in the large-scale *Government Commission on Schools* which the post-war Social Democratic Government set up in 1946, and which presented its proposals for a revised school system in 1948. This was the programme that was adopted, with minor modifications, by Parliament in 1950.

Pedagogic progressivism coincided only in part with the socio-political variety and stemmed from older traditions, partly native to Sweden and partly of foreign origin. Several of Sweden's nineteenth-century pedagogic theoreticians and practitioners can be seen as the forerunners of this progressivism and from around the turn of the century it acquired strong support from the growing discipline of pedagogic psychology, both in Sweden and abroad. The writings of the Americans *John Dewey* and *W. Kilpatrick* had exercised a great influence on pedagogic thinking ('learning by doing'). A corresponding influence was exercised by foreign, mainly German, activity school educationists (such as *O. Glöcher* and what was known as the *Vienna School*). In Sweden, too, several distinguished and influential industrial school educationists emerged in the wake of the new psychology of pedagogics, including *Elsa Köhler* in Gothenburg and *Arvid Gierow* in Helsingborg.

It was the working approach adopted in schools in accordance with the pedagogic progressivism that came in due course, in the 1940s, to influence educational thinking in Sweden. Co-operation between teachers and pupils, interdisciplinary school-work and the co-ordination of theoretical and practical studies emerged as methodological solutions suitable for the new school, favourable examples of this pedagogic progressivism becoming evident in the Folk High Schools and in the study circle activities of the organisations for popular education. What happened in the 1940s - and this provided a basis for the wide-embracing reform in Swedish education from 1950 onwards - was that the two types of progressivism met in a political

education programme. As being the stronger of the
two, socio-political progressivism came to dominate
even from this point. The decisive questions were
organisational, and related to the length of
schooling, the organisation of different lines of
study, and choice of studies. The methodological
solutions, i.e. individualisation, differentiation,
structure of subjects, and size and heterogeneity of
classes, had to be provided within the organisational
frameworks set. The solutions, it was thought, were
after all there, in pedagogic progressivism and its
examples of individualisation and co-operation in
groups.

From around 1950 the task to be tackled was to
fuse these two types of progressivism, an attempt
which, as we shall see, has met with only partial
success: the process is still going on and it
continues to excite debate. Socio-political
progressivism has achieved its breakthrough, in so
far as it has given Sweden a uniform school
structure, extended education for all, and an
educational system in which the organisational
division of students takes place only after the
completion of compulsory schooling, i.e. an entire
new school structure. Educational reform,
ultimately, is always a political question. The
pedagogic element can make its voice heard, but to
have any impact it must acquire a political
anchorage. The main anchorage in the present case
was acquired by socio-political progressivism, with
its considerations of equality, social justice, and
democracy. The pedagogic solutions came in second
place.

This brings us to the third type,
administrative progressivism: this is a phenomenon
which is consequent upon the two former types, is
secondary (in that it presupposes the former two)
and is created by an integration of the first two.
It is precisely this fusion of mutually independent
if not actual conflicting theses that is the
necessary condition for realisation of the reform,
which will only succeed if the third type of
progressivism is achieved. This applies at all
levels in the educational machinery, the local and
the central, and to both teaching and administrative
staff.

The word 'administrative' suggests a static
bureaucracy, an executive realisation of established
principles without innovation. Progressivism needs
its instrumentation, its administrative apparatus.
It is in the applicability of this administrative

apparatus to change that administrative progressivism lies: it would be equally possible to speak
of the 'administration of progressivism'. A new
definition of administration is thus required here:
it is not only what is once and for all given, what
is established, that can and should be administered,
it must also be possible to administer a change.
The characteristic feature of this sort of
progressive administration is in fact that it
presupposes action, decision-making and checks in
a situation in which the premises for change are
often unclear. The administrative apparatus is
usually required to do at least the following three
things:

  (i)   Interpret the aims of educational policy:
        the decisions of the *Riksdag* and
        Government are often generally and
        diffusely formulated. The aims set up
        allow different interpretations and
        different practical arrangements. The
        political arm is often perfectly aware
        of this, and thus leaves the detailed
        interpretation to administrative agencies
        at the central and local levels.
  (ii) Adopt a position when aims conflict:
        political decisions concerning the school
        system and education can be mutually
        incompatible, or at least be comprehended
        as such. It is here the task of the
        administrative apparatus to clarify the
        situation and itself adopt a position
        concerning conflicting aims and arrive at
        mutually compatible interpretations.
  (iii) Set priorities between different aims:
        often political decisions cannot be fully
        implemented with the monetary funds or
        other resources made available in the
        decision. Here, the administrative
        apparatus is required to set priorities,
        to rank, and to set up the timetables and
        resource schedules that the political arm
        refrains from.

     In this way the administration becomes a power
per se: to implement decisions becomes the same as
interpreting decisions, or making subsidiary
decisions. A reform that stops simply at a
political, verbal expression of will is no reform.
Implementation is a responsibility for both the
central and local administration and communication

between these two levels is of major importance.
Local education committees, school managers and
teachers are surrounded by conservative forces and
will often fail to implement what is new unless they
receive support from the central administration.
The administrative responsibility in Sweden for the
experiments with comprehensive schools during 1950-
1962 and the transfer to this new system was
concentrated in the *National Board of Education*.
At the local level new districts were organised,
within which the previous different school boards
for 'parallel' schools in 1958 were replaced by a
unified board. In 1962 school laws and statutes
were made the same for primary and secondary
education, for academic and technical-vocational
education and in 1968 the new teacher training was
started, with different categories of trainees in
the same institutions.

STRATEGIES OF POLICY IMPLEMENTATION

In terms of *political strategy*, for a reform
decided upon actually to be achieved presupposes a
large number of support activities to assist
individual school districts, schools, and groups of
teachers. However, no support inputs will have any
real effect unless they are based on a firm line of
educational policy that has both a central and local
anchorage. Some examples of this will be given
below. The decision in 1950 was worded obscurely,
in a spirit of compromise, and it was interpreted
differently by the devotees and opponents of the
reform out in the schools. The former considered
that the new school had already been decided on
and that the experiments were solely to establish
how best it should be organised. The latter
considered that the decision was conditional and
that the new school would be introduced only if it
proved to function satisfactorily during the period
of experiment. If not, they assumed that the old
lower secondary schools would be retained and even
expanded.
        This dual interpretation of the decision at the
local level was a real problem during the first
experiments. This problem was gradually eliminated
by a series of political decisions. The first of
these was taken in 1953, when the *Riksdag* approved
a programme for the expansion of schools at the
lower secondary level, which said that the increase
in the number of places at lower secondary level was

to be achieved via 'experiments with nine-year comprehensives'. The old separate secondary schools were not allowed to expand. Growth was assigned to the new school, which also received the necessary state grants for this purpose. The second important decision by the *Riksdag* was taken in 1956 when it adopted a clear position as to the future of the new nine-year comprehensive and put an end to all talk that the new school was to be introduced only if experimental activities gave good results. The new nine-year comprehensive, the *Riksdag* decided, had definitely to be introduced and the experiments were designed solely to show how this school could best be organised, above all with regard to the division of students over different lines and courses during the last three years. At the same time, the *Riksdag* decided that experiments should be terminated in 1962, and that during the ten-year period 1962-1972 the new comprehensive school should be introduced in place of the parallel school system throughout the country in accordance with a specific plan.

The third important decision by the *Riksdag* was taken in the following year, 1957. It was then decided that a politically composed state commission should evaluate the experiment, and present detailed proposals concerning the structure of the new school. The most important question arising in this context concerned the diversification of students in grades 7-9, i.e. at the lower secondary level. The *Riksdag* further decided that a comprehensive scientific report on the experiments should be compiled by the NBE in co-operation with the *Institute of Educational Research* at the *Stockholm School of Education*. These three important political decisions by the Swedish *Riksdag* gave not only the central NBE unit charge of experiments, but also the local education authorities, school managers and teachers notice of how activities were to be structured. Decisions on policy were also being continuously made by the local education authorities. In this context it was of great importance that such local decisions corresponded with central decisions, i.e. that an attempt was also made locally to achieve an organisation in which the parallel school system was replaced by a comprehensive school system. Each year during the experimental period 1950-1962, the *Riksdag* discussed how many municipal authorities could be permitted to start experiments with the new comprehensive school, and decided the scale of such activities. During this entire period, more municipalities wanted to

take part in the experiments than could be allowed
to do so for economic and other reasons.

An important decision regarding state grants
was taken by the government in 1955 which made it
possible to have smaller classes at the lower
secondary level. The problem related primarily to
grades 7 and 8, since it was assumed that grade 9
would be divided into separate lines. In grades 7
and 8 the maximum number in a class was thirty-five
(as in the older '*realskola*' and the girls' schools),
if students were divided up according to choice of
subject and if the local education authority
retained students with different choices of optional
extras and alternative courses in the same class the
maximum was lowered to thirty. No division was then
made in the subjects and courses common to all
students. This system of state grants favouring
experiments with mixed-ability classes led an
increasing number of authorities, in the late 1950s,
to apply the comprehensive school principle with
mixed-ability grouping not only in grades 1 to 6 but
also in grades 7 and 8. It has been said that the
mixed-ability classes were bought at the price of
smaller classes.

In terms of *administrative strategy*, the new
school also received the support of special experts
and a network of both personal and other inputs was
created. These inputs included the following:

(1) Instruction courses for teachers, teacher-
training staff and headmasters from
municipalities intending to start
experimental activites.

(2) The *NBE Experimental Division* employed
consultants who visited the experimental
schools, led courses, and assisted in
planning and evaluating experiments.

(3) As activities expanded, the central
consultants spent more and more time at
the NBE and support to the local
authorities and experimental schools was
increasingly detailed to regional
consultants. These were teachers,
teacher-training staff and headmasters who
participated on a part-time basis in the
planning, follow-up and evaluation of
experiments in individual schools.

(4) NBE, through its central project-leaders
and consultants, had held continuous
deliberations with the producers of
teaching aids in Sweden regarding the

production of textbooks and other aids for
students in the experimental schools.

(5) Schools were also assigned special
municipal directors of studies to handle
the pedagogic aspects of the experiment.
As from 1955, their salaries were paid
from state grants.

(6) To assist teachers in the experimental
schools in planning their activities,
special course-planning days were arranged
in each experimental authority at the
beginning of the academic year.

(7) Over the years, a rich flow of official
documents relating to the new school
emerged and pamphlets with articles,
experimental reports, and scientific
studies were also published. The NBE
operated a special publications activity
to support the experiments, including the
periodical *På försök (Experiment)* which
from 1952 was published quarterly and
circulated to all experimental schools.

(8) Since 1962 the NBE has been receiving
special educational research and development grants (R&D), of which about half was
spent to pay for research pursued at
different kinds of university and college
departments. From 1962 to 1976 the grant
grew from 2 million kronor to 36 million
kronor, which was equivalent to about 60
per cent of all the specially ear-marked
funds for educational R&D in Sweden.
After 1976 these funds were reduced.
Parts of the money have gone directly to
the local school authorities.

(9) In 1962 an in-service training organisation under NBE and some regional centres
were established for the introduction of
the new school. Sweden was divided into
six further training regions, each with
its own department for this purpose.
Resources for in-service training were
also assigned to the country's twenty-four
County School Boards. Each county was
given a further training officer, some ten
further training consultants employed on a
half-time basis, and certain funds to
carry on and pay for a regional in-service
training activity. Another significant
factor was that as from 1962 the schools
were given the opportunity to use one of

the school year's forty weeks for the
in-service training of teachers.

There was a great diversity of in-service
training programmes during the 1960s, when Sweden
changed over from the old to the new educational
system although space does not permit the mention
of more than two of these: one ensured that all of
Sweden's primary school teachers and secondary
school mathematics teachers were informed about the
'new mathematics' during the years 1967-1970. Two
vehicles were used to convey this information:
firstly the five study days per year mentioned
above and secondly a series of weekend courses or
holiday courses. Use was made of centrally produced
teaching aids publications giving information about
the New Mathematics. The other further training
programme was designed to let primary school
teachers assume responsibility for the teaching of
English. This project, known as *JET (Junior English
Teaching)*, ran from 1968 to 1972. It absorbed a
comparatively high proportion of the state funds set
aside for the in-service training of teachers.
English was introduced as a compulsory subject
in primary school as from 1962 and by that time the
majority of teachers in the class-teacher stage had
acquired, either from their formal education or from
their enrolment in in-service training programmes,
the competence to teach English in primary school.
However, many teachers, about 12,000, had not been
able to acquire this competence through their own
efforts and through efforts made by the NBE and its
subordinate, regional further training units, as
well as a number of municipalities, numerous in-
service training courses were arranged in English
teaching. In order to take part in such training
the individual primary teacher was given leave of
absence from his or her classroom duties. The
broadcasting media, radio and television, mounted
special courses in English, for which special
extension-course material was also produced. A
special testing procedure was organised through the
NBE. By the end of the in-service training period,
all but about 2,000 teachers had acquired the
competence that these courses were meant to provide.
Personnel training within the school area
during the 1970s has contained two main ingredients
which form integral parts of a rolling reform
activity. The one is staff-team further training
for the primary school; the other is school manager
training for all headmasters in the comprehensive

school.

SOME OUTCOMES

It is not within the scope of this chapter to
examine the outcomes of the overall Swedish
educational policy since 1950, which would be a very
complicated task. Goals are usually not clearly
defined and evaluation criteria are subject to
different interpretations, whilst restricting forces
as well as support activities are susceptible to
differing judgements and other factors. A
comparison of outcomes of education in Sweden today
with outcomes earlier (even before the reform start
in 1950) is for many reasons not meaningful.
Evaluation criteria change. Another type of
evaluation might be more meaningful: are the results
in Sweden - with its egalitarian goal setting -
comparable to the results in countries with a less
egalitarian policy?
     A first and simple question is: 'Does more mean
worse?' An international study of this was made by
Postlethwaite[2], defining the outcomes as the 'total
yield'. Using data from an international study in
1963 in mathematics he defined this 'total yield' as
the mean result per nation of mathematical knowledge
of each individual when he/she leaves the school.
His conclusion was that 'more does *not* mean worse'.
The broadening of recruitment (in Swedish terms:
the democratisation of education with access to
further studies) did not end up in a lower mean
achievement. Another question is: 'Are the
especially talented students hindered in their
progress by being taught together with students of
lower talent?' (This was one of the crucial
questions in the Swedish differentiation debate in
the 1950s.) In one of the *IEA* studies the student
results in Sweden (with a broad recruitment and with
high-ability and low-ability students in the same
setting) was compared with corresponding results in
the Federal Republic of Germany and some other
countries with a fairly strong selection of students
for further education. It was found that (a) the
mean results at the end of secondary schools were
higher in countries with a strong selection of
students (for instance West Germany with only 9 per
cent cohort to the final examination '*Abitur*')
compared to countries with a broad recruitment to
this schooling (USA, Japan, Sweden), but also that
(b) the 'best 1 per cent', the 'best 5 per cent', or

even the 'best 9 per cent' of the entire age cohort
were at least as high in countries with a broad
recruitment as in countries with a restricted
selection[3]. These results support the hypothesis
that the best students are not hindered in their
attempts for high achievements by a broadening of
opportunities. A parallel question is if the
'poorest' are helped by being together with students
in general. Again the IEA studies with international comparisons[4] say that the poorer seem to be
as poor in a 'comprehensive' education structure as
in a selective one. Thus good and poor results seem
to appear at the same amount or frequency in
comprehensive and in selective systems.

All the above concerns the student outcomes on
an individual level. And here the Swedish
egalitarian drive seems to have had little effect.
If we turn to the school level, however, some
results seem to appear. Table 6.2 shows the results
of a comparison in the IEA study[5] of the variation
of schools in literature knowledge in five countries,
England, Finland, Italy, Sweden and the USA for 14-
year-old students. The differences between 'good'
and 'poor' schools varied in these countries. All
five countries have both high-achieving and low-
achieving students (middle column, indicating the
between-student variance). The left-hand column is
an estimation of how schools vary in mean results.
High figures here tell that there is a great
difference between 'good' and 'poor' schools. Here
Sweden proves to have the lowest between-school
variance, thus, in this respect, Swedish schools are
more alike than schools in the other four countries.
In the right-hand column we can see how the between-
school variance is related to the total variance.
Here the Swedish figure is the lowest (15 per cent),
which means that Sweden is the most homogeneous
country in this respect.

There is certainly room for discussion on
whether this is good or bad for Sweden: official
Swedish policy says that students should have the
same opportunity to get a good education, regardless
of socio-economic status and geographical location
and in respect of this goal the result must be seen
as good. Sweden has roughly the same proportion of
'good' and 'bad' students as the other four
countries, but these are not concentrated in
specific schools to as great an extent as in the
other four countries.

Rather similarly, there is hardly any
difference in prestige or status between different

Table 6.2: Literature Knowledge According to IEA, 14-year-old Students

Country	Standard deviation		Between-school variance in percentage of total variance
	Schools	Students	
England	2.1	4.1	26
Finland	1.7	3.4	25
Italy	1.8	3.2	31
Sweden	1.5	3.8	15
USA	2.1	4.2	25

Source: A.C. Purves, *Literature Education in Ten Countries, Stockholm, 1973, pp.292-4.*

universities and colleges with the same kind of higher education. The integration of academic, general and technical-vocational education in the upper secondary school seems to have had a corresponding effect of levelling the attractiveness of different study programmes so that the traditionally pre-university study areas of specialisation are no longer the most attractive. Some vocational specialisms, for instance the electro-technical and the nursing specialisms, now get students with higher qualifications from the compulsory school than students to the science, humanistic or social study specialisms. Classes in the science specialism are now hard to fill, while classes in the agrarian-forestry specialism have twice as many applicants as there are places. Obviously there are other reasons for this 'equalisation' than an egalitarian school policy, such as job opportunities after school.

The same trends are now seen also in higher education. It is now more difficult, in terms of entrance qualifications, to become a nurse or nurse assistant than to become a student of science at the university and it is more difficult to get a place in primary teacher training than to get a place in the school of law, etc. This all means that the old prestige pattern is being changed just as at the same time conditions of work, salaries, job security, vacations, pensions, etc., are rapidly changing.

This all means that the equalisation trend in education has some effects, even if achievement of the egalitarian goal in a broader sense certainly depends on a large number of other societal circumstances than education.

CONTRACTION POLICIES

One experience of the development of a new policy after 1950 is quite obvious: the school has become expensive. The following table relating to costs for compulsory, upper secondary and adult education, including costs for school administration, indicates that the school expenditures in 1980 were six times as high as in 1950, when the reform activities started. This relates partly to the increased number of students, but also expenditures per student and year were four times as high in 1980 as in 1950 (all in constant prices). Over the same years the general standard of living increased, but not by as much as the costs for education (GNP, middle column). The columns to the right show how the costs were shared between the state and the municipalities, with the latter's share eventually overtaking that of the former.

Table 6.3: Expenditures on Schools in Sweden, 1950/51 to 1982/83, in constant prices (1950/51=100)

School year	Expenditures		Gross National Product	Expenditures in percentage of Gross National Product		
	Total	Per pupil		State	Munici- pality	Total
1950/51	100	100	100	1.3	1.0	2.3
1954/55	147	121	112	1.7	1.4	3.6
1958/59	185	140	124	2.0	1.6	3.6
1962/63	226	173	148	2.0	1.6	3.6
1966/67	301	227	180	2.5	1.7	4.2
1970/71	352	250	213	3.0	2.0	5.0
1974/75	432	278	238	2.8	2.5	5.3
1978/79	562	361	236	3.5	3.2	6.7
1979/80	640	411	242	3.6	3.6	7.2
1982/83	631	401	241	2.8	3.0	5.8

Source: National Board of Education: Budget for respective years.

In Table 6.4 we see that the Swedish costs for schools seem to be the highest in the western industrialised world. Some comparable countries are missing from the table: Australia, Canada, Switzerland and the United States. According to corresponding statistics from 1973 none of these countries spent as large a proportion of GNP as Sweden. Thus it seems likely that Sweden has the most expensive national school system of the world.

Table 6.4: Part of Gross National Product (GNP) spent by OECD Countries on Schools and Higher Education. Deviation in percentage from average figures ('Typical country').

Country	Percentage of GNP for education			Deviation in percentage from 'Typical country'		
	School	Higher education	Total	School	Higher education	Total
Austria	3.72	0.79	4.51	-10	-16	-9
Belgium	4.88	1.11	5.98	18	17	21
Denmark	4.60	1.19	5.78	11	25	17
Finland	5.24	0.86	6.10	27	-9	24
France	2.78	0.54	3.32	-33	-42	-33
Great Britain	4.53	1.45	5.98	10	53	21
Italy	3.60	0.57	4.16	-13	-40	-16
Japan	3.40	0.50	3.90	-18	-47	-21
Netherlands	4.70	2.43	7.13	14	156	45
New Zealand	3.70	1.29	4.99	-11	36	1
Norway	5.18	0.96	6.15	25	2	25
Sweden	6.22	1.37	7.58	50	44	54
West Germany	2.77	0.59	3.36	-33	-38	-32
'Typical country'	4.14	0.95	4.93	-	-	-

Source: *Educational Expenditures in the 1970s. World Bank paper, 22 September 1981, by M. Zymelman, Education Department, CPS Staff (Draft).*

Why did it become so expensive? An analysis of costs shows that the capital costs (school building, teacher training) are not especially high in Sweden. But the running costs are. And here the major part

comes on the staff salaries. Again, salaries per
teacher are not especially high, but the number of
teachers is high. The student/teacher ratio is
only 13. Classes are not especially small, but
there are many extra resource teachers for special
provisions to handicapped, to pupils with special
problems, to immigrants, etc. And classes are split
up into groups in foreign languages and mathematics
in order to facilitate teaching of the heterogeneous
student population. The mixed-ability grouping has
made the school expensive. This is the price for
the egalitarian policy, the guiding principle all
since 1950. An important event in 1976 was that the
long Social Democrat period of government was broken.
A coalition of the Conservative, Liberal and Centre
parties took over. After some subsequent internal
changes of this government the Social Democrats were
back again in late 1982.

Due to an overall economic recession in the
period after 1976, and especially after 1980, there
has been a period of contraction also for schools
and higher education. Costs for these cannot
increase as before. Nor even can they remain on a
constant level. They have to be reduced. In this
ambition there is no real difference between the
political parties. The need for saving of money is
stressed by the Social Democrats as well as by the
other political parties.

The trend towards a reduction of costs did not
show up until 1980/81. From this year the state
grants were reduced. To keep the standard the local
authorities have been forced to increase their own
expenditures. There are so far no obvious signs of
changes in teaching and school standards in general
due to this contraction. They might appear in years
to come. Everybody seems to be aware of the dilemma
of saving money in public education. There are at
least three risks with this: (1) it is easier to
save money in the teaching of low-achieving students
than for students in general, (2) expenditures per
student are larger in small schools than in big
schools, therefore it is tempting to merge
small schools into bigger ones in sparsely populated
areas in the countryside, and (3) technical-
vocational training is more expensive per student
than general education, which makes the former type
more susceptible for saving. A reduction of costs
for schooling thus runs the risk of striking those,
who in policy of equality were given priority. This
way of saving might create 'inequality' or at least
stop a movement towards equality. Evidently there

is a need for new models of educational development, models where improvements not automatically presuppose more money, models where available resources are used in a new way. The future will show if and how this can be achieved.

NOTES

1. A.M. Fris, *Policies for Minority Education. A Comparative Study of Britain and Sweden* (Studies in Comparative and International Education, No.7, Institute of International Education, University of Stockholm, 1982).
2. N. Postlethwaite, *School Organization and Student Achievement* (Almqvist & Wiksell, Stockholm, 1967).
3. T. Husén, *Svensk skola i internationell belysning, I. Naturorienterande ämnen* (Swedish School in International Comparison. I. Science) (Almqvist & Wiksell, Stockholm, 1973).
4. A.C. Purves, *Literature Education in Ten Countries*, International Association for the Evaluation of Educational Achievement (Almqvist & Wiksell, Stockholm, 1973).
5. Purves, *op. cit.*

OTHER USEFUL REFERENCES

Bergendal, G. (1978), *Reflections on Educational Policy from an Employment Perspective - With Particular Reference to Admission to Post-secondary Education*, OECD, Paris (SME/ET/78. 41).
Bierschenk, B. (1967), *Theorie und Praxis der Oberstufe der Schwedischen Grundschule*, Schroedel, Hannover.
Dahllöf, U. (1970), *Svenska skolreformer under 25 år* (Swedish school reforms during 25 years), Gothenburg.
Gurgdies, E. (1975), *Schulreform und Chansengleichheit. Ergebnisse der schwedischen Gesamtschulreformen*, Verlag J.W.H. Dietz, Berlin.
Hörner, H. (1970), *Demokratisierung der Schule in Schweden*, Weinheim, Berlin; Beltz, Basel.
Husén, T. and Boalt, G. (1968), *Educational Research and Educational Change*, Almqvist & Wiksell, Stockholm.
Jüttner, E. (1970), *Der Kampf un die schwedische Schulreform*, Diss, Berlin.

Marklund, S. (1980), *The Democratization of
    Education in Sweden. A UNESCO Case Study*,
    Studies in Comparative and International
    Education, No.2, Institute of International
    Education, University of Stockholm.
Marklund, S. and Bergendal, G. (1979), *Trends in
    Swedish Educational Policy*, The Swedish
    Institute, Stockholm.
Marklund, S. and Söderberg, P. (1967), *The Swedish
    Comprehensive School*, Longmans, London.
Orring, J. (1968), *School in Sweden*, SO-förlaget,
    Stockholm.
Paulston, R.G. (1966), 'The Swedish Comprehensive
    School Reform', *Comparative Education Review*,
    10, 1, New York.
Sjöstrand, W. (1970), *Frihet och jämlikhet. Två
    grundbegrepp inom 60-talets svenska pedagogik*
    (Liberty and equality. Two basic concepts in
    Swedish education in the 1960s), Gebers,
    Uppsala.
Skolöverstyrelsen, *Anslagsäskanden för åren 1950/51
    - 1980/81* (National Board of Education, Budget
    Plans for 1950/51 - 1980/81).
—— *Läroplan för grundskolan 1962, 1969 och 1980*
    (Central Curriculum for the Basic School 1962,
    1969 and 1980), Stockholm.
—— *Läroplan för gymnasieskolan 1970* (Central
    Curriculum for the Upper secondary school
    1970), Stockholm.
Statistiska Centralbyrån, *Statistisk Årsbok*, åren
    1950-1980 (Statistical Yearbook of Sweden,
    Years 1950-1980), Stockholm.
Wiesner, K. (1974), *Bildungspolitik und Gesellschaft
    in Schweden. Darstellt unter besonerere
    Berücksichtigung der Einführung der Gymnasie-
    schule als Berufsgrundschule*, Jobst Schultze,
    Hamburg.

Seven

THE UNITED KINGDOM

Marten Shipman

The legal basis of the Education service in England and Wales remains the 1944 Education Act. This was implemented as part of the post-1945 organisation of public services into the Welfare State. The thinking behind the legislation that reorganised social welfare had been spelled out in the *Beveridge Report* published in 1942. This was concerned with overcoming the 'evil giants' of Want, Disease, Ignorance, Squalor and Idleness specified by Beveridge[1].

The major principle that was incorporated into the public services that implemented the Beveridge Report in the late 1940s was universalism. The social services were to involve everyone. All should contribute to their cost. All should benefit. This was seen not only as efficient, but a way to achieving social justice and a sense of community. This principle was to remain without serious political challenge for over twenty years from 1945, in the Education service as elsewhere. The assumption that the provision of universal public services would eliminate poverty, promote equality and reinforce social coherence dominated the political centre of politics in the United Kingdom in the formative period of the welfare state including the education service after 1944.

If it is easy to detect the dominant thinking behind social policy in the post-war UK, it is nevertheless difficult to be precise about either the way that policy was implemented within the Education service, or to identify the agents responsible. The service is often described as a 'partnership' of central and local government, and teacher unions. All three exert pressure for educational change. Teachers not only affect change through their representatives on national

committees and in informal consultations, but
develop the curriculum within their own schools.
Another popular description of the service is 'a
national system, locally administered'. *Local
Education Authorities* (LEA) have responsibility
for the day-to-day running of the service. They
appoint the teachers, resource the schools and have
responsibility for the curriculum and its teaching.
There are 104 LEAs and while their financial
positions are limited in their variety by central
government grants taking local needs and resources
into account, they have pursued contrasting
educational policies. Indeed, many of the major
developments in post-war education in the UK have
been pioneered within LEAs such as the West
Riding of Yorkshire, Leicestershire, Inner London
and Coventry and through the leadership of their
chief education officers such as Clegg, Mason,
Briault and Aitken.

THE DEVELOPMENT OF EDUCATIONAL POLICY

The 1944 Education Act strengthened the role of
central government. Part 1, Section 1 (1) of the
Act defines the duties of the Secretary of State
for Education as '...to promote the education of
the people of England and Wales... and to secure
the effective execution by local authorities under
his control and direction...of national policies
for providing an education service in every area'.
Yet in contrast to many European countries, the
direct controls exercised by the *Department of
Education and Science* (DES) are restricted to
approving building programmes by LEA and determining
the numbers of teachers in training. There is no
control over the appointment of teachers or over
what they teach. Indeed, the strongest control is
indirect, through the provision by central
government of over half the money spent by local
authorities where Education is the most expensive
service. Thus in contrast to the USA where
central government provides under 10 per cent of
funds for education, financial pressure from the
centre can, in the long term, force changes at the
local level.
    This diffused distribution of power in the
Education service in the UK is taken even further
within the universities where central government
provides the money, but its allocation between the
institutions is determined by an autonomous
organisation of academics, the *University Grants*

Committee. Within higher education this has
enabled universities to develop independently. But
this independent local action also occurs within
further education and the schools maintained by LEAs.
Up to 1960 there was little disagreement over policy
at any level. There had been only slow development
in the 1920s and 1930s, and the 1939-1945 war left
a backlog of building and teacher recruitment.
This and the need to implement the 1944 Education
Act, particularly secondary education for all, was
the major concern between 1945 and 1960.

   At the end of this immediate post-war period
around 1960 the structure of a universal education
in three stages was visible. All children completed
both primary and secondary schooling. Under the
immediate post-1945 Labour government three kinds
of secondary school had been established so that
about a quarter of all children went at 11 years to
selective grammar schools and the rest to
unselective secondary modern or to the few
technical schools. In 1960 there were only 130
comprehensive secondary schools.

   The gap in the provision of three stages of
education for all was in further and higher
education. In 1960 only 40 per cent of children
aged 14 to 17 were in full-time education in the UK
compared with 94 per cent in the USA. Only 6.5
per cent entered higher education compared with
37 per cent in North America. For working-class
children the contrast was even greater, only 2
per cent entering higher education in the UK
compared with 20 per cent in the USA. Proposals in
the 1944 Act for county colleges to cater for those
leaving secondary schools had not been implemented
and the expansion of full-time public sector
further education had been slow.

   There were three important policy aspects in
this immediate post-1945 development of Education.
First, there was little disagreement between the
major political parties over the direction of
change. The Labour Party was in favour of
secondary school reorganisation to abolish
selection and a move to comprehensive schooling.
But up to 1960 it moved slowly to win support for
reorganisation. There was still strong opposition
to the ending of grammar schools within the Party.
The Conservative Party supported this gradualist
policy and as long as the rate of reorganisation
remained slow there was a degree of consensus.

   The second aspect was the reluctance of the
Department of Education and Science to plan the

service beyond ensuring that the building programme
was adequate. This became a public issue in 1975
when OECD published a critical analysis of the
planning role of the DES[2]. The Expenditure
Committee of the House of Commons investigated this
planning role of the DES in the following year[3].
In evidence, Sir William Pile the Permanent
Secretary at the Department maintained that
planning did not go beyond '...the sheer mechanical
business of calculating costs and scale of things.'
Planning was largely restricted to ensuring that
the buildings, the resources and the teachers were
available. The system was seen to depend on
policies generated from a variety of sources and
through all those involved acting sensibly. This
absence of a strong central government planning
role meant that policies concerning the content
of education and its relation to economy and society
were left to LEAs and the teachers. By 1960
the teacher unions had assumed a right to determine
the curriculum and in 1963 were successful in
stopping the DES from setting up a committee to
study curriculum matters[4]. Educational policy was
not only diffused. By 1960 that diffusion had been
accepted, despite the wording of the 1944 Act
which suggested a powerful role for central
government.

The third aspect was the complexity of the
checks and balances in the service. This not
only involved government and teachers. Secondary
school curricula continued to be dominated by
public examinations and by 1960 these were spreading
into non-selective secondary schools. Further
education was restricted by employment practices
and trade union insistence on long apprenticeships.
The universalist potential of the maintained system
was itself constrained by the link between the
independent schools and the universities. This
diffusion of power meant that there was no single
dominant source from which change could be
organised. Neither was there the appeal to a
constitution that could have involved the law to
exert leverage on the Education service.

The most remarkable example of this difficulty
in pinpointing the sources of power in Education in
the UK is the control of the curriculum. The 1944
Act seems to place responsibility with the
Secretary of State. Yet Crosland and Boyle, both
ex-Secretaries of State for Education, denied that
it lay with them[5]. Indeed, if a question was
asked about the curriculum of a school in the House

of Commons, the answer would be that this was not
the concern of the Minister. The responsibility
for day-to-day running of the schools lay with LEAs.
Yet no LEA in 1960 would have maintained that they
determined the curriculum of the schools for which
they were responsible. This responsibility was
placed with school governors. Yet these too would
have denied that it was their duty, for they
expected the headteacher and his or her staff to
decide what was to be taught. Up to 1960 this and
other issues about who controlled Education could
remain unresolved given the agreement over the
direction of the gradual changes in the service as
the 1944 Act was implemented. But once that
agreement came to an end, these questions of control
had to be answered.

By the end of the 1970s the DES was playing a
more active role in setting the agenda for the
debate over educational policies among the other
partners. That debate was launched in 1976 by
the then Labour Prime Minister, James Callaghan.
He had previously received a report, since known
as the 'Yellow Book', prepared within the DES
which was critical of developments in maintained
schools. The Great Debate that followed was
organised and documented by the DES and it has been
followed by many official publications on the
curriculum, the organisation of schools and on
accountability. This central government activity
has kept the debate going. Slater and Tapper[6] see
this as an attempt by the DES to use the current
economic crisis to justify greater central government intervention, relegate the other 'partners'
and monopolise policy-making.

This view of the DES as a bureaucracy, actively
legitimating its position as policy-maker, is
plausible given the flow of publications from the
DES and the demands for responses from LEAs.
There is now a *Departmental Planning Organization*
and an *Assessment of Performance Unit*. But this
view assumes a degree of independence for the DES
as a government department, particularly from the
Treasury, and a coherence in its planning that is
difficult to detect in practice. Kogan, himself
an ex-DES official, points out that recent policies
hardly smack of a bureaucratic dynamic and that
ministers are playing a lively part in initiating
policies[7]. Certainly DES agencies such as the
Assessment of Performance Unit show few symptoms
of possessing a unified bureaucratic ideology.
The more active planning role seems to result from

the prodding of the Secretaries of State for
Education rather than from educational bureaucrats
who have cornered the market in ideas. Nevertheless,
this increased central government role in
determining the direction of change in areas of
Education which had, before 1970, been assumed to
be the preserve of LEAs and the teachers is the
political context of the account of recent policy
developments which follow.

POLICY AT THE PRIMARY SCHOOL LEVEL

The publication of the report of the Plowden
Committee *'Children and their Primary Schools'*[8] and
its endorsement by central government seemed to
have defined a clear policy for primary schools.
Indeed the word 'Plowden' came to sum-up a child-
centred, progressive schooling, where children
were allowed to develop free of the constraints
of specialised, academic curriculum or didactic
teaching. The developments in schools were not
planned centrally. They were mostly the result of
initiatives by individual school staffs, often
under the influence of innovative local authority
advisors. These were grassroots developments
brought together in official reports and endorsed
by government.
     Looking back at the Plowden Committee it is
clear that it gave an impression of widespread
innovation that was very restricted in practice.
Thus Simon[9] looking at the evidence across the 1970s
concluded that only one major change had taken
place, the ending of streaming and its replacement
in primary schools by mixed ability groups. The
open-planned, child-centred, progressive school
remained a rarity. This was a significant
commentary on difficulties in determining the
influences on policy in education in the UK.
Following the Plowden Report, local authority
advisors and *Her Majestys Inspectors* (HMI) from the
DES promoted the progressive primary school image.
Teacher training, the publishing industry and
academics reinforced the progressive pressure.
Innovation seemed to be accelerating to the
extent of creating a panic and a backlash in the
form of five *Black Papers*[10] strongly critical of
the swing to the 'Plowden' style. Yet in this one
area where central and local government, the
teacher trainers and the academics seemed to be in
agreement, change in the desired direction turned
out to be restricted. Teachers may have initiated

the progressive movement in a few schools, but
they seemed to have resisted any rapid spread.

An illustration of how the checks on innovation
worked came in 1976 with the publication of the
Auld Report on the William Tyndale Junior and
Infants Schools[11]. The headteacher and some of the
staff of this school had introduced a radical
curriculum in the early 1970s. Inner London had
falling primary school rolls by this time and
parents began to remove their children from the
junior school to other schools which had room.
Some teachers in the school opposed the headteacher.
The managers of the school tried to intervene. The
local authority inspectors took over the school and
the staff were suspended. Finally the Inner
London Education Authority set up an enquiry and,
after receiving its report, dismissed the
headteacher and his deputy, and moved other
teachers from the school. In this case the reforms
introduced were considered to be too radical and
too badly organised by the LEA. They upset
parents and the managers of the school. The case
helps to explain why progressive primary schooling
was restricted through the checks that were brought
to bear on any innovative staff. They could argue
that they were only carrying through policies
recommended in the Plowden Report and endorsed by
DES and LEAs. But the speed of change can not be
fast and the anxieties of parents, inspectors,
administrators and eventually politicians can act
as brakes on radical policies.

By the late 1970s official policies for
primary schooling had changed. Her Majesty's
Inspectors surveyed primary schools and reported in
1978[12]. The emphasis in this report was on the
basic skill subjects, on the need to pay attention
to the able child, for the matching of curriculum
to the ability of the children, to the need for
organisation in classroom and for good management
in schools. In 1978 the DES announced the terms
of reference for the Assessment of Performance
Unit to assess standards in schools nationally[13].
Local Education Authorities were also increasing
their testing and inspecting to ensure that
standards were not falling. The Prime Minister
had expressed his concern about the direction of
change in the schools in 1976 and the DES published
a consultative document in 1977 that was to be
the first of many official documents on schooling
and the curriculum[14].

This activity by the DES at the end of the

1970s is a recurring theme in the remainder of this
account.   There is no question about the intention
of central government under both Labour and
Conservative governments to play a more positive
role in policy-making.   This coincided with
financial constraints as the economy faltered and
with falling rolls in schools.   Much of this
activity was directed at primary schools.   By the
end of the 1970s the ending of secondary selection
had enabled LEAs to abandon the tests at eleven
years that sorted children out for the grammar
schools.   But this had also removed the one set of
indicators, however inadequate, on the performance
of primary schools.   The Black Papers, the doubts
expressed by the Prime Minister, the concern over
the William Tyndale case, an emphasis on the need
for structure, standards and evaluation in teacher
training and critical publications on primary
schooling, were symptoms of a concern that change,
however modest, had not been unquestionably and
universally beneficial.   The rapid change in policy
was clear.   The increased role of central government
was also apparent.   But there was no official
pronouncement or legislation spelling out this
policy.   Change came throughout the service, among
all the partners and it seemed to be supported by
parents.   But it is still conjecture when the
balance of the influences on policy are analysed.

POLICY AT THE SECONDARY SCHOOL LEVEL

Most of the modest changes in primary schooling
came from initiatives within the schools.   In the
secondary sector there were both increasing
external pressures for change and powerful internal
conservative forces.   The former were concentrated
on the 11 to 16 curriculum once all children went
through secondary school.   The outstanding change
across the twenty years from 1960 was that
comprehensive schooling was extended to all but a
few areas.   Selection and selective schools were
largely abolished.   But there was also increasing
concern with the content of education, particularly
as unemployment among young people increased in the
late 1970s.   The curriculum changed slowly, but at
the end of the period, even in comprehensive
schools, looked very similar to that of the old
selective secondary schools prior to the
reorganisation.   That conservatism seems to have
resulted from two powerful constraints on the
schools, the reluctance of parents to see their

children penalised in the labour market by not being able to take public examinations in traditional subjects, and the failure to move forward on examination reform either at 16 or 18 years.

The crucial breakthrough in the movement towards comprehensive secondary schooling came in 1965 when in *Circular 10/65* the then Labour Minister of Education and Science asked all LEAs to submit plans for reorganisation on comprehensive lines. The Labour party had been re-elected in 1964 and at that point decided to implement its policy of ending selection for secondary schooling, spelling out that there would be no funds for secondary school building that was not for comprehensive reorganis- ation. The financial control held by central government over LEAs was used to ensure that in time selective secondary schools would be reorganised on comprehensive lines. In 1965, 8.6 per cent of the secondary school population was in comprehensive schools. Ten years later this was well over 50 per cent and at intake few children were receiving selective schooling in the maintained sector. By the end of the 1970s there were over 3,000 comprehensive schools and only 253 grammar schools.

Labour Party policy had been consistent, but implementation had been slow. Many party leaders saw the selective grammar schools in which they received their education as the path to upward mobility for the working class. They had come up that way and they were reluctant to see this opportunity suddenly replaced by universal comprehensive schooling where the effects on the chances of the poor were unknown. But by the mid-1960s the Labour Party was ready to act and had partially succeeded in changing the public attitude towards comprehensive schools. Even more important, there had been a strong reaction against the technical reliability of the selection tests, their effect on the primary school curriculum and their impact on children. The negative reasons for the policy shift may have been stronger than the positive attractions of comprehensive schooling. But by the 1970s there was only isolated resistance among LEAs, Labour and Conservative to ending selection.

The response of LEAs to comprehensive reorganisation was varied. Some areas such as inner London and Coventry had already led the way. Some of these were Conservative local governments. In

different areas, different parties within the
Education service provided the major thrust[15].
While Labour governments pressed hard for
reorganisation from 1965, Conservative governments,
while not actively discouraging, allowed LEAs to
move slowly. Some LEAs had reorganised in the
1960s. At the start of the 1980s, one LEA, Kingston
upon Thames, still had no comprehensive schools.
The teacher unions took different positions, but the
largest union, the National Union of Teachers was
actively pressing for comprehensive schools from the
mid-1960s. Parents began to take a greater interest
in schooling as comprehensive reorganisation spread
and their own children were affected. The more
dramatic cases resulted in parents using the law to
try to stop reorganisation. But the 1960s were also
a period when parental pressure groups were
proliferating and many of these were pressing for
universal comprehensive schooling. As in many
European countries the ending of selective
secondary schooling created increased parental
concern, and education was becoming a political
issue after years when all parties were mainly in
agreement.

By the late 1970s attention was switching
from reorganisation to the curriculum of secondary
schools. First, the new comprehensive schools
often streamed children so that selection was
practised within rather than between schools.
Second, the grip of public examinations continued
despite many attempts to reform at both 16 and 18
years. These two factors focused attention on
the curriculum for the majority who would not go
on to higher education. The third factor was the
worry over poor economic performance and the rise
in unemployment after the oil crisis in the
early 1970s. These general issues were heightened
by the specific problems for the schools arising
from the low attainment of minority groups such as
Blacks and children from the unskilled working
class, and of girls, particularly in the inner
cities.

The coincidence of major reorganisation,
concern about the curriculum and falling school
rolls brought Education into the political limelight
in the mid-1970s. But while both major political
parties sensed the public concern and the
political mileage, their policies divided after the
long post-1945 period of consensus. While the
Great Debate on Education was launched by a Labour
administration, and the DES and particularly Her

Majesty's Inspectorate, began to play a more
positive part in discussion over the curriculum,
it was the Conservative government elected in 1979
that broke the agreement over the general direction
of change, particularly in secondary schooling.
The presence of Rhodes Boyson, a consistent
critic of progressive schooling, in government, at
the DES, was a significant indicator of the changed
political climate for education.

The most striking policy shift was to re-
introduce a measure of selection through the
provision of assisted places in independent schools.
This was defended as promoting the chances of the
able poor, particularly in inner cities.
Undoubtedly these able children were penalised
academically in being a small minority in
comprehensive schools that could not sustain an
academic curriculum. But these were just the
schools that were struggling, and by removing even
a few able children, the government was seen as
undermining comprehensive schooling before it had
time to settle down. This was particularly
important with the prospect of falling rolls
causing small sixth forms to decrease to non-viable
levels.

The most sustained pressure from central
government came as a flow of publications, surveys,
assessments and policy statements on the curriculum
and standards of attainment. These tended to be
critical of mixed ability grouping, integration
across subjects, non-specialist teachers and the
introduction of the social sciences into schools.
The government pressed for a national consensus
on the curriculum in the national interest. It
also pressed for more attention to be paid to
the relation between school and work. All these
influences reinforced the constraints over the
teachers' freedom to innovate. This remained
constrained by public examinations. The definition
of the curriculum by the DES further tightened the
grip on curriculum development. In 1982 the Schools
Council, responsible for curriculum development,
was reorganised and its resources cut. Finally,
the Education Act of 1980 forced schools and LEAs
to give parents more information on the schools and
their curriculum. Central government was playing
a more positive and largely conservative role. It
was also altering the balance of influence between
the 'partners'.

The ability of LEAs and the teaching profession
to oppose central government policies was

restricted by economic stringency. The central government cut the amount of money available to the Education service as school rolls fell. The steady rise in public expenditure was reversed and the amount of local authority expenditure paid for by central government grant was cut. LEAs and teachers had to concentrate on running the existing service with reduced funds. Saving jobs took first priority for the teacher unions. In the early 1960s the DES was stopped from setting up a group to discuss the school curriculum by a combination of teacher union and LEA opposition. In the 1980s the DES was pressing hard for a core curriculum, was regularly testing through the Assessment of Performance Unit and had cut back funds from independent innovating agencies such as the Schools Council.

POLICY IN FURTHER AND HIGHER EDUCATION

It is necessary to separate the independent, university sector of higher education from the maintained further education sector in the UK. The forty-six universities in the UK receive their money largely from central government, but through the University Grants Committee, which is a body of academics allocating the sum received to the various universities. Most of the remaining institutions receive their money direct from local authorities and are hence under their financial control. There is however a further division within the maintained sector. The Polytechnics, Colleges of Education and Colleges or Institutes of Higher Education are usually described as providing higher education, while the 800 other Further Education Colleges offering full and part-time courses mainly at sub-degree level are labelled further education. There are in addition some 6,500 evening institutes.
    Burgess[16] has described this university tradition in the UK as follows.

> The autonomous tradition is aloof, academic, conservative and exclusive. People and institutions acting in this tradition and with this view of their purpose think it right to hold themselves apart, ready if necessary to resist the demands of society, the whims of government, the fashions of public opinion, the importunities of actual or potential students.

To Burgess the emphasis on preserving, extending and disseminating knowledge in the universities necessitates exclusiveness. Only those deemed to be capable of benefiting are accepted. The intellectual order is protected, ordered and nurtured. Furthermore, autonomy allows the universities to remain as centres for independent criticism of the state and of the economic and political order. The exclusiveness of the universities has served as a brake on rapid expansion. In the maintained sector of higher education, the service institutions such as Polytechnics are organised to be responsive to vocational, professional, economic and social pressures. But the established prestige of the universities has led to many Polytechnics and Institutes of Higher Education trying to move in the academic direction and dropping their lower level service courses. In the face of this supply-side resistance to an expanded higher education serving a comprehensive secondary school system, expansion has been slow. Furthermore, on the demand side there has been neither sustained political action for expansion, nor the pressure groups that marked public concern for reform in the school sector. The results can be seen in Table 7.1:

Table 7.1: Percentage Enrolment of Students by Selected Age Groups: EEC 1970/1 - 1977/78

| | 1970/1 | | 1977/8 | |
	17-18 yrs	20-21 yrs	17-18 yrs	20-21 yrs
France	31.6	12.2	54.5	15.8
Germany	23.7	12.7	35.7	16.5
UK	26.1	12.8	31.5	14.0

Source: *Eurostat, Education and Training 1970/1-*
1977/8, Table 1/7, p.186 (1980)
Statistical Office of the European
Communities.

Demand-side restraint on expansion in higher education was also uneven across social classes. The chances of working-class children reaching higher education increased as the sector expanded. But the differential recruitment, particularly to universities, remained. This can be seen in

Table 7.2. The reasons for this are complex.
But the exclusiveness of the universities probably
contributed. Furthermore, the O and A level school
examinations that dominate the secondary school
curriculum are university examinations and help
sustain the academic emphasis, originating within
unversities, inside secondary schooling even when
these have been reorganised on comprehensive lines.
Indeed, the resistance to change within the
universities has been mirrored by the extraordinary
difficulty in reforming public examinations since
1920. These were designed to select a few for
higher education and have remained as the major
influence on all children in secondary schools for
sixty years. Major reforms have repeatedly
foundered.

Table 7.2: Social Class Background of Students in
Higher Education: by Country

		Social class group					
		A	B	C	D	E	Others
England and Wales	1961	61.0	13.0	–	–	26.0	–
	1970	46.0	27.0	–	–	27.0	–
France	1960	55.2	34.4	5.8	–	4.6	–
	1974	42.5	39.2	6.4	–	4.9	–
Germany	1961	34.2	29.0	3.6	14.7	5.4	–
	1972	24.7	34.4	5.9	19.7	12.5	2.3

*Source: G. Neave, Patterns of Inequality, National
          Foundation for Educational Research
          (Windsor, 1976).*

The expansion of higher education in both the
university and the maintained sector was also
restrained by the resources made available. The
universities have not been insulated from
government attempts to economise in the public
sector of the economy. The Robbins Report[17] had
recommended that '...courses of higher education
should be available to all those who are qualified
by ability and attainment to pursue them and wish
to do so'. In the ten years from 1967 to 1977 the
number of university students increased from
55,900 to 77,800. But in the 1980s Government
cut the resources available and universities, along

with the maintained sector of higher education, was
planned to shrink.

Central government policy after the Robbins
Report was clarified by defining a binary system
for higher education, retaining the independent
universities on one side and the maintained
polytechnics and colleges under LEA control on the
other. The justification for this division was
that the public sector had to be held responsive to
economic and social changes and subject to LEA
control. Particularly in teacher training within
colleges and polytechnics, the principle of being
responsive has led to dramatic expansion under
central government direction in the 1960s,
followed by drastic contraction in the 1970s and
1980s. The existence of independent universities
has probably increased the determination of
central government to retain control over the
maintained sector with its emphasis on science,
technology and professional training. Neither
political party has been willing to move from the
binary pattern.

It was in further education outside the
universities that the main expansion has taken
place since 1946. From then to 1970 the number of
part- and full-time students rose from one and a
half million to over three million. In the White
Paper, *Education: A Framework for Expansion*[18]
this growth was planned to continue. This was
achieved, but the number of institutions actually
fell from 1970 to 1980. This was largely due to
closure of evening institutes and the reorganisation
of teacher training where many Colleges of
Education were closed, merged into Polytechnics or
re-named Colleges or Institutes of Higher Education.

The area receiving most attention has been
industrial training. Throughout the post-1945
period there have been continuing efforts to
develop an effective organisation of industrial
training that would meet shortages of skilled
labour and raise the general level of skill among
school leavers not going on to higher education.
As unemployment rose in the 1970s proposals to
plan a coherent system became more frequent.
From the publication of *Training for the Future*
in 1972[19] to *A New Training Initiative* from the
Department of Employment in December 1981[20] there
were a succession of moves to improve the quality
of training and to increase the number of students
on courses.

By the end of the 1970s the improvement in the

quality of training was the objective of the many
policy documents that were published. In 1979
there were three consultative papers on this theme,
Education and Training for 16 to 18 year olds[21], *A
better start in working life*[22] and *Providing
Educational Opportunities for 16 to 18 year olds*[23].
In the following year, the Government's Central
Policy Review Staff reported on education and
training to improve industrial importance[24] and
there was the major report by Finniston on the
training of engineers[25]. The policy common to all
these and many other reports in the 1970s and
early 1980s was the need to raise the level of
skill among those under training in further
education. This continued a succession of such
efforts, particularly since the 1964 Industrial
Training Act, which had promoted integrated courses
of training and further education for apprentices,
and led to the establishment of Industrial Training
Boards to develop the courses and associated
programmes at work.

In the early 1970s the efforts to raise the
level of skill of those entering employment or in
apprenticeships widened with the setting up of
the *Technician Education Council* (TEC) in 1973 and
the *Business Education Council* (BEC) in 1974.
These councils were given a common objective by
the government, to plan, administer and keep
under review the unified courses for training
technicians and others of similar position in
industry and business.

Below the technician level the policy was
the same, to establish organisations to launch
new courses that would raise the level of skill
available in employment. The most important
developments came from the *Manpower Services
Commission* (MSC) established under the Employment
and Training Act 1973. One executive arm of this
Commission, the Training Services Division,
concentrated on the link between education and
training. An example of its work was the
programme of Unified Vocational Preparation to
develop and assess courses of vocational preparation
for those in work where there was no opportunity
for further education or systematic training on the
job.

The number of reports and developments intended
to implement a policy of improved preparation for
work is an indication of the priority given to this
post-school area of education. The continuing
flow of reports also indicated how difficult it has

been to build up the momentum and get the balance
of training and education right. But by the end of
the 1970s rising unemployment produced another
acute problem for further education, and for the
schools where many unemployed 16 to 18 year olds
would stay on when faced with unemployment. The
major developments in this area were organised
through another arm of the MSC, the *Youth
Opportunities Programme* (YOP). YOP came into being
in 1978 following the Holland Report, *Young People
and Work*[26]. It has grown rapidly to meet rising
unemployment. It is responsible through the MSC
to the Secretary of State for Employment, not to
the DES. The attraction of this link is that
action does not have to be mediated through the
local education authorities. the MSC is well-
funded and can initiate and support action through
administrative action. The DES has few
administrative functions, no local offices and
does not promote or directly fund curriculum
developments. Given the speed with which
unemployment rose at the end of the 1970s and in
the 1980s, the urgent action was taken outside
the Education service by an agency of the Department
of Employment. On the positive side this made
quick action and a rapid expansion of programmes
possible. On the negative side it by-passed
local, democratically-elected, councils. It also
left the schools unaffected, despite the
organisation of programmes that affected the whole
16 to 19 group.
     The divorce between the Youth Opportunities
Programme and the schools, even though they are
dealing with the same age group and are both
concerned with the impact of unemployment on the
young, is likely to leave the schools without a
major role in the education of the majority of the
16 to 19 group. The freedom of action of schools
is restrained, not only by the public examinations
that still determine most of the curriculum for
all children, but by falling rolls and reduced
resources that are limiting their freedom to act.
Efforts to bridge YOP courses and work in school
are rare. An exception is the City of Coventry:
MSC funded activities have been actively developed
and it is proposed to plan the organisation and
curriculum of secondary schooling to unify the
school sector, work in FE and the programmes for
unemployed youth. Here the school population is
seen to be dividing into three parts. One-third
will go on to full-time further or higher

education. Another third will enter work and
consequently need further education and training.
A further third will be unemployed and will need
further education on lines already developed within
the city. The implications are seen to be a
need to review the whole of secondary schooling,
not just that concerned with the 16 plus age
group. One aim in this review is to ensure that
the three groups will not receive a completely
separate education.

Initiatives such as that launched in Coventry
are rare. There is a national policy and the
intention under *A New Training Initiative*[27] is
that all unemployed 16 year old leavers will
receive one year of full-time training. Some
100,000 extra students were planned to begin this
training in further education colleges by
September 1983. The initiative also included
proposals for expanded opportunities for the 17
year old unemployed. This initiative means a rapid
expansion of further education, funded from the
Department of Employment, involving newly recruited
staff in organising new forms of courses, many
away from the colleges at places of work.

In the policies designed to improve the quality
of training and to cope with unemployment that
dominated the 1970s and early 1980s there was a
clear preference for skill-based courses. The
traditional mix of subjects taken at college and
apprenticeship based on working alongside skilled
men, was being replaced by courses where the skills
required for the work were mapped out in advance
and linked to planned work experience. This applied
to the new technician courses as well as the
initiatives for the unemployed to prepare them for
possible work. Thus the planning involved
identifying the core skills involved in various
types of work, building these into a course and
backing this by work experience where the skills
could be practised.

The speed of developments in the further
education sector to cope with unemployment and the
need to raise the level of skill in the workforce
is indicated by the publications recommending new
schemes that have come as a flood across the 1970s
and into the 1980s. The pace had quickened in
each decade since the 1940s. But this followed a
century of developments in maintained Education
when the priority for training and its status had
remained low. The policies to expand opportunities
and improve training for work came under the

pressure from poor economic performance and from
rising unemployment among youth. By 1980 this
work-related side of further education was the one
area of Education where expansion and curriculum
development was rapid. While the Education
service, including higher education, was being
cut back in line with falling school rolls,
training services were being rapidly expanded with
funds provided by the Department of Employment.

Looking for the policies behind further and
higher education in all their variety is bewildering.
First, there are the administrative differences.
There is an independent sector, albeit financed
indirectly by central government, and a maintained
sector of higher education. Second, there is a
further division between the Department of
Education and Science responsible for the
institutions catering for the more able going on
to full-time and extended higher and further
education, and the Department of Employment,
through the MSC, responsible for the training of
school leavers who are likely to be unemployed
and for many developments in vocational training.
Third, these two government departments have
totally different administrative and financial
arrangements.

The consequence of this diversity is that
there is no policy that embraces the 16 to 19 age
group as a whole, despite the unfortunate division
into those who go into higher education, those
who leave school for work and those who leave for
unemployment and training. A comprehensive
secondary schooling is followed by a most unequal
post-school education, for students entering
higher education are grant-aided, while those
attending MSC courses receive only a small
allowance for a brief course. With an independent
university sector, local authority financed further
and higher education, and MSC courses under the
Department of Employment there are plenty of
proposals for change, but no coherent policy.

Perhaps the most unfortunate aspect of this
confusion is the failure to involve the secondary
schools. Inevitably the rise in unemployment
and of MSC courses of training has affected the
attitudes of those approaching the age for
leaving school. The logic of this is that the
secondary school curriculum can no longer be
geared to the needs of the most able third
through the influence of public examinations
across the whole curriculum of schools. Yet few

initiatives have come from the schools. The most
obvious policy given the prospect of continued
high unemployemnt would be to raise the school
leaving age to 17 or 18. Yet this is not even
discussed as a possibility. With an unreformed
curriculum the teachers find it very difficult
catering for existing 16 year olds. The prospects
of holding even older students, however rational
that step now seems, is too much for teachers or
policy-makers to contemplate given the way
secondary schools are organised.

EDUCATION, ECONOMY AND POLITICS

The outstanding factor behind government policies
for Education in the UK since the mid-1970s has
been the steady contraction of resources. To
overcome economic stagnation successive governments
have limited the growth of the public sector,
where Education is one of the biggest spenders.
Falling school rolls have provided a justification
for this trimming. There has also been surprisingly
little political pressure on government to reverse
this policy, suggesting that the power base of
Education may have been undermined by criticisms
of the way the service was developing. These
were increasingly heard just as the economic
crisis became acute in the 1970s.
    The economic situation deteriorated further
for Education in the 1980s. A reduction of eight
per cent in expenditure on Education between 1980
and 1984 was announced in the *Public Expenditure
White Paper* of 1982. Rigid and underestimated
allowances for inflation will probably have added
another cut of two to three per cent. Overspending
local authorities will be 'taxed' so that they lose
grant as a penalty. Faced with these cuts and
penalties, LEAs found it increasingly difficult
to plan local services, particularly as two-thirds
of the money spent on Education went to paying
salaries. LEAs were unwilling to face the
opposition of the teacher unions to redundancies,
and economies elsewhere were not only difficult,
but could not be achieved year after year without
cutting back the money for books, teaching
materials and support services to the point where
the children would suffer.
    The attempt to restrict public sector
expenditure started under a Labour Government and
was pressed further by the post-1970 Conservative
administration. The consequence was first to

break the consensus between central and local
government. Chief Education Officers in particular
complained that their jobs were made impossible by
successive cuts. Secondly, the shortage of
resources shifted the location of decision-making
to central government. LEAs had to wait for the
level of central government grant before making
decisions, and when this grant was cut year after
year, local freedom to innovate was restricted.
Central government began to exert increased
pressure on the schools through a flood of
publications on the curriculum in the late 1970s.
These came just as the schools were having to
adjust curriculum to match the staff they had lost
once those leaving were not replaced. Many LEAs
introduced policies to secure a basic curriculum
by planning the distribution of staff. By 1980
it was clear that the autonomy of teachers to
plan their own curriculum and of LEAs to re-
structure their schools was disappearing.

The coincidence of a restrictive economic
policy for Education and of increased activity
by central government to influence the curriculum
and to monitor standards, can be explained in
different ways. Some writers have seen the
intervention as a deliberate attempt by central
government to re-assert its authority over the
service[28]. Others have analysed the situation in
terms of the growing bureaucratisation of
educational power, with the DES deliberately
legitimising its position in order to manage the
context in which policy is made[29]. Fowler[30]
sees the centralisation of decision-making as
the consequence of structural contraction. But
all agree that policy-making has moved away,
or been removed, from the teachers in their
schools and through their unions, as well as from
LEAs, to central government.

There have been many protests about this
contraction of the Education service. Significantly
few of them have concentrated on the long-term
effects on the economy. This is surprising given
the prominence given to the economic role of
Education in promoting economic growth in the
expansion up to the 1970s. Similarly, while
Education was seen as the avenue through which
social justice would be achieved by promoting
increased upward social mobility in the 1960s,
there was little emphasis on this function as
contraction began to bite ten years later.
Confidence in Education as the engine for economic

recovery and social justice had faded.

The reasons for the collapse of confidence in Education as a means of achieving greater social justice lie in the evidence on the failure of the service to increase the opportunities of working class children to move into higher education and the professions when compared with those from the middle class. There was an increase, but it was due to expanded numbers entering rather than any proportionate increase in the chances of the poor[31]. Indeed, by the end of the 1960s faith in a universal system of social services had been weakened by evidence on persisting inequality, ill-health, unemployment and bad housing. Across the 1970s positive discrimination was adopted by both central and local government to concentrate funds where they were seen to be most needed to help the deprived. The universal principle of social welfare and education was seen to have left too many in a deprived condition.

This policy of positive discrimination in education involved action research projects, central government funds for local initiatives, and LEA resourcing of schools to help teachers in deprived, largely inner city areas. In total the impact was minimal, in line with the marginal funds involved, but the Inner London Education Authority for example not only launched action research projects and improved staffing in schools in deprived areas, but resourced its schools on the basis of roll and deprivation assessed on a set of social indicators including such factors as family size, number of one-parent families, social class, number taking free meals, measured behaviour and a number of indicators of the material condition of the school. Nationally, and in most cases locally, the investment in positive discrimination was small. But the policy did focus attention on the need to do something to boost the chances of the inner city poor, many of whom were children of ethnic groups whose parents had come to the UK in the 1960s.

By the end of the 1970s confidence in positive discrimination as a policy had waned. Many programmes had been funded for limited periods and LEAs short of funds found it increasingly difficult to take over the financing of these when their temporary funding ended. By the start of the 1980s the major remaining national programme was the Inner City Partnerships bringing together

central and local government to fund projects in
inner city areas. Ten years before, Education was
the focus of many intervention projects. Now it
played only a small part in the partnership
schemes. Even the inner city riots of 1981 and
the rising unemployment among youth brought no
great pressure for investment in new educational
projects. Planning the survival of the existing
school system seemed to be taking priority over
new developments. Indeed, many of the organisations
set up to promote new developments such as the
Centre for Educational Disadvantage and the Schools
Council were either closed, threatened with
closure, or reorganised. Above all, HMI, who in
the early 1970s seemed to have adopted an
innovatory, advisory role, switched back to
inspecting, surveying and critical reporting by
1980.

It is possible to explain why the claims for
Education as a motor for the economy became muted
by the 1980s. The economy was stagnant and there
had been no apparent pay-off from the increased
investment in Education across the 1960s and into
the 1970s. Investment had to be switched from a
universalist policy of expanding educational
opportunity in the hope that a raised general level
of qualification in the country would boost the
economy, to a specific focus on the skills
necessary for the renewal of industry as the
computer revolution had its effect, and to
cushion the impact of mass unemployment,
particularly among young people. Once again it can
be seen in global terms as a shift from universalist
policy to specific, selective policies. This
seemed to be both a symptom of loss of faith in
the power of Education to boost economic growth and
a response to the need to cut back expenditure.
Universalism was an expensive policy in Education
and confidence in it, as in other public services,
seems to have declined.

In Education at the start of the 1980s there
were many factors weakening the bargaining position
of the service in the annual public expenditure
survey exercise. The claims of the health and
social security services were boosted by the
rapidly growing numbers of over 65s in the
population, compared with falling numbers of
school-aged children. Services for the unemployed
had absorbed increasing funds at a time when the
total amount available to public services was
being cut. The Falklands battle strengthened the

claims for defence spending. The local tax base
was too weak to support the existing educational
services and there was little money available for
developments. Significantly in a service where
teachers' salaries take the major part of the
funds available to local authorities, the numbers
in training were still being cut back ten years
after these cuts first started. This control of
numbers in training was a direct responsibility
of central government and the policy of continuing
cuts spelled out a pessimistic message for the
service as a whole.

As this essay was being written there were
discussions about possible new financial
arrangements for Education. These included the
proposal to pay teachers from central rather than
local government, and another to include a specific
grant for Education rather than keeping it within
the block grant determined by central government
to support all local expenditure. These proposals
were under discussion because LEAs found themselves
unable to sustain their existing service and
frustrated in their efforts to respond to new
needs. In turn these difficulties within local
education authorities washed over into schools.
School-based initiatives were increasingly
difficult to launch as the marginal changes that
were possible with the reduced funds made available
had to go to reorganisation to cope with loss of
staff, reduced capitation and emergencies such as
increased numbers staying-on in preference to
becoming unemployed. In many cases the problems
could not be handled at school level. School-
based curriculum development gave way to LEA
policies to staff schools to secure a basic
curriculum that was worked out in county or town
hall, because individual schools could no longer
secure the balance required by recruiting
replacement staff or adding to their establishment.

When the location of power in a public service
is decentralised, financial stringency can force
decision-making back to the centre. Local
administration in Education and the freedom of
teachers to innovate are both limited by the need
to wait to see what resources will be available
to retain existing arrangements. New developments
are unlikely and central government, through
agencies such as the Manpower Services Commission,
has been given the responsibility for urgent
innovation.

The context for educational policy-making in

the UK did not change solely as a consequence of
financial restraint imposed as part of an economic
package to deflect resources to the private sector
of the economy. That restraint was imposed by
central government on an education service where
policy was being made, not only by central
government and in 104 local education authorities,
but in each of over 25,000 maintained schools and
nearly 1,000 colleges and institutes for further
education. The staff in each of these maintained
their right to develop organisations and curricula.
Financial restraint reduced the scope for local
action and increased the opportunity and necessity
for central government to play a more prominent
part, not only in controlling existing institutions,
but in funding new courses outside education to
help the growing number unemployed.

It is impossible to detect whether the
increased role taken by central government over
such areas as the school curriculum, which had
previously been the preserve of the professionals,
is being forced on a reluctant partner or is the
implementation of an intentional policy to
restore central influence to that suggested in the
Education Act of 1944, which remains the legal
basis of the service. The most convincing
explanation is probably that the political will
to increase central government control has been
present since the mid-1970s and has been put
into practice by both Labour and Conservative
governments. Financial restraint reinforced this
trend. But the moves to ensure central government
influence over educational policies sprang from
the same economic crisis that led to the cut in
resources to the public sector, including
Education. In expansive times policy-making
and implementation can remain decentralised. When
the expansion ceases Education becomes one possible
cause for concern about the causes of economic
failure. The contraction of resources and
increased central control of developments are both
political solutions to the same economic problem.

DEVELOPMENTS IN EDUCATIONAL POLICY IN THE UNITED
KINGDOM

There was a clear break in the political consensus
over the Education service around 1960. Up to
then, post-war reconstruction and the implementation
of the 1944 Act went ahead with apparent agreement
between the main political parties and the

administrative and professional interests. There
was no discernible national groundswell of unrest
among parents, employers, pupils or students.
Education had rarely been the subject of sustained
political dispute. Its high priority for public
funds was unchallenged.

There have been many symptoms of the breakdown
of this consensus since 1960. Unrest among
students in higher education and older pupils in
schools, parents going to law to challenge new
policies, criticism by employers about the
attainment of school leavers, local and national
politicians pressing for increased professional
accountability, industrial action by teachers, all
point to disagreements within the service, over its
importance and over the direction of developments.
This concern over the trend of educational policies
has been accompanied by alterations in the balance
of influence between the three parties in the
'partnership' (central government, local
government and the organised teachers), and between
these and parents, employers and local interests
that form the consumers of Education. Educational
policies became the focus of central and local
political concern.

Public interest in Education was increasingly
reflected in interest groups which proliferated
across the 1960s. The broadest issue attracting
such groups was the right of parents to exert
influence over educational policy, particularly at
the school level. This may have come largely as a
result of comprehensive secondary schooling, when
articulate, politically aware middle-class
parents had to use the same schools as the poor
for the first time. There is however no doubt
that over twenty years from 1960, parents pressed
for more information, for more choice in the schools
to which they could send their children and for
more say in the way they were taught. The pressure
groups came from political right and left. The
Campaign for Comprehensive Organisation was
matched by the *Campaign for Academic Standards*
opposing further comprehensivisation. Probably
the most influential has been the *Campaign for the
Advancement of State Education* (CASE) pressing
for such policies as the abolition of corporal
punishment, the acceleration of the move to
comprehensive secondary schooling and more
parental participation in school government.

In one case, the provision of some form of
education before statutory schooling started at

five, the pressure groups had a remarkable success.
The *Pre-school Playgroups Association* was started
by mothers frustrated by the absence of maintained
provision. This filled the gap left by the
failure to expand nursery schooling before entry
to school at five. In 1981 some 40 per cent of
the 3-4 year old age group in England received
some nursery education in maintained schools. By
then the voluntary playgroups had established a
permanent place in the education service, despite
opposition from the teacher unions in the early
stages when they were seen as a threat to
professionalism. Over the more general issue of
obtaining an increased say in the running of the
service, resistance has been harder to overcome and
progress slower. This arises from the difficulty
in securing change in a service where power is
distributed among many different parties. The
'partners' were used to dealing with each other.
Their constituencies were clear. Central and
local government were bound by legislation,
were informed by political parties and their
bureaucracies were in close contact. Similarly,
the teacher unions were organised to obtain the
views of their members and to feed these views
into government at local and central level. When
parents and others began to press for a place in
these decision-making arrangements, the traditional
bases for policy-making were challenged. The key
issue for tracing the shift in influence within
the education service is over the government of
schools, where the interests of parents, teachers,
administrators and central and local politicians
come together.

The Education Act of 1944 intended each school
to have a governing or managing body. In practice,
many LEAs grouped schools so that they shared
governing bodies and for primary schools there was
very often a single managing body for the whole
authority. In the 1960s parental interest was
increasing articulated through pressure groups
such as CASE, the *National Association of
Governors and Managers* and the *National Confederat-
ion of Parent-Teacher Associations*. This increased
pressure to influence the government of schools
was only part of a broader movement to influence
the education given to children. When the *Plowden
Committee* reported on primary schooling in 1967,
17 per cent of schools were reported as having
Parent-Teacher Associations[32]. Ten years later
there were 35 per cent[33]. At the same time much

of the resistance to parents entering primary
schools had diminished and in the 1980s the
involvement of parents in the early learning
of reading had become a popular innovation.

The political response to the increase in
public interest in the running of schools was not
long delayed. By the mid-1960s the Conservative
Party had produced the idea of a *Parents' Charter*.
A private members bill on this subject was
presented in the House of Commons in 1974. The
Labour government, then in power, responded in
1975 by setting up the Taylor committee to review
the arrangements for the management and government
of maintained schools, including their relations
with the parents of pupils and the community around
the school. This Committee reported in 1977[34]. It
dealt with two main issues, the powers that should
be exercised by governing bodies and their
membership.

The Taylor committee recommended that LEAs
should be required not only to ensure that each
school had a governing body, but that this should
consist of equal representation from parents,
teachers and members of the community, to be
balanced with an equal number of representatives
selected by the LEA. Predictably there was strong
resistance from LEAs and from teachers. The
former, responsible to the local electorate,
opposed the proposals as a threat to local democracy.
The latter responded by condemning the proposals
as bogus because lay people could not share in
management that had to be professional. When a
conservative government finally legislated to
reform the government of schools in the Education
Act of 1980 there was only a requirement that LEAs
provide places for parents and teachers on governing
bodies not to balance these interests and their
own representation.

This long debate over the government of
schools illustrates the complexity of policy-
making procedures in the United Kingdom. The
existence of a 'partnership' meant that any
attempt to redistribute power was resisted by one
or more of the partners. The debate over the
government of schools was part of the wider debate
over the control of the curriculum that has been
discussed earlier. There is no doubt that since
1970 the central government has been exerting its
right to discuss the school curriculum.
Simultaneously it has tried to give parents a say
in the government of schools and more choice in

selecting a school for their children. To change
the balance of influence, central government not
only legislated to give parents a place on
governing bodies, but legislated to increase the
flow of information to the public about the schools
in their area. This was the effect of the 'Great
Debate' launched by a Labour government in the
mid-1970s. It was also the subject of part of the
Education Act of 1980 which spells out the duties
of LEAs and schools to provide information to the
public about schools.

This attempt to increase the information
available to the lay public about the curriculum
and organisation of schools, and the possibility
of a more informed lay public has been seen as the
most important feature of the attempt to obtain
wider participation in the affairs of schools[35].
The proliferation of pressure groups in the 1960s,
the moves towards a Parents' Charter in the 1970s,
the Great Debate over the curriculum and the
attempts to increase parental choice in the service
have altered the balance of influence in educational
policy-making. To this has to be added the
diminished power of the teachers in a situation of
falling school rolls, where parents can empty an
unpopular school, where the ability of LEAs to
find resources for the schools has been restricted
and where teachers have lost a lot of their
bargaining power because ground has to be
surrendered when faced with the alternative of
losing jobs. The political balance has been
altered. But this has come about not only through
political action, but through an economic climate
that has altered the bargaining position of those
involved.

There is a tide for more participation in the
formation of educational policies at both local and
central government level in the United Kingdom.
Parents and employers are increasingly recruited
to committees that were once the preserve of the
professionals. They are now represented on the
governing bodies of schools. They are receiving
the information that will help them exert influence.
But it would be wrong to see this as a flood,
sweeping parents and others into positions of
influence over the curriculum of schools. The
historical development of education in the United
Kingdom was 'top-down'. It gives scope for local
initiatives by LEAs and by individual schools.
Teachers can act independently. But the service
is run by insiders and the influence of parents and

the local community remains slight. In the last twenty years other voices have been heard in the national system locally administered. But the decentralisation of responsibility that is the feature of the service in the UK has left policy-making firmly in the hands of the traditional partners.

NOTES

1. W. Beveridge, *Social Insurance and Allied Services* (Cmnd 6404, HMSO, London, 1942).

2. OECD, *Educational Development Strategy in England and Wales* (OECD, Paris, 1975).

3. House of Commons Expenditure Committee, *Policy Making in the DES* (HMSO, London, 1976).

4. R. Manzer, *Teachers and Politics* (Manchester University Press, Manchester, 1970).

5. M. Kogan, *The Politics of Education* (Penguin, Harmondsworth, 1971).

6. B. Salter and T. Tapper, *Education, Politics and the State* (Grant McIntyre, London, 1981).

7. M. Kogan, 'Changes in Perspective', *Times Educational Supplement* (15 January 1982), p.4.

8. Department of Education and Science, *Children and their Primary Schools* (HMSO, London, 1967).

9. B. Simon, 'The Primary School Revolution: Myth or Reality' in B. Simon and J. Willcocks (eds), *Research and Practice in the Primary Classroom* (Routledge and Kegan Paul, London, 1981).

10. C.B. Cox and A.E. Dyson (eds), *A Black Paper* (Critical Quarterly Society, London, 1969a); C.B. Cox and A.E. Dyson (eds), *Black Paper Two* (Critical Quarterly Society, London, 1969b); C.B. Cox and A.E. Dyson (eds), *Black Paper Three* (Critical Quarterly Society, London, 1970); C.B. Cox and R. Boyson (eds), *Black Paper 1975* (Dent, London, 1975); C.B. Cox and R. Boyson (eds), *Black Paper 1977* (M. Temple Smith, London, 1977).

11. Auld Report, *The William Tyndale Junior and Infants School* (Inner London Education Authority, London, 1976).

12. Department of Education and Science, *Primary Education in England* (HMSO, London, 1978a).

13. Department of Education and Science, *Report on Education: Assessing the Performance of Pupils* (HMSO, London, 1978b).

14. Department of Education and Science,

Education in Schools. A Consultative Document
(Cmnd 6869, HMSO, London, 1977).

15.   P.H. James, *The Reorganisation of Secondary Education* (National Foundation for Educational Research, Windsor, 1980).

16.   T. Burgess, 'Bias is of the Essence' in D. Warren Piper (ed.), *Is Higher Education Fair?* (Society for Research into Higher Education, Guildford, 1981).

17.   Robbins Report, *Higher Education* (Cmnd 2154, HMSO, London, 1963).

18.   Department of Education and Science, *Education: A Framework for Expansion* (HMSO, London, 1972a).

19.   Department of Education and Science, *Training for the Future* (HMSO, London, 1972b).

20.   Department of Employment, *A New Training Initiative* (HMSO, London, 1981).

21.   Department of Education and Science, *Education and Training for 16 to 18 Year Olds* (HMSO, London, 1979a).

22.   Department of Education and Science, *A Better Start in Working Life* (HMSO, London, 1979b).

23.   Department of Education and Science, *Providing Educational Opportunities for 16 to 18 Year Olds* (HMSO, London, 1979c).

24.   Central Policy Review Staff, *Educational Training and Industrial Performance* (HMSO, London, 1980).

25.   Finniston Report, *Engineering: Our Future*, Report of the Committee of Enquiry into the Engineering Profession (Cmnd 7794, HMSO, London, 1980).

26.   Holland Report, *Young People and Work* (HMSO, London, 1977).

27.   Department of Employment, *A New Training Initiative*.

28.   For example, D. Lawton, *The Politics of the School Curriculum* (Routledge & Kegan Paul, London, 1980).

29.   Salter and Tapper, *Education, Politics and the State*.

30.   G. Fowler, 'The Politics of Education' in G. Bernbaum (ed.), *Schooling in Decline* (Macmillan, Basingstoke, 1979).

31.   A.H. Halsey, A.F. Heath and J.M. Ridge, *Origins and Destinations: Family, Class and Education in Modern Britain* (Clarendon Press, Oxford, 1980).

32.   Department of Education and Science, *Children and their Primary Schools*.

33. R. Cyster, P. Clift and S. Battle, *Parental Involvement in Primary Schools* (National Foundation for Educational Research, Windsor, 1979).

34. Taylor Report, *A New Partnership for Our Schools* (DES/HMSO, London, 1977).

35. G. Baron, 'Pressures for Change in School Government' in G. Baron (ed.), *The Politics of School Government* (Pergamon, London, 1981).

Eight

THE UNITED STATES OF AMERICA

James W. Guthrie and Judith Bodenhausen

The United States of America maintains an education
'system' which is probably more diverse, disparate,
decentralised, and dynamic than any other in the
world. This system depends little upon national
government to make educational policy or to provide
financial support for education institutions.
Instead, governmental authority for American
education is distributed primarily among the fifty
states which, in turn, delegate administrative
responsibility to thousands of local school
districts. The consequence is fifty systems of
public, tax-supported, lower and higher education in
which policy is made by fifty sets of state
officials, governors, legislatures, judges, state
boards of education, and their counterparts in
thousands of local communities. As if this were not
sufficiently complex, there exists a parallel system
of private or non-public institutions, generally
outside of government, for both higher and lower
education.
        Decentralisation has permitted development of
a wide array of institutions. Local districts in
America vary in size from small one-room schools to
huge urban systems, such as New York City with
almost one million students. Some public school
districts operate only elementary schools, others
only secondary schools, yet others operate both
types. There exist 'community colleges' which offer
two years of post-secondary instruction. Beyond
this are both colleges and universities ranging in
size from small four-year liberal arts institutions
to huge university systems with one or more campuses
offering instruction in a staggering number of
liberal arts subjects as well as graduate and
professional fields. Here again, almost everything
that exists through public financial support is

mirrored in the private sector.

Given such decentralisation and diversity, the comprehensive nature of America's educational institutions may come as a surprise. Formal education encompasses almost every segment of the population in terms of students' age, interests, and ability levels. In excess of 58 million students are formally enrolled in both lower and higher education institutions[1]. It is increasingly typical that an American child will begin nursery school or pre-school at age three or four. Thereafter, 90 per cent of an age cohort will graduate from secondary school and more than 50 per cent will attend a post-secondary institution. Literally millions of adults attend vocational and avocational non-degree classes. (This does not take into account those adults attending proprietary (profit-making) schools, generally for vocational training purposes.) All these institutions together employ approximately 4.5 million individuals working in more than 100,000 buildings. When one considers pupils and employees, and the members of their immediate family, American education directly involves 25 per cent of the total population.

Despite the extent to which education is generally pursued by Americans, US systems of education are riddled with paradox. Schooling is intended to benefit those who are gifted, those who are handicapped, and all those in-between. The old, the young, the élite, as well as the poor are all targets of specific school programmes. Education is expected at once to ensure social cohesion as well as cultural diversity; academic achievement as well as vocational relevance; moral virtue as well as individual self-enhancement. Schools are expected to be free of politics yet responsive to public clients; sensitive to national needs, yet subject to the desires of local citizens; and controlled by lay persons while staffed with professionals. All such expectations are to be met in a national climate of values which stresses, however incompatible, equality, liberty, and efficiency. More complicated yet, education policy is the con-commitant responsibility of all three levels of government, federal, state and local. Given this complexity, the wonder is that education works at all in America.

How did such a diverse institutional system evolve? What are the publicly held values which shape this system? What is its present structure and financial status? With what major policy

problems has the system been confronted within the
last quarter century, and with what issues is it
likely to be occupied in the near future? These are
the topics around which the remainder of this
chapter is focused. However, before embarking upon
such descriptions and analyses, we wish to extend a
caveat. We are confident in capturing the major
policy trends and functional dynamics that have
occurred in the United States over time and believe
our prognostications regarding the future are
reasonable. Nevertheless, given the remarkable
complexity of the American system, significant
counter trends and anomalies may sometimes be
sacrificed for the sake of generalisation.

HISTORIC EVOLUTION

The first American educational ordinances were
enacted by the Massachusetts colonial legislature,
then called the General Court, in 1642. These
statutes re-affirmed the family's primary
responsibility for providing the ability to read
and vocational training for children. They also
established a public responsibility for education.
If a household failed to provide for a child's
education, the town's elected officials, known as
selectmen, were required to remove the child from
the home and place him or her in a suitable
apprenticeship situation[2]. Similar compulsory
education laws subsequently were enacted by all the
New England and middle-Atlantic colonies except
Rhode Island. These early compulsory education
statutes prescribed minimum standards, but did not
prescribe schools. It became apparent, however,
that formal instruction would be needed to provide
the amount and kind of education deemed necessary by
colonial leadership. Thus, beginning in 1635, a
number of the towns in Massachusetts and other New
England colonies established schools. By 1647,
eleven of the sixty towns in New England voluntarily
established and were managing and supporting town
schools[3].
    In 1647, the Massachusetts General Court
enacted the first legislation referring to schools.
This act required all towns of fifty or more
families to provide a teacher of reading and those
of one hundred families to provide a Latin grammar
school. This legislation became known as the '*Old
Deluder Satan*' act, and its explicit purpose was to
ensure that everyone in the Bible Commonwealth be

able to read and understand the principles of religion and the capital laws.

During the Colonial period, laws were enacted that established the authority of the state legislature to determine whether towns should be required to maintain schools, the kinds of schools, lengths of term, means of control and support (including the innovation of subsidies from taxation[4]), and qualifications of teachers. In so doing, the Massachusetts General Court initiated a principle that education is a function of the State. Deliberately, however, the legislature emphasised the town as the unit of local school administration. Town meetings, comprised of those who had the right of local suffrage, were the source of local authority.

As towns grew in size and complexity, matters relating to education were increasingly delegated to town selectmen. In 1692, the Massachusetts General Court granted to selectmen the power to supervise schools and employ teachers. The selectmen, in turn, began to delegate educational responsibilities to special school committees comprised initially of their own members and later expanded to include others who were not selectmen.

In 1789, the Massachusetts General Court established by law many of the actual practices that had developed in the State, by a statute that provided for regular attendance and for the visitation and inspection of schools[5], placed responsibility for certification of teachers with the selectmen, rather than town ministers and preachers, gave legal recognition to the school committee as an official group charged solely with control and maintenance of local schools, and officially recognised the district as a level of community organisation involved in the establishment and control of schools.

The act of 1826 in Massachusetts made compulsory the maintenance of school committees for all towns. This legislation required the selection of a committee that would not be part of the regular town government, but would have a special function of school governance. It also established the principle of lay control; nowhere did it mention ministerial, professional, or educational standards for membership on the committee, and throughout the colonial and early national period, laws in Maine, Vermont, New Hampshire, and Connecticut followed the example set by Massachusetts[6].

In the more diverse southern and mid-Atlantic

colonies, education initially developed along different paths than in the more northerly New England. For example, southern residents depended heavily upon private tutors and English schooling for the children of the upper classes and many children from poor families attended church-supported pauper schools. Thus, public schools were substantially slower to develop. Nevertheless, the New England school pattern eventually came to dominate in these regions as well. As the rich new western lands were opened to settlement, and large numbers of persons moved from the original thirteen colonies (as well as from Europe) the New England tradition of public education exerted a strong influence over federal policies for the new territory. The federal ordinances of 1785 and 1787 reserved the 16th section of land in each township for the 'maintenance of public schools within townships', thereby establishing in each new state a tradition favouring public support of education[7].

In the mid-nineteenth century, at the urging of social reformers, the Massachusetts legislature established a state board of education, created the office of State Superintendent of Schools, and established a state normal school for the preparation of teachers. The legislature also required towns of specified size to maintain a high school, and, in 1852, passed the nation's first compulsory school attendance law. By 1865 all states outside the South had enacted similar legislation.

At the turn of the twentieth century, the United States was in a period of dramatic population growth and intensified industrialisation. Public school systems, common schools, had become an integral part of every community in all states. The national population had increased to 72 million, and there were nearly 110,000 local school districts. State government bore the major burden of over-seeing educational policy. The primary movement in this regard consisted of efforts to consolidate small rural school districts into larger operating units. Proponents argued that larger school districts would be more efficient economically and could offer students a wider range of academic programmes. Consequently, between 1900 and the beginning of the Second World War, the number of US school districts was reduced almost fourfold to less than 30,000. Concomitant enrolment increases meant that the resulting districts were not only larger geographically but also contained many more

schools and students. This was the beginning of
bureaucracy in American education.

The ever larger size of school districts
rendered them increasingly difficult to be managed
by elected lay school board members. Whereas once
there had been an elected school board member for
every 138 citizens, by the Second World War it was
already the case that, on average, each school
board represented literally thousands of
constituents. Such conditions promoted the
preparation and employment of professional school
managers.

The twentieth century use of professional
school administrators was encouraged by another
movement: the so-called '*Progressive Era*' in
American politics began at about the turn of the
twentieth century. In an effort to overcome the
machine politics and rampant graft and corruption
then existing in many large cities, state and local
political charters were reformed so as to rid the
system of what was then described as 'an excess of
politics'. One result was to insulate school
governance from the main stream of partisan
political activity. Professional superintendents
were ceded even greater authority, and school boards,
if continued at all in an elected fashion, were
admonished not to cross the 'boundary' between
policy and administration.

Professional administrators were encouraged
even further by the widespread incorporation into
education, prior to the Second World War, of so-
called *scientific management principles*. This was
the era of efficiency where time-and-motion studies
were promoting substantial productivity gains in the
private sector. The assertion on the part of
scientific management proponents in education was
that schools could be made equally productive by
following private sector management patterns. The
movement, in retrospect, does not appear either to
have reduced school costs or enhanced pupil achievement. What it did do, without question, was to
promote the authority of professional school
managers[8].

Thus, immediately before and for some time
after the Second World War, the United States
possessed a decentralised system of education with
overall state authority, strong historic roots in
delivering school services based on local districts,
and a burgeoning bureaucracy of professional
administrators.

CONTEMPORARY STRUCTURAL FEATURES OF AMERICAN EDUCATION

American lower and higher education have substantially different traditions, policymaking processes, operating standards, and organisational cultures. Hence we undertake a separate description of each system.

Lower Education

Approximately 2.1 million, 36 per cent, of three and four-year olds in the United States attend what are known as nursery or pre-schools[9]. Attendance is generally for two or three hours a day. If both the mother and father have full-time employment, attendance may be for a longer time period and portions of the school activity take on the function of child care. Only a small percentage of this schooling is publicly provided, namely federally funded pre-school programmes for children from low income families. On occasion, employers provide the service, but this is not yet common. More frequently, pre-schools are private and parents pay fees. Now that it is increasingly the pattern for mothers to be employed outside the household and 70 per cent of US women between the ages of 25 and 65 are employed, pre-school enrolments can be expected to grow even more.

<u>Public Schooling</u>. By age five or six, youngsters are generally enrolled in a *kindergarten*. In 1981, there were 3.2 million kindergarten students, 94 per cent of the age cohort. This service generally is publicly provided and is typically part of an elementary school. Private kindergartens exist, frequently as an extension of a nursery school of pre-school day care operation. However, approximately 90 per cent of elementary and secondary students are enrolled in public schools, and it is with kindergarten that this American pattern of public school dominance begins to emerge.

American elementary schools typically begin with kindergarten and extend through to at least grade six (school grades are numbered from 1 for ages 6-7 up to 12 for ages 18-19). Some elementary schools, depending upon the grade configuration model adopted by their school district board of trustees, may encompass grades seven and eight as well. These two patterns together accounted for

27.8 million students in 1981.

Schools typically commence at approximately 8 or 8.30 a.m. Kindergarten will frequently be only one half day. Grades one through three may end at 1.30 or 2 p.m. Grades 4 and above (ages 9+) typically will extend until 3 p.m. or later. American schools operate five days a week and are closed on Saturdays and Sundays.

The overwhelming majority of elementary students are in so-called 'self-contained' classes, that is they are instructed throughout their school day by the same teacher. Subject-matter includes reading, mathematics, social studies, science, physical education, etc. but in the course of the school day the youngsters do not typically change classrooms.

In local school districts which adhere to what is described as a 6:3:3 grade configuration plan, six years of elementary schooling, three years of junior high school, and three years of high school, students enter '*Junior High School*' at the beginning of the seventh grade. Junior high was conceived historically as a transition from the self-contained classes of elementary schools to the fully developed departmentalisation of senior high schools. In practice, however, contemporary junior high schools are themselves almost always fully departmentalised.

For the seventh, eighth, and ninth grades (ages 12-15), a student will take approximately six classes a day, moving from teacher to teacher for each of the approximate 50 or 55 minute classes. Courses generally include English, a combination of grammar, composition, and literature; mathematics; science; history or social studies; physical education; and 'electives' chosen from fields such as drama, music, art, or vocational subjects such as woodshop, sheetmetal, or mechanical drawing.

By the end of junior high school, the ninth grade, students have been encouraged to regard achievement evaluation quite seriously, and formal report cards containing grades and performance ratings are issued to the homes, generally every six weeks throughout the nine month school year.

The secondary school day is generally from 8 a.m. until 3 or 3.30 p.m. Whereas the elementary school frequently is within a few streets of the students' homes, by the time of junior high, schools draw upon a larger attendance area, and a student may have to walk anywhere from one or two miles or may actually ride a publicly provided bus

to school. The latter will especially be the case
in rural areas.

A few districts operate '*Intermediate Schools*'.
These typically encompass only grades seven and
eight and offer departmentalised instruction and are
seen as a transition to secondary school. In these
instances, students attend ninth grade at the local
high school, and do not go to a junior high.

In 1981 there were 14.6 million students
enrolled in secondary schools. Secondary schools
encompass either grades 9 through 12, where students
previously attend either K-8 or K-6, 7-8 schools
(K, for Kindergarten, precedes grade 1). Where
junior high school is the dominant pattern, then
secondary schools contain grades 10-12. These are
fully departmentalised with students typically
having a six or seven period day. The basic
curriculum continues to consist of English,
composition and literature; mathematics; science;
history; and courses on government (sometimes known
as 'Civics'); and an expanded list of electives.

Either by design or *de facto* students will
generally be 'tracked' by the time they reach
secondary schools. Indeed, this system of academic
streaming or segregation may have begun in the
junior high, and critics of American schooling
assert that it begins, even if subtly, in the
elementary years. Those planning to attend a four
year college will generally be in an academic track
with intense attention paid to literature, foreign
language, higher mathematics, and sciences such as
physics and chemistry.

Students whose academic plans are not well
formulated, or who do not do well in school, may
find themselves in a middle track which has a
diluted academic curriculum. Upon graduation they
may attend a *community college* or even a *state
college* which does not have stringent entry requirements. Students may also be in a third track with
a preponderance of vocationally-oriented courses.
However, most vocational preparation in the United
States takes place on the job, or in an apprenticeship programme. American secondary school
vocational education has not generally been judged
as successful.

Non-public Schools. Parallel to the public, tax-
supported lower education system is a private
system. These private pay, non-tax supported,
institutions also stretch from pre-school through

secondary school. Since 1975 actual enrolments in
private schools have remained stable, but as a proportion of the total K-12 population they have been
increasing. By the mid-1980s, non-public school
enrolments accounted for 11 per cent of total US
K-12 enrolment. The overwhelming part of the non-
public system, 65 per cent, consists of schools
operated by Catholic churches. Additionally, other
religious denominations operate schools, Lutheran,
Episcopal, Seventh Day Adventist and Jewish
prominent among them. The most rapidly growing
private elementary schools are so-called *Christian
schools* characterised by a rigid discipline code and
relatively fundamental interpretations of the
Protestant Bible.

Additionally, there exist non-sectarian private
schools. Indeed, many of the most prestigious
private schools, *preparatory schools*, are of this
nature. They specialise in preparing students for
entry into top ranked colleges and universities.
They are few in number and enrol but a small percentage of students, but they exert disproportionate
influence upon school practices because of their
traditions and generally élite clientele.

Higher Education

Higher education institutions comprise approximately
2,000 colleges and universities, which had in 1981
more than 7.5 million students enrolled as full-
time students and an additional 3.2 million enrolled
part time.

As with America's system of lower education,
these colleges and universities include an unusually
wide variety of institutions in terms of history,
purpose, size and quality. Higher education consists of both public and non-public institutions.
The first to have been established were the non-
public, but currently it is the public post-
secondary institutions which by far have the large
enrolments. In 1980, 70 per cent of college
enrolment was in public institutions. These include
community colleges which generally serve a local or
regional population. They provide two years of
academic coursework for those desirous of trans-
ferring to a four-year liberal arts programme.
Entry qualifications for community colleges
generally require only graduation from an accredited
high school. Successful completion of a two-year
academic community college curriculum qualifies one
for entry into the upper division, final two years,

of a four-year college.

Community colleges offer two other kinds of programmes. One is a vocational programme oriented specifically to employment in a trade or skill such as a computer programmer, dental technician, cosmetologist, or restaurant manager. Also, community colleges usually offer a wide variety of avocational courses. These are not for credit toward a degree and more generally centre upon subjects simply of interest to the takers, e.g. literature, art, drama, music and domestic crafts. Overwhelmingly, community colleges are supported publicly, only a few are privately operated.

The backbone of America's post-secondary education system is comprised of four-year *liberal arts colleges*. These were initially concentrated on the east coast and were privately operated. In the twentieth century they expanded geographically and many public institutions have been established as well. The public liberal arts colleges frequently originated as a *normal school* established initially for the preparation of elementary teachers. Growing post-secondary student populations justified expansion of these into full fledged liberal arts colleges. These colleges are supported primarily by funds from state legislatures. In 1983, there were approximately 1,000 of these schools.

In 1862, Congress enacted the first Morrill Act. This bill, sponsored by Justin Morrill, US Senator from Vermont, provided federal government land to states to establish colleges and universities, hence the label *Land Grant College*. Congress subsequently provided additional resources in a second Morrill Act, 1897, and these endeavours substantially encouraged the expansion of America's state systems of higher education. Most Land Grant Colleges are public, such as the *University of California* or the so-called 'Big Ten' universities located in mid-west states. However, a few private colleges such as the *Massachusetts Institute of Technology* (MIT) in Cambridge, Massachusetts, and *Cornell University* in Ithaca, New York, were assisted when state legislatures provided the land grant federal aid to a non-public institution.

As a consequence of the federal government land grant incentives, it is now the case that each of the fifty states contains at least one major university offering graduate study in a wide variety of academic and professional fields. There continue to exist a significant number of private

universities also noted for their uncommonly high
academic productivity, e.g. *Stanford*, *Harvard*, *Yale*
and *Princeton*.

In addition to the public and non-public system
of community colleges, liberal arts colleges and
great universities, there is a loosely knit system
of training schools which prepare secondary school
graduates for a wide variety of occupational
endeavours. These schools, some proprietary and
others non-profit, offer a wide variety of courses
for fields such as secretarial training, computer
programming, visual arts, radio broadcasting and
manual work such as construction equipment operation.
Statistics are not readily available about such
undertakings, but it can reasonably be estimated
that they enrol between 10 and 20 million students.

UNITED STATES EDUCATION ADMINISTRATIVE AND POLICY STRUCTURES

Values serve as a substrate which nourishes and
influences public policy. In order to do so,
however, values must be transformed into proposals
and the translation depends partially upon the
practicalities of government. Thus, we offer here
a brief description of the structures responsible
for educational governance in the United States.

Limited National Government Role

In an effort to avoid strong central authority, the
United States *Federal Constitution* widely dispersed
power over three governmental branches: legislative,
executive and judicial, and three levels: local,
state and federal. Education was a function
consciously omitted from the federal government's
immediate aegis. The provision of schooling was
left legally under the control of state government,
and there it continues to reside. State legislature possess *plenary*, meaning ultimate, authority
for both higher and lower education.

State Government and Education.

States in the
United States mirror federal governmental arrangements[10]. Each of the fifty states has three
branches of government. The lengths of term and
qualifications of publicly elected members may vary,
but the general authority of state legislative
bodies is similar. The executive branch in each

state is headed by an elected governor. Additionally, each state has a judicial system with several
levels of trial and appellate courts culminating in
a state high court.

Most state legislatures have a standing
committee in both the upper and lower house which
specialises in education legislation. Additionally,
there may exist a non-partisan legislative analyst
office responsible for providing members of all
parties and in both houses with research reports on
matters before the legislature. In populous states
such as California and New York legislatures have
committee staffs responsible for research and
analysis.

The executive branch, headed by the Governor,
contains several agencies with educational
responsibility. Chief among these is the *state
education department*, headed by a *chief state school
officer* (CSSO). This official is sometimes elected
from among citizens of the state. In other
instances, the CSSO is appointed by the Governor or
by members of the state board of education. This
latter authority is a quasi legislative body
situated in the executive branch responsible for
establishing education policy within boundaries
established by the state constitution and legislature. In some instances, state board of education
members are elected and in other instances they are
appointed by the Governor.

Conflict can result when the CSSO has a
different electoral base of authority than the state
board of education, e.g. when the latter is
appointed by the Governor and the CSSO is elected
statewide. In a few instances the state board of
education may have authority over both higher and
lower education. More typically, there is a
separate governing board for each.

It is often the case that a Governor will have
a special advisor for education matters. Also,
within the executive branch, there typically is a
state equivalent of the federal *Office of Management
and Budget* responsible for state revenue projection,
spending plans, and overall co-ordination of
executive branch policy and activity. This
directing body will advise the Governor regarding
education policy and generally will play an
important role on fiscal matters regarding education.

The state education department, staffed by
professional educators, is the major agency
responsible for communication with and supervision
of local school districts. The state education

department distributes state funds to local
districts, ensures that the latter comply with state
educational regulations, provides technical
assistance in implementing state policies, compiles
assorted statistics on education, and may collect
information regarding student academic achievement.
Public higher education institutions being many
fewer in number generally are not subjected to close
administrative scrutiny by state agencies.

<u>Local School Districts</u>. Historically, the
approximate 15,000 local school districts,
distributed quite unevenly among the fifty states,
have been responsible for day-to-day delivery of
educational services.   Some states, such as
California, Nebraska and Texas, have more than
1,000 such local administrative units.   At the other
end of the continuum, southern states typically
organise lower education along county boundaries,
rather than around municipalities, and thus have
many fewer, and geographically larger, local
districts.
      A local district is governed within the legal
authority granted to it by a state's constitution
and statutes, by a *school board*.   These bodies are
typically elected from the citizenry at large
within the geographic boundaries of the school
district.   Elections tend to be non-partisan and
are hotly contested only in times of conflict, such
as with racial desegregation, or in large urban area
areas.   In a small per cent of the US school
districts, school board members are appointed by a
mayor or by local judges.
      In the abstract, local boards are responsible
for setting school district policy.   In fact, since
the late nineteenth century advent of professional
school administrators, such boards seldom are well
enough informed or have sufficient time to engage
in much policy setting.   Their members are almost
always citizens serving without financial compensation and they typically meet but two to four
times a month.   The result is that the majority of
significant decisions are made by school district
and school managers.   In the period since the
Second World War, collective bargaining between
school management and labour has permitted teachers
also to have a voice in school district matters.
On balance, however, school boards, generally
constituted of five or seven members, are
restricted to decisions regarding the selection and

retention of the superintendent, selection of school sites, establishing teacher salaries through the bargaining process and, perhaps, setting the property tax rate for generating local revenue.

Each local district will have a *superintendent* as a chief executive officer. In large districts such as New York City or Los Angeles, the superintendent may have hundreds of additional administrators as assistants. In a small rural district, the superintendent may also serve as the district's school principal and may even be responsible for instructing students. More typically, there will exist a district central office where the superintendent and a modest number of administrative staff will attend to local functions such as budget planning and administration, hiring, overseeing maintenance, distribution of supplies, and an assortment of other duties associated with communication and community relations. Local school boards have virtually no policy setting role for non-public schools or for higher education institutions.

At each school site there is typically a *principal* who is the head of the instructional staff and in charge of the school. If the school has a large enrolment, the principal will frequently be assisted by one or more vice-principals. The principal, or a member of his or her staff, will be responsible for evaluating teachers, ensuring student discipline, ordering supplies, overseeing building maintenance, and relations with parents.

Whereas state-level courts have a major role in establishing directions for schools, by interpreting state constitutions and statues, local courts are not significant actors on this dimension.

Higher Education Administration. In populous states where publicly supported post-secondary education occurs on more than one campus there usually is a *State Board of Higher Education* or a *Board of Regents* responsible for higher education policy. These boards operate within the policy boundaries created by the state legislature. Each campus will have a chief executive officer, a president or chancellor, who will be in charge locally. There exist few administrative ties between higher and lower education systems.

Federal Agencies. The federal government contributes only five per cent of US lower education and 15 per cent of higher education revenues. However, the federal government's influence in education policy is disproportionate to this level of financing. With but minor exceptions, the federal government does not itself operate education institutions. Thus, its policies are implemented through state and local education agencies. Federal policies must be enacted by Congress and are then administered by the federal Department of Education centrally located in Washington DC and having nine regional offices. Federal policies are generally directed at ensuring that the nation's school systems and colleges do not neglect national needs. For example, matters connected with manpower training, enhancement of economic productivity, and ensuring equality of educational opportunity are prime targets for federal higher and lower education policy. At the higher education level, the federal government is the nation's major supporter of scientific research and provider of student financial support.

Federal courts are responsible for a substantial shaping of the nation's education system. For example, until 1954, 13 states operated segregated public school systems, one for black students, another for white. The US Supreme Court's decision in *Brown v. Board of Education*[11] began the process of dismantling these dual systems.

THE AMERICAN EDUCATIONAL POLICY PROCESS

Describing the political processes by which US public policy is created is much like peeling an onion. There seemingly is always another layer. Education as a particular dimension of the overall public policy process is no exception. The actors include members of the public generally, interest groups and their representatives, members of the education profession, and numerous public officials. Federal, state and local governments are all involved. Within any level of government, all three branches, executive, legislative and judicial, can also be involved. Why is schooling compulsory? Why are not the age ranges of compulsory attendance the same among all states? Why is schooling compulsory, but attendance need not be at public schools? How can schooling be compulsory but, under specified circumstances, parents may be permitted to

instruct their children at home? These questions
illustrate the kaleidoscopic complexity of the
American educational policy process.

Education and Politics
Americans are not comfortable considering the linkage between education and politics. Indeed, much
of the ethos of professional education is filled
with the need to sustain a separation between
political activity and public schooling. Historians
and political analysts refer to this condition as
education's 'apolitical myth'. For decades the myth
suffused the literature of professional education
and coloured the public's view regarding education
policy[12]. Much of this myth can be traced to
'Progressive Era' reforms which, at the turn of the
nineteenth century, attempted to separate education
policymaking from the mainstream of partisan
politics. The illegal graft and corruption which
characterised politics in many American cities in
the latter part of the nineteenth century spilled
over to the management of public school systems.
The awarding of teaching positions by school board
members to electoral campaign supporters and illegal
rebates on supply and repair contracts were all too
common. The diagnoses of these ills was that
education suffered from an excess of partisan
politics.
     The proposed cure was to insulate school
decisionmaking from mainstream electoral undertakings. The practical outcome was to reinforce
special government, local governing boards which had
public schools as their exclusive purview. School
boards were to have their own taxing authority so as
to be free of municipal political machines. School
board members were to represent the entire city, so
as to render them publicly more visible, and their
selection was to be accomplished by relatively non-
partisan procedures, such as appointment or by
running for office in a politically unaffiliated
manner. When elected, the voting was to occur at
times different from municipal officials. State
boards of education and other education officials
were also made non-partisan and chief state school
officer positions were sometimes made appointive.
By the second decade of the twentieth century, the
apolitical myth and its practical consequences were
firmly entrenched both in statute and in the
American cultural outlook toward education, and

education politics had a somewhat unique course at the state and local level.

Whatever the public perception, the reality was, and to a growing degree is, that education is part of the political system. An undertaking which commands in excess of 7 per cent of Gross National Product, touches the lives of more than fifty million students, employs more than four million individuals, and is looked upon as a major institution responsible for inculcating societal values can hardly expect to be unnoticed by the political system.

Systems Theory

The application of systems theory to political processes has provided a model useful for capturing much of the complexity of contemporary policymaking. The systems model describes the linkage between the subsystem responsible for the authoritative allocation of values, the political system, and the broader society and its other subsystems, such as those concerned with the economy and religion. Figure 8.1 schematically models the political system and its relationship to the broader social environment[13].

Figure 8.1: Model of a Political System

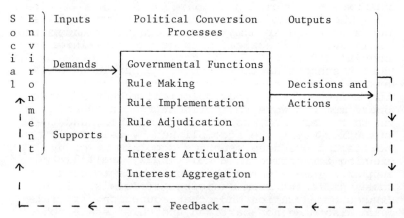

The Environment. It is difficult to specify the boundary and the political system. Where is the distinction between economics and politics to be

drawn? A nation's monetary or fiscal policy can
easily influence the actions of elected officials
and political parties and vice versa. Distinguish-
ing the boundaries for the educational policy
system is even more complicated. It is the case
that much of educational policy at the federal and
state levels is a product of the general political
system responsible for overall public policy. Thus
it is easy for education policy to become embodied
in political party campaign platforms or a
presidential candidate's political promises. For
example, in 1976, the *National Education Association*
(NEA) openly supported the presidential candidacy of
Jimmy Carter. Subsequently, President Carter
advocated formation of a federal cabinet level
Department of Education. This was widely viewed as
a reward to the NEA for its electoral support.

In many local communities, education takes the
form of special government. That is the system of
a locally elected board of education responsible
only for public school policy renders the boundary
setting process somewhat neater than at the state
and federal levels. Even locally, however, the
matter is not altogether simple. Though not
technically responsible for schools in the narrowest
legal sense, an elected mayor might advocate the
position of local constituents and oppose the
closing of a neighbourhood school. The mayor, even
if acting only through persuasion, might exercise
substantial informal influence in such a situation.

The boundary between the larger social system
and the portion of the political system responsible
for educational policy is a permeable membrane
through which substantial exchanges occur. Across
the boundary comes *inputs*. The policy system acts
upon these and transforms them into policy *outputs*.
The latter, outputs, are themselves fed back into
the social system and subsequently serve to
influence the environment and future demands and
supports.

Schools, at the most simple level, can be
viewed as processing inputs and converting them into
outputs. The educational system can be seen as
receiving expectations from society to socialise
students into the ideology and mechanisms of the
political system. Students are mandated to attend
school. Schools are supported by public resources,
taxes. The societal expectation for political
socialisation is a policy *demand*. Tax revenues can
be viewed as a *support*. Schools process such
supports and demands and produce an output. In this

instance output takes the form of a politically
socialised population which is itself then the
source of successive demands and supports. Output
influences the environment, hence the 'feedback'
loop included in Figure 8.1.

Inputs. Political *demands* made upon the
educational policy system by the larger environment
take several forms. Demands are classified as
extractive, *regulatory*, *participatory*, or *symbolic*.
Extractive demands can be exemplified by a public
expectation for vocational training, restoration of
music or art courses in the curriculum, or for
construction of a new neighbourhood school.
Regulatory demands are exemplified by the judicial
ruling to dismantle racially segregated dual school
systems or to mandate that students not be dismissed
from school without a 'due process' hearing.
Participatory demands can be illustrated by the
judicially supported requests of parents of handicapped students that their children be better served.
The request that schools teach the pledge of
allegiance and flag salute or honour a dignitary
such as Martin Luther King by commemorating his
birthday as a school holiday are demands for
symbolic displays.

Supports. These comprise the other component of
policy inputs. *Material* items constitute support,
e.g. tax receipts, trained teachers, school
buildings and school supplies. In addition, it is
necessary to have non-materials supports such as
obedience and deference in order to transform
demands into outputs. For example, if there were
no societal deference to the flag, or to the
significance of Martin Luther King for American
history, then flag salutes and holidays would be
empty undertakings. Similarly, parental obedience
to school policy mandates such as compulsory
attendance is necessary for the system to sustain
itself.

Outputs. As mentioned, the educational policy
process converts inputs, demands and supports into
outputs. We have already illustrated a range of
outputs such as new or added school services,
regulations regarding attendance, provisions for
added participation, and symbolic displays. These

234

outputs are fed back into the larger political
environment where they serve subsequently to
influence successive sets of demands and supports
upon the educational policy system.

Conversion Processes. Transforming demands and
supports to outputs requires both political and
governmental actions. Political actions, in this
context, are comprised of *interest articulation* and
interest aggregation. The former comprises a means
by which policy expectations are transported across
the boundary between the larger society and the
educational policy system. No matter how widespread
or intense a public desire may be, until it is
expressed in some practical fashion it cannot easily
be acted upon to translate into an output. For
example, if parents desire the school day to be
longer, or if they want the state to relieve
property taxes by funding a larger share of school
support, then these expectations must be voiced.
This is the process of interest articulation and it
can occur in many ways. It may take a form so
simple as a telephone conversation with an elected
official or a letter to the editor of a newspaper.
It may take the form of an electoral campaign
position by a candidate for school board or for a
state legislative position. A political party may
incorporate an expectation in its campaign platform.
However it happens, the result is to introduce into
the conversion process an idea which is potentially
eligible for transformation into a policy output.
     It sometimes is the case that even when
articulated, interests must be packaged, shaped, or
bundled together so as to attract sufficient support
to undergo enactment. For example, demands for
greater equality in the delivery of school service
are frequently packaged with demands for greater
school efficiency. In this manner a coalition can
be built which encompasses sufficient supporters to
gain enactment. This process is known academically
as interest aggregation. Politicians know it as
political side payments.

Governmental Functions. There exists three means by
which demands, once articulated, and supports, can
be converted by government into outputs. The three
governmental functions within a political system are
rule making, rule implementation and *rule adjudi-
cation*. Typically these are thought of as being

performed by separate branches of government,
legislative, executive and judicial. In fact,
practical divisions are nowhere so neat. Legislative bodies influence rule implementation, for
example, when they conduct oversight hearings. Or
a local school board, presumably a rule making body,
in selecting a superintendent exercises the
potential substantially to influence rule implementation. Similarly, a court periodically will undertake a rule implementation function when the judge
directly oversees a school racial desegregation plan
or orders a court master to devise a new school
finance plan. Generally, however, in the United
States, each of the three branches of government
concentrates on the function constitutionally
assigned to it.

Inputs from the society, environment, penetrate
the boundary of the political system and are
potential grist for the conversion process to transform into policy outputs. Whether or not a particular input is in fact converted depends upon many
complexities such as the potency of the demand and
the availability of supports. To a substantial
degree, the success of a demand may depend upon the
degree to which it is aligned with one or more of
the three value streams which undergird the United
States public policy.

PUBLIC VALUES AND PUBLIC SCHOOL POLICY

American culture contains three strongly held values
that significantly influence public policy: equality,
efficiency and liberty. Government actions regarding national defence, housing, taxation, anti-trust
regulation, racial desegregation, and literally
hundreds of other policy dimensions, including
education, are motivated and moulded by one or more
of these three values[14].

Equality, liberty and efficiency are viewed by
an overwhelming majority as conditions that government should maximise. These three values are
considered 'good', 'just' and 'right'. Belief in
them has historical roots that are deeply embedded
in American's common heritage. This belief
permeates the ideology promulgated by political
parties, legends, schools and other social
institutions.

Despite widespread public devotion to these
values as abstract goals, the ultimate fulfilment of
each value is virtually impossible. At their roots,

the three desired conditions are inconsistent and
antithetical. Exclusive pursuit of one violates or
eliminates the others. Imagine, for example, that
government in an effort to increase equality,
nationalised the construction industry and then
mandated that housing production be standardised.
Presumably all citizens above a specified age would
be guaranteed a government produced home. Only one
kind or perhaps few variations upon that type of
building would be manufactured. Consequently, all
eligible consumers would be provided with identical
products and would by definition have equal housing.
An added degree of efficiency would be achieved by
the high volume of manufacture possible with
extraordinarily uniform products. Unit costs of
houses might possibly be reduced, however, liberty
would be sacrificed. The absence of variety in
housing would severely restrict or totally prevent
choice. In the absence of choice, there is no
liberty. Moreover, in time, lack of competition
might discourage the search for new production
techniques and thus impair economic efficiency.
Would the absence of inequality be worth the
presumed loss of freedom and efficiency? What
emerges is that pursuit of equality exclusively will
restrict or eliminate liberty and efficiency.
Conversely, complete attention to either liberty or
efficiency diminishes the other values.
Consequently, efforts to re-arrange society so as to
maximise one of the three values are constrained by
forces designed to preserve the status quo. This
dynamic equilibrium among the three values
constantly shifts, with the balance at any particular point fixed as a consequence of a complicated
series of political and economic compromises.

It can be argued that liberty is the highest
of the three values. Efficiency for its own sake
has little meaning. The justification for desiring
that an endeavour be undertaken efficiently is to
conserve resources that could then be used for
other endeavours, thus expanding choice. Similarly,
equality *qua* equality appears hollow. Few if any
persons desire absolute parity with their peers.
Rather, equality of wealth and circumstances can be
viewed as a desirable means to the end of expanded
choice for everyone.

Among the eighteenth century leaders of the
United States, education was viewed as a means to
enable the citizen to participate as an equal in
the affairs of government and was thus essential to
ensure liberty[15]. It was not until the nineteenth

century that education began to assume significance
in economic terms. The increasing demands of an
industrial technology necessitated an educated work
force; henceforth, schooling was taken as an
important contribution to economic efficiency. By
the twentieth century, intensified technological
development and economic interdependence made formal
preparation a *sine qua non* for an individual's
economic and social success. Consequently,
education assumed new importance from the standpoint
of its role in maximising equality.

Post-war US Education Policy
Beginning with the 1954 *United States Supreme Court*
decision *Brown v. Board of Education*, and continuing
with the increase in federal government education
programmes of the 1960s and the school finance
reform efforts of the 1970s, a major portion of
twentieth century education policy has been
directed at achieving greater equality. Consequently, we begin our discussion of values and
school policy by concentrating on equality.
Subsequently, we will discuss efforts following the
Second World War to achieve greater efficiency and
liberty.

Equality
Post-Second World War education policy reforms
focused upon equality have followed three particular
dimensions: efforts to gain more equal client access
to educational services, more equal distribution of
state financial resources, and more equal employee
access to decisionmaking.

Access to Services. The United States Supreme
Court's 1954 decision in *Brown v. Board of Education*
was among the most significant in the history of
the nation. This case not only had the particular
consequences of disallowing the previous constitutional legitimacy of racially segregated school
systems, it also unleashed a substantial nationwide
movement to redress civil rights grievances on other
dimensions, e.g. voting, housing and employment.
The *Brown* decision and the furor which surrounded
subsequent governmental efforts to implement it are
probably the single most significant policy issue in
post-Second World War American education. By the
mid-1980s, school systems in Southern States which

238

previously had been racially segregated by law were reasonably well desegregated. Controversy centred more frequently upon northern cities and western cities where racial segregation of schools assumed more subtle forms, frequently *de facto* rather than *de jure*. Though not now as intense a policy issue, school racial desegregation remains an important concern even three decades after the initial *Brown* decision.

Handicapped Students. Throughout most of US history, severely handicapped individuals have not had equal access to publicly provided educational services. In the early 1970s, several judicial decisions[16], relying heavily upon the US Constitution's Fourteenth Amendment 'equal protection' clause, enjoined state legislatures to provide equal school access for handicapped individuals. These court decisions facilitated the 1975 congressional enactment of the *Education for All Handicapped Children Act* (Public Law 94-142). This statute provides substantial federal funding to assist state and local school districts in the provision of educational services to handicapped students.

Bilingual Students. Beginning in the 1960s, the United States began to experience a substantial upsurge of migrants. Initially, it was individuals arriving from Puerto Rico and Cuba but subsequently populations from Mexico and Central America dominated. Following the Vietnam War, many Indochinese refugees also emigrated to the United States. The situation varied by geographic region. New York City experienced large numbers of Puerto Rican immigrants. Miami became home for tens of thousands of Cuban refugees. San Francisco was the relocation site for many thousands from mainland China, Vietnam and Latin America. Increasing numbers of school-age children could not speak English or had only a limited grasp of English. Indeed, by the mid-1980s, ten per cent of California's students were either non-English or limited-English speaking. Court cases, particularly *Lau v. Nichols*, proclaimed the legal right of such students to receive effective instruction and equal access to educational services[17]. A federal programme was initiated to provide funding to assist in these instructional efforts. Many states also enacted

categorical financial aid programmes to provide
assistance to local school districts for bilingual
education. Though few now deny the need to provide
bilingual students with appropriate assistance, the
form that such aid should take is increasingly
controversial. The political question is the degree
to which bilingual education should assist in
explaining and sustaining students' cultural
heritage, be it Hispanic, Asian, etc., versus more
simply enabling the student to learn English as
quickly as possible. This is likely to be a
controversial educational policy issue for the
remainder of the twentieth century. The problem is
exacerbated by the scarcity of public resources in
the 1980s[18].

  Migrant Education. American agriculture depends
to a substantial degree upon the labour of individuals and families willing to move in keeping with
seasonal crop patterns. Children of such workers
were, and to some degree remain, neglected by the
school systems into which their parents periodically
move. In order to assist local school districts
better to educate such students both the federal
government and a number of states have enacted
financial categorical aid programmes.

Distribution of Resources. Three major efforts have
transpired since the Second World War to redistribute financial resources in education so as to
provide greater equality of educational opportunity.
Two of these efforts are sponsored by the federal
government. These are the *Elementary and Secondary
Education Act* and *student financial aid* programmes.
The former is aimed at lower education and the latter
at higher education. The third effort at achieving
greater resource equality is the school finance
movement which has been a judicially oriented reform
strategy aimed primarily at state level resource
allocation.

  Compensatory Education. In the mid-1960s
President Lyndon B. Johnson launched a social reform
campaign known as 'The War on Poverty'. A significant struggle in this 'war' was to compensate
selected students for the educational deficit with
which they entered school. The outcome was enactment of the 1965 *Elementary and Secondary Education*

Act[19]. This statute was, and continues to be, the
federal government's major education programme in
terms of resources. Annual congressional
appropriations exceed $3 billion. Funds are
allocated to states, and subsequently to local
school districts, based on the numbers of children
from low income households. Funds are used to
provide intensified instruction, generally in the
elementary grades.

Post-secondary Student Aid. The United States
relies upon three major federal government
sponsored programmes to assist college students
financially. One of these, the *Serviceman's Re-
adjustment Act*, enacted following the Second World
War, is important historically. However, it is not
primarily an equal opportunity measure in that it
was, and to a degree still is, available to veterans
based on the years of their military service, not
necessarily upon their financial need. The other
two programmes, the *Guaranteed Student Loan Program*
(GSLP) and *Basic Educational Opportunity Grants*
(BEOG) are designed to assist students based on
their parents' income level. The BEOG programme
provides federal funds to low income post-secondary
students to pay schooling costs. The Guaranteed
Student Loan Program provides federal subsidies to
commercial lending organisations, e.g. banks, to
defray interest on student loans. This provides low
and middle income students with loans at interest
rates lower than otherwise would be the case. Upon
graduation students are responsible for beginning
repayment of the loan. The administrative arrangements in all instances are between the student, the
college at which the student is enrolled, and the
bank making the loan. There is little direct contact
between students and the federal government. These
loan programmes are intended to ensure that students
are not denied access to higher education for lack
of family or personal finances.

School Finance Reform. Since the early part of
the twentieth century, the school finance revenue
generation and distribution arrangements in most
American states have resulted in unequal taxing
burdens and disparate expenditures. In the 1950s
legal scholars constructed a means for questioning
the constitutionality, both federal and state, of
these financing arrangements. The outcome was

disappointing at the federal government level. The US Supreme Court ruled in *Rodriguez v. San Antonio* that such unequal state systems were not in violation of the US Constitution[20]. However, state courts thereafter often judged such systems to violate state constitutions[21]. Consequently the period from 1970 to 1980 was witness to the greatest school finance reform movement in any concentrated period of American history. The outcome, though not uniform across states, is a substantially greater equality in the provision of school support and taxing burden than was previously the case[22].

In that higher education institutions are funded directly by the state in most instances, these equal protection cases did not apply to them. The exception to this statement is those community districts historically aligned with K-12 school districts and continuing to utilise property tax revenues as a source of support.

Equal Access to Decisions. The twentieth century growth in professional school administration, increased size of school districts, both in terms of pupil enrolments and geographic distances, and bureaucratisation of large city school systems, contributed to the post-Second World War growth of lower education teacher unions. Particularly in large school systems, teachers increasingly came to view themselves as disenfranchised by their inability to participate in decisions regarding the terms and conditions of their employment. An answer to this sense of powerlessness was to organise collectively so as to be able to intervene in the decisionmaking process by bargaining directly with the school board. This movement began most visibly in 1955 in New York City and thereafter spread quickly to other east coast cities and eventually to the entire nation. It is now the case that collective bargaining takes place, either sanctioned by statute or informally, in every state. By the 1980s, US teachers were unionised such that the *National Education Association* (NEA) and its state and local affiliates had more than 1.5 million members and the *American Federation of Teachers* (AFT) had approximately 300,000 members.

Efficiency
Efforts to render schools more productive, to maximise output at a specified resource level, are

not unique to the post-Second World War period under
consideration in this chapter. Raymond Callahan[23]
and David Tyack[24] have each written insightful
descriptions of the 'Cult of Efficiency' that
pervaded American education at the beginning of the
twentieth century. This earlier effort assumed that
adoption of scientific management principles would
earn for schools the mantle of legitimacy then
accorded private sector business endeavours. More
recent efficiency movements have also attempted to
pattern schools after business. However, in the
struggle to make schools 'accountable', contemporary
reformers, frustrated by the inability of technocratic procedures to increase educational
productivity, evolved two additional stages, testing
and fiscal containment. This section traces each
of the three stages, beginning with the technical-
industrial accountability model.

The 1957 Soviet space success, Sputnik,
triggered substantial criticism of America's public
schools. They were tried quickly in the press and
found guilty of defrauding the United States of
technological supremacy. Congress responded by
enacting the 1958 *National Defense Education Act*
(Public Law 85-864), intended to buttress
instruction in science, mathematics and foreign
language. Cynics were quick to observe that
America's schools were remarkably responsive: a year
later, 1959, the United States launched its first
successful space capsule. Whatever the objective
performance of America's schools at the time, the
seeds of public dissatisfaction had been widely sown.
Moreover, as the space programme began to accomplish
even more amazing feats, the question continued to
be asked, how is it we can put a man on the moon
while the student on the street cannot read, write
or count satisfactorily?

Against this backdrop of unfocused public
dissatisfaction with school productivity, there
appeared the 1966 *'Coleman Report'* with its widely
misinterpreted finding regarding school resources
and student achievement[25]. Whereas Coleman and his
colleagues were careful to circumscribe their
conclusion, intending only to say that schools
appeared to have little influence on achievement
independent of the social class conditions of
individual students, laymen frequently were quick to
assume that this meant schools had no effect and
that added dollars for schools would be wasted.

243

<u>Technocracy</u>. If student achievement was disappointing, and dollars spent in the conventional pattern had little influence, then the time had come for new strategies. Efficiency proponents were quick to suggest that many private sector management techniques, if appropriately applied to schools, could provide answers, by which they meant higher student performance and lower costs. Thus, the latter part of the 1960s and the early portion of the 1970s witnessed numerous efforts to apply technocratic management strategies to public education[26]. Techniques such as *Program Performance Budgeting Systems* (PPBS), *Systems Analysis*, *Program Evaluation and Review Techniques* (PERT) and *Management by Objectives* (MBO) had been honed during the Second World War, polished in the private sector during the post-war period, and propelled to their greatest prominence with the American space programme successes of the 1960s.

In 1967, the year following publication of the Coleman report and its conclusions regarding school effectiveness, President Lyndon B. Johnson issued an executive order facilitating implementation throughout the federal executive branch of *Program Performance Budgeting*. America's education has long been subject to the rapid adoption and subsequent dissolution of fanciful fads, and PPBS was to be no exception. If the *Department of Health, Education and Welfare* (HEW)[27], including the *Office of Education*, had to implement Program Planning Budgeting, then surely so could school districts. Also, if it was good enough for the Defense Department and the federal government, then just as surely it would benefit schools. Education publications were quick to trumpet the virtues of the new management techniques. Consulting firms rapidly packaged the new management tools for sale to local school district superintendents and school boards who, even if they did not know what PPBS and PERT were, certainly knew they needed them. It was difficult to resist such a popular steamroller.

States, frustrated at not being able to dictate increased school output, began legislatively to intrude on school processes. *Competency-Based Teacher Education* (CBTE) became yet another crest on the accountability wave. Literally dozens of states began requiring that teachers be trained with an eye toward those instructional techniques that were most effective with students. Once they had mastered these professional techniques, then they would be licensed to teach and certified as competent. The idea was badly flawed. There existed few scientifically proven instructional skills[28]. Teaching continued to be far more of an art than a science. Despite exaggerated claims of many teacher trainers and the impetus given to the idea by federal conferences on the topic, the scientific base of pedagogy was simply too thin to justify competency-based teacher education, and the idea generally was short-lived.

Testing. For all the publicity, money and effort, the technocratic accountability movement appeared by the early 1970s to have produced little by way of results. The score card used by the public continued to reflect failure. Standardised test results had been declining since the mid-1960s. Annually the *College Entrance Examination Board* (CEEB) reported that scores on *Scholastic Aptitude Tests* (SAT) were lower than the preceding year[29]. If new management techniques could not reverse the sorry situation, then what could? One answer to the question was to utilise more tests. The assumption behind the strategy was that by subjecting student performance to the glare of public scrutiny educators would be induced to work harder or more effectively.

Beginning in 1964, the federal government contributed to the testing movement by appropriating funds to a *National Assessment of Education Progress* (NAEP)[30]. After the initiation of the NAEP, a number of states began mandating statewide testing programmes. Frequently these tests were tied to the awarding of high school graduation certificates. Proficiency standards and minimal competences were important phrases frequently reflected in legislation. By the latter portion of the 1970s, 35 states had adopted a form of testing to encourage or ensure higher school productivity. Educators resisted on grounds that the tests were insufficient to capture the full range of school purposes and that overuse of examinations would distort the ends of education. A backlash of sorts occurred. Several states, New York prime among them, enacted 'truth in testing' bills. Despite such criticisms, the public generally continued to believe that tests were accurate measures of school output. A spring 1980 Gallup poll revealed that 75 per cent of the public was favourably disposed to testing; an even higher proportion of minority group members hold such views[31]. Nevertheless, as the 1970s drew to a close, nationally administered test scores continued to reflect a decline.

Fiscal Containment. School districts have lived with taxing limitations for more than a century. Conventional school finance plans permit local school boards to maintain taxing discretion only within a ceiling; if the tax rate is to be higher, it necessitates voter approval. Beginning in the 1970s, however, a new strategy began appearing with increasing frequency: state limitations on spending. In 1972, in an effort to avoid a court ruling in the previously mentioned case, *Serrano v. Priest*, the California legislature imposed a ceiling upon school districts. This spending limit, when coupled with declining enrolments, meant that for the first time, some districts annually found themselves in the position of having the same or a smaller total operating budget than the previous year. Ten other states followed suit in adopting spending ceilings.

Efficiency proponents contended that if school could not be made more productive, then at least it should be possible to limit the amount of public money wasted. The spending limit wave began to build and spilled over beyond the boundaries of public schooling. By the mid-1970s, spending limitation campaigns for all local public services had been organised and succeeded in 25 states. Several state governments had spending ceilings imposed upon them, and serious sets of proposals were made not only to require annually that federal spending be balanced against revenue, but also to limit federal spending to a specified proportion of the Gross National Product (GNP)[32].

The fiscal containment movement met with a measure of success. A Rand Corporation survey revealed that total government spending as a function of GNP grew steadily from 1929 to 1975. By that year government spending, including schools, equalled 35 per cent of the total value of all goods and services produced in the United States. From 1975 to 1979 this percentage fell to 32.6 per cent. The share of lower education (that is, grades K-12) in GNP also declined from its 1975 level, from 7 to 5 per cent of GNP. As a per cent of total government spending, education had fallen from 30 per cent in 1956 to 27 per cent by 1975 and even lower by 1979[33].

To some degree, efforts to achieve greater equalisation need not directly conflict with reforms

aimed at influencing school processes or outputs.
At least occasionally, proponents of equality and a
more rigorous school curriculum, for example, 'back
to basics', can co-exist and may even co-operate.
However, attempts to achieve greater school
efficiency by limiting inputs of school dollars are
seldom compatible with equity reforms. School
reform is difficult to impossible in an atmosphere
of fiscal containment. Without additional resources,
equity necessitates a redistribution, taking from
some to give to others. Fiscal containment policies
militate against surpluses in the absence of which
equity can come only from redistribution. Altering
a plan to redistribute resources such that there are
not simply winners and even bigger winners (or at
least winners and those held harmless), but rather
winners and losers, invites intense political
conflict. It is such conflicts that frequently give
birth to proposals for greater liberty or choice,
the topic to which we next turn.

<u>Liberty</u>
Freedom to choose from among alternatives is a long-
respected component of American culture, schooling
included. Since its colonial inception, America's
education system has been characterised by
substantial diversity. Choices existed whereby
parents and citizens could satisfy their preferences
for schooling. In *Pierce v. Society of Sisters*
(1925)[34], the US Supreme Court affirmed the right
of parents to select from among both public and
private school alternatives. Even within the public
school sector, efforts have consistently been made
to ensure that even though schooling was compulsory,
schools themselves were nevertheless responsible to
the clients they served. Responsiveness was intended
for public schools to facilitate choice, to be a
proxy for liberty in a system that otherwise held a
monopoly position for most parents and students.
    Post-Second World War efforts to ensure or
enhance liberty for public schools have taken two
primary forms: (1) proposals to encourage greater
privatisation of schooling, and (2) reforms intended
to render public schooling more diverse and more
responsible to clients.

<u>Privatisation</u>. The mid-1950s Supreme Court school
desegregation decisions precipitated numerous
reactions. One outcome, white efforts to avoid

247

racially desegregated schools, took various forms:
violent resistance, civil disobedience, legal
subterfuge, delay and escape. This latter strategy
resulted in the greatest surge in non-public school
enrolments in the twentieth century. By 1968, the
time by which court-ordered desegregation was at its
most intense nationwide non-public school enrolments
climbed to 14 per cent of the total school
population[35].

This growth resulted primarily from the
formation of hundreds of 'white academies' in
southern states. Prince Edwards County, Virginia,
attempted to aid such segregated schools by closing
its public schools[36]. Mississippi rescinded its
compulsory school attendance law and attempted to
arrange state tuition payments for students attending segregated private schools. These and similar
efforts were eventually found to be illegal. Under
the pressure of court decisions, Internal Revenue
Service investigations, and sheer economics, white
academies began to close.

By 1975, the nationwide proportion of students
enrolled in non-public schools had been halved, to
only 7 per cent. Undoubtedly white fears of racially
mixed schools had been at least partially assuaged,
and this accounted for the closing of many segregated
private schools. However, no sooner had non-public
school enrolment proportions declined to 7 per cent
than they began once again to ascend. By 1980 it
was estimated that non-public school enrolments had
rebounded to between 10 and 11 per cent of total
kindergarten through to twelfth grade enrolments.
Growing public popularity moved legislative proponents in states such as New York and Pennsylvania to
enact state aid provisions benefiting these schools.
Such aid took various forms: direct aid to non-
public schools for supplies and to cover costs of
state-mandated operations such as testing, transportation to students, and state income tax credits,
and deductions to households paying private school
tuition. Whatever the political popularity or moral
rectitude of such provisions, they systematically
have been found to be constitutionally unacceptable[37].

Non-public school advocates enjoyed, at least
initially, greater success in their efforts to
obtain federal financial aid. In an extraordinarily
adroit move, Johnson administration education
officials were able to fashion a compromise between
the *National Education Association* and the *National
Catholic Welfare Conference* that permitted enactment
of the 1965 *Elementary and Secondary Education Act*.

Simultaneously frustrated by the inability to obtain judicial approval for a major state aid to non-public schools plan and heartened by the ESEA federal assistance breakthrough, non-public school aid advocates subsequently attempted an even more dramatic strategy, congressionally approved tuition tax credits. A concerted tuition tax credit coalition effort was mounted beginning in 1977. Proponents put forth bills that would grant to households a federal income tax credit proportional to non-public school tuition payments. The plans, if enacted, would cost the federal treasury several billion dollars annually in foregone tax revenues. Throughout the 1970s and into the 1980s, these revenue deficits were sufficient to dampen congressional enthusiasm for the idea[38].

There remains yet another avenue by which privatisation proponents attempted to gain public support: voucher plans. Governmental aid to students, who then select the school of their choice, was popularised for higher education with the advent of the so-called 'G.I. Bill' following the Second World War[39]. In 1955, Milton Friedman, the Nobel prize-winning economist, advocated a similar strategy for returning efficiency and responsiveness to lower education[40]. Friedman's idea began to receive greater attention during the onset of the efficiency movement in the 1960s. Finally, one small local school district, *Alum Rock*, in the area of San Jose, California, consented to undertake a diluted voucher trial. The Alum Rock trial concluded with mixed reviews[41]. Privatisation critics asserted that vouchers were imperfect, and proponents contended that the experiment was flawed and that inability of private sector schools to participate rendered the experiment invalid.

Responsiveness. The 1960s and 1970s encompassed a period of intense public school criticism. One dimension of these complaints was that American schools were insensitive to the preference of clients, parents and students. Public policy diagnosticians attributed the illness to excessive influence by educational professionals, administrators and teacher organisations. The prime remedy was judged to be a restoration of local control, greater citizen participation. Toward this end, four reform surges took place between 1955 and 1980:

(1)   the so-called 'community control'
       movement,
(2)   efforts to establish 'alternative schools',
(3)   administrative decentralisation, and
(4)   school site management and parent advisory
       councils.

Community Control. In the early 1970s, the
Ford Foundation sponsored a study of New York City
schools[42]. The report recommended that steps be
taken to disaggregate the huge New York City school
district into presumably more manageable subunits.
Three experimental *community control* districts
emerged and rapidly became the focus for
substantial conflict. Eventually, the New York
Legislature enacted a bill that divided the city's
schools into 31 elementary districts with elected
boards subject to the overall authority of the city's
central school board. Each of these subdistricts
contained more pupils than the overwhelming majority
of school districts throughout the United States.
Community control proponents were dismayed that the
new subbureaucracies would be touted as a way to
return schools to the 'people'. Moreover, early
political analyses asserted that newly elected local
boards were heavily dominated by citizens supported
by teacher unions[43]. Much discussion was given to
similar disaggregating proposals in other city
districts, but little came of it practically.

Alternative Schools. This concept, much like
accountability, was and continues to be a semantic
umbrella of sufficient breadth to encompass numerous
schooling ideas, some of them antithetical. In the
1960s, several notable authors wrote stinging
critiques and asserted that public schools were
debilitatingly uniform, repressive, stifling of
student and staff creativity, and administered in a
mindless fashion[44]. Alternative education was
proposed as a reform. British primary schools were
frequently cited as a model for students' early
years, wherein relatively unstructured learning
experiences would more easily assist in the transition from home to scholarly activities. Many
parents removed their children from public schools
to place them in private *alternative schools*.
Public school systems themselves, unwilling to
forego their market share easily, established public
alternative school experiments. By the end of the

1970s, the movement had run its course, and several of its major ideologues had revised their opinions, confessed a change of heart, and advocated more structured schools[45].

Administrative Decentralisation. Large city school districts underwent a wave of *decentralisation* during the 1960s and 1970s. The general justification was that disaggregation would permit schools to be more responsive to clients and employees. The typical pattern was to divide the district into several administrative subunits, each with an administrative officer nominally in charge of all schools in the subdistrict. Districts varied with regard to the degree of decisionmaking discretion permitted to these subunits. In most instances, fiscal authority continued to be centralised. Personnel administration also typically remained a central office function. Curriculum planning and instructional emphasis were often permitted to vary in accord with the tastes of the subdistrict administrator. Only in New York City was disaggregation accompanied by political reform, namely the election of subdistrict school boards. In other cities, the central school board continued to be the policymaking body for the entire district. Consequently, critics contended that decentralisation accomplished little more than added costs and the insertion of yet another bureaucratic layer between local schools and 'downtown' decisionmakers. It was difficult, outside of city school central offices and subdistrict administrators, to identify those favourable to the reform[46].

School Site Management. The relative failure of community control, alternative schools, and administrative decentralisation, encouraged yet a fourth effort to infuse schools with greater citizen participation. This additional reform was described in detail initially by a New York State reform commission that utilised the label *school site management*[47].
The plan intended both to gain a greater measure of lay control and to provide more 'accountability' by using the school, rather than the district, as the basic decisionmaking unit for personnel and curriculum. School district central offices would continue to handle fiscal and business matters and serve as planning, co-ordinating and

record-keeping bodies. A *parent advisory council* (PAC) at each school would be responsible for selection and evaluation of the school principal and for advising that officer on curriculum, instructional, and personnel matters. Principals were envisioned as being on multi-year contracts, the renewal of which was subject to parent advisory committee approval. Within specified boundaries, the principal and parent advisory council would have discretion over funds budgeted for the school by the central office. Each school's budget allocation was to be determined by a set of uniform decision rules, including criteria such as number, grade level and achievement records of pupils assigned to the school. The parent advisory council would issue an annual evaluation report including plans for the subsequent year.

Several states adopted parent advisory council components for their state categorical aid programmes. Portions of the idea also were favourably received by federal authorities, which began to include parent advisory council requirements for schools receiving categorical aid funds under programmes such as ESEA, Title I, Emergency School Assistance Act (ESAA) and bilingual categorical funds. The idea became so pervasive that school administrators were soon to ask that the parent advisory councils undergo consolidation lest principals' nights consist of one council meeting after another and little else.

Aside from the widespread adoption in form, there is slight evidence regarding the effectiveness of the idea. In many instances, little budget discretion was ceded to parents, collective bargaining agreements with teachers continued to render most decisions a central office matter, parents claimed they were too easily co-opted by administrators, and few principals were attracted to the idea of their job security being tied to parental approval. These factors inspired the impression that the reform was widely adopted but not yet of consequence[48].

CONCLUSION

Almost every reform has demonstrated that isolated pursuit of one value is virtually impossible. The coalition building necessary to define, fashion and implement a widespread reform almost always necessitates concessions to proponents of yet another value stream. Successful school finance reform coalitions to 1980 were most often formed by proponents of equality and efficiency. Hence, in state after state, redistribution of spending and taxing authority has been accompanied by productivity reforms such as statewide achievement testing, spending limits, state-prescribed teacher-training procedures, state-mandated teacher-pupil ratios, and additional reporting requirements. The outcome in almost every instance has been reduced decisionmaking discretion for local school authorities. Whether or not this consequence will, in time, foster counterpressures for reform on the dimension of liberty remains to be seen.

NOTES

1. The annual operating cost of this 'system', both public and non-public and higher and lower education, in 1983 was in excess of $170 billion.
2. See L. Cremin, *American Education: The Colonial Experience: 1607-1786* (Harper & Row, New York, 1970).
3. M. Jernegan, *Laboring and Dependent Classes in Colonial America: 1607-1783* (University of Chicago Press, Chicago, 1931), p.82.
4. D.B. Tyack (ed.), *Turning Points in American Educational History* (Blaisdell, Waltham, Mass., 1967).
5. *The Acts and Resolves, Public and Private, of the Province of Massachusetts Bay*, Vol.I, Acts of 1789, Chapter XIX, cited in L. Cremin, *The American Common School* (Teachers College, Columbia University, New York, 1951), p.130.
6. *Ibid.*, pp.136-7.
7. *Ibid.*, pp.88-90.
8. This movement is explained by R. Callahan, *Education and the Cult of Efficiency* (University of Chicago Press, Chicago, 1962) and D.B. Tyack, *The One Best System* (Harvard University Press, Cambridge, 1974).
9. These and other enrolment statistics in this chapter are taken from *Current Population Reports* of the US Census Bureau of the US Department of Commerce.
10. One state, Nebraska, is something of an exception having only a unicameral legislature.
11. 347 U.S. 483, 495 (1954).
12. See Tyack, *The One Best System*.
13. This explanation of a political systems

model is based upon D. Easton, *A Framework for Political Analysis* (Prentice-Hall, Englewood Cliffs, 1965).

14. For more on this topic, see J.W. Gardner, *Excellence: Can We Be Equal and Excellent Too?* (Harper & Row, New York, 1961).

15. See F. Rudolph (ed.), *Essays on Education in the New Republic* (Harvard University Press, Cambridge, 1969).

16. *PARC v. Commonwealth* 834. F.Sup.Ct. 1257 (ED Pa. 1971) 343 f.Sup.279 (ED Pa. 1972) and *Mills v. Board of Education* 348 f.Sup. 866 (PCC 1972).

17. *Lau v. Nichols* 94 Sup. Ct. 786 (1974).

18. See the 1 May 1983 report on education of the Twentieth Century Fund, New York City.

19. Combined in the Education Consolidation Improvement Act in 1981.

20. *Rodriguez v. San Antonio* 411 U.S. 1 (1973).

21. State cases such as *Serrano v. Priest* 18 Cal 3rd 729.

22. The effort to obtain greater equality of resource distribution through the judicial process is summarised by M.W. LaMorte and J.D. Williams in 'Court Decisions and School Finance Reform', a paper delivered at the 1983 annual meeting of the American Education Research Association in Montreal, Canada, 11 April 1983.

23. Callahan, *Education and the Cult of Efficiency*.

24. Tyack, *The One Best System*.

25. J.S. Coleman *et al.*, *Equality of Educational Opportunity* (US Government Printing Office, Washington DC, 1966).

26. D. Martin, G.E. Overholt and W.J. Urban, *Accountability in American Education: A Critique* (Princeton Book Company, Princeton NJ, 1976).

27. In 1979, the federal executive branch was altered to make The Office of Education of cabinet rank. When it became The Department of Education, then HEW became the Department of Health and Human Services.

28. R.W. Heath and M.A. Nielson, 'The Research Basis for Performance-Based Teacher Education', *Review of Educational Research*, vol.44, no.4 (Fall, 1974), pp.463-84.

29. J.H. Thomas, 'Declining Test Scores: The State's Reaction', *Compact*, vol.9, no.6 (Dec. 1975), pp.9-12.

30. For a history of the formative years of NAEP see R.W. Tyler, 'National Assessment: A History and Sociology' in J.W. Guthrie and E. Wynne, *New*

Models for American Education (Prentice-Hall, Englewood Cliffs, 1971).
    31. Spring 1980 Gallup poll on public acceptance of testing reported in the February 1980 issue of *School and Community*.
    32. The 1978 *Congressional Quarterly Almanac* covering the second session of the 95th Congress (Congressional Quarterly 1979) contains an extensive description and analysis of these spending limitation proposals at the federal level. Similarly, John Augenblick has summarised state legislative actions in 1978-79 in an Education Commission of the States Report F 79-4, July 1979.
    33. A.H. Pascal and M.D. Menchik, *Fiscal Containment: Who Wins? Who Loses?* (Rand Corporation, Santa Monica, 1979).
    34. 268 U.S. 310.
    35. US Department of Health, Education and Welfare, *A Century of U.S. School Statistics* (Washington DC, 1974).
    36. *Griffin v. County School Board* 377 U.S. 218 (1964).
    37. P.S. Duffy, 'A Review of Supreme Court Decisions on Aid to Nonpublic Elementary and Secondary Education', *The Hastings Law Journal*, vol.23, no.3 (March 1972), pp.966-89.
    38. See J.S. Catteral, *Tuition Tax Credits: Fact and Fiction* (Phi Delta Kappa, Bloomington, 1983).
    39. The Serviceman's Readjustment Act Public Law 78-346.
    40. M. Friedman, *Capitalism and Freedom* (University of Chicago Press, Chicago, 1982).
    41. D. Weiler, *The Public School Voucher Demonstrations: The First Year at Alum Rock* (Rank Corporation, Santa Monica, 19 June 1974).
    42. Authored principally by M. Fantini, the report was entitled *Reconnection for Learning*.
    43. M. Gittell, *Participants and Participation: A Study of School Policy in New York City* (Center for Urban Education, New York, 1967).
    44. See, for example, J. Kozol, *Death at an Early Age* (Houghton Mifflin, Boston, 1978).
    45. J. Kozol, *Children of the Revolution* (Delacorte, New York, 1978).
    46. G.R. LaNoue and B.L.R. Smith, *The Politics of School Decentralisation* (Lexington Books, Lexington, Mass., 1973).
    47. J.W. Guthrie, 'Social Science, Accountability and the Political Ecomony of School Productivity' in J.E. MacDermott (ed.), *Indeterminancy in Education* (McCutchan Publishing Corporation,

Berkeley, 1976).

48. *Improving Education in Florida: A Reassessment* - Prepared for the Select Joint Committee on Public Schools for the Florida Legislature (Tallahassee, 1976).

Nine

WEST GERMANY

W. Schwark and A. Wolf

HISTORICAL BACKGROUND

After the Second World War, the foremost educational
concern of the three western occupying powers was to
bring about, by means of re-education, an ideological
transition from National Socialism to democracy in
the German people. However, in spite of diverse
ideas as to how this was to be achieved, and in view
of the immense problems of reconstruction, it was
soon agreed among American, English and French
educational politicians that such a transition could
not just be arbitrarily imposed, but would have to
come from the Germans themselves. At the end of
1945, subsequent to the denazification of the
teaching force and the expurgation of National
Socialist influences from educational material,
schools and colleges were again in operation. The
tripartite vertically-scaled school system which had
existed before the National Socialist period was
again adopted, even though American educational
experts had recommended the horizontally-graded
comprehensive system as a means of accelerating the
process of democratisation. A subsequent revival,
however, of Christian and humanistic ideals and
values within the educational subject-matter then in
use acted as a counterbalance both to discredited
National Socialistic ideas and also to the Socialism
of the East.
    With the founding of the Federal Republic
(*Bundesrepublik*) in 1949 this initial phase of
recovery and reconstruction was succeeded by a
period of co-ordination in the education sector. In
1949 the 'Permanent Conference of Education
Ministers' (*Ständige Konferenz der Kultusminister*)
in the regions (*Bundesländer*) was formed, in spite
of the cultural autonomy vested in the individual

regions, with the object of maintaining a relative
uniformity in the education system. In 1955 it
agreed upon a standard code of procedure applicable
to questions of school administration and
organisation. The 'German Committee for
Educational Cultural Affairs' (*Deutscher Ausschuss
für das Erziehungs- und Bildungswesen*), in office
between 1953 and 1965, made known its views on
questions of improvements and standardisation of the
school system in a series of reports. These aimed
at a greater equality of educational opportunity for
pupils coming from a variety of social backgrounds.

Even by the end of the fifties it was becoming
evident that, compared with other countries, science
and technology in the Federal Republic were lagging
behind. The qualified work-force had, at the same
time, been similarly affected. It was therefore
essential that a re-orientation of the educational
field should take place by the beginning of the
nineteen-sixties if further economic growth was not
to be endangered. A phase now began in which
educational resources were being mobilised. The
'Council of the Arts, Science and Research'
(*Wissenschaftsrat*), formed in 1957, put forward an
overall plan for the advancement of science and
learning (*Wissenschaft*), and initiated new areas of
emphasis in the now considerably expanding field of
higher education. It was felt that a rationalisation of the educational process would enable the
greatest possible number of undergraduates to
improve their final qualifications. In both
teaching and research the assessment methods of
behavioural theory and their didactic application to
testing procedures became standard practice. In the
schools, the existing eight-year elementary school
(*Volksschule*) course was, in 1964, split into a
four-year course at a primary school (*Grundschule*)
and a five-year course at a secondary school
(*Hauptschule*). The small rural schools were widely
replaced by larger middle schools (*Mittelpunktschule*).
Intensive publicity and a greater mobility between
the various types of school led to an increase in the
quota of successful candidates in the school-leaving
examination (*Abitur*). New opportunities via the
'second road to education' were offered by colleges
and evening institutes where students with practical
job-experience could catch up on the school-leaving
examination and higher studies. Other ways of
obtaining further vocational qualifications were
opened up by the 'people's universities' (*Volkshoch-
schule*), by academies in the social, administrative

and economic fields and by training centres run by trade unions and industry.

Since the sixties some of the legal authority in matters of educational policy has gradually been shifting in the Federal Republic from the regional to the national government. The 'German Council for Education', formed in 1965, was designed to bring political decision-making and academic requirements more fully into accord with one another. In 1970 - one year after the Socialist-Liberal coalition came to power - it passed a 'Structural Plan for the Education System', thereby initiating a phase of fundamental educational reform. Its chief aim was to make equality of opportunity truly effective in the realms of education, and here the comprehensive school (*Gesamtschule*) was recommended as being the best possible means for achieving this aim. In 1970 the Government submitted a comprehensive report on education, as well as the draft of legislation standardising the structure of higher education. This came into force in 1976. A 'National-Regional Commission' (*Bund-Länder-Kommission*) dealing with educational matters prepared an overall blue-print for education which was published in 1973. The 'Legislation for the Statutory Support and Further-ance of Education' (*Bundesausbildungsförderungsgesetz* - BAföG) of 1971 provided for state support for those embarking upon educational and training courses.

The great educational reforms, however, in spite of initial success, came to a halt at the half-way stage. Economic crises and structural problems arising since the mid-seventies have prevented their implementation. Comprehensive schools exist only in individual regions and have only been set up on an experimental basis; the aim of equal opportunity has not been achieved. A basic consensus of all participants (i.e. state, regions, communities, economic and educational experts) is lacking with regard to aims, areas of emphasis and ways of implementing the reforms. Thus then, after periods of reconstruction and co-ordination, of mobilisation of resources and efforts at educational reform, a phase of development stagnation has now set in; a fact which even the trend towards 'inner reform' in schools and colleges cannot obscure.

Table 9.1: Phases of Educational Policy since 1945
(*Phasen der Bildungspolitik seit 1945*)

1945-1949	1949-c.1960	c.1960- c.1968	c.1968- c.1975	from 1975
Phase der Restaura- tion, des Wiederauf- baus. Re- education- Tendenzen	*Phase der Koordinie- rung der Bildungs- politik der Bundeslän- der*	*Phase der Mobilisie- rung der Bildungs- reserven*	*Phase der Versuche umfassen- der und grund- legender Bildungs- reformen*	*Phase der Stagna- tion der Reform- versuche*
Phase of Restoration and Re- building. Re-education Tendencies	Phase of Co-ordination of Edu- cational Policies of the Länder (Regions)	Phase of Mobilising of Edu- cational Reserves	Phase of Experi- mentation Relating to Edu- cational Reforms	Phase of Stagnation of Edu- cational Reforms

Source: Arnold and Marz, 1979, pp.16-22.

THE PRIMARY SCHOOL

It was under the Weimar Republic in 1920 that, for the first time, the four-year primary school became a distinct entity within the elementary school framework. It was to include all children from all the various social classes and attendance was made compulsory. Specific guidelines, having a democratic schooling as their aim, regulated the curriculum. The central theme to which all subjects were to be related was that of '*Heimatkunde*' - a knowledge of local history and geography. A 'popular' education was to be imparted, by which the child's area of experience began with family and neighbours and was gradually expanded to include the immediate locality, the country and finally the 'world'. Additional instruction in the native language, in number and in music served the same purpose, as did the '*Heimatkunde*' itself. Primary education had above all to be concrete, and had to involve the 'head, heart and hand' of the child in the process.
    During the period between 1933 and 1945 the

National Socialists distorted the idea of 'popular education' in order to make it conform to their ideology. The *'Volks- und Rassengemeinschaft'* dominated the teaching content and was reflected in the reading and arithmetic books of the primary school. After the Second World War, individual regional governments revived the primary school concepts of the Weimar Republic. *'Heimatkundlicher Gesamtunterricht'* - general instruction in local knowledge - became the guiding principle of primary schooling. Only gradually during the nineteen-fifties and sixties did greater specialisation begin to infiltrate the primary school curriculum.

During this time, however, considerable changes were taking place with regard to the children's environment and general experience of life, and in the demands made upon them by the modern industrial society. Therefore, when the primary schools became separated from the secondary schools in 1964 they called for new ideas more in keeping with the changing conditions. The old 'local knowledge' centred system needed to be replaced by one that was subject-orientated. The basic concept of the local primary school has, since the end of the sixties, been deeply affected by many different factors. These include trends towards greater specialisation, greater equality of educational opportunity, a speeding-up of the learning process combined with more specific 'pre-school teaching' and, finally, a movement towards more freedom and scope for the child in actual lesson material and methods.

Now that a 'popular education' is no longer adequate as the aim and end of the primary school, it has been superseded by a reshaping of the curriculum along more scientific lines, taking special account of the natural sciences. Today's approach to mathematics involves far more than elementary operations in arithmetic, and the new school subject, 'Integrated Studies' (*Sachunterricht*) which has replaced the old *'Heimatkunde'*, includes instruction in basic science. For these reasons the primary school resembles far more a fully differentiated 'primary grade' rather than just a stepping-stone between the thinking and experiences of the young child and the teenager. The initial bias in favour of the sciences in the primary school curriculum has, in the meantime, been counter-balanced by an increase in humanistic and musical instruction. Instead of single isolated subjects being taught, courses are given ranging over whole areas of the curriculum, thus overlapping subject boundaries.

Now that the former somewhat rigid concept of 'aptitude' has been superseded by a more dynamic one, the task of awakening talent (and thereby giving children from different social backgrounds equal opportunities both in and outside school) has largely devolved upon the primary school. The primary school is expected to put into practice a creative and social curriculum which is also concerned with topical problems. In four years (six years in Berlin, Bremen and Hamburg) it is expected to lay the foundations for the first form of the secondary school to facilitate the transition to intermediate (*Realschule*) and grammar (*Gymnasium*) schools and, at the same time, to integrate the increasing number of children from foreign workers' (*Gastarbeiter*) families. This excess number of responsibilities threatens to overload the primary school. It is for this reason that many educationalists today are again demanding more time and more 'elbow-room' to be given to a 'child-centred' curriculum, so that the primary pupil, instead of his school life being made a misery, feels ready to venture into unfamiliar areas of learning.

THE SECONDARY SCHOOLS

(a) Development
From the period of the Weimar Republic until 1964 the school system in Germany was divided up into separate sectors according to the type of school. The vast majority of pupils remained in the eight-year elementary school after completing the four-year primary school course, and then left to enter the adult world of work. Only a few transferred after the fourth year from the elementary to the intermediate or grammar schools, both of which were fee-paying and therefore inaccessible to most classes in society. This vertically-scaled system with the primary school as its base reflected the social classes in the population. In general, working-class children attended the elementary schools, middle-class children (of salaried workers and lower officials) attended the intermediate schools and upper-class children (of higher civil servants and academics) attended the grammar schools. These three types of school set great store by their independent status, having nothing in common except the fact that they manifestly all functioned as

West Germany

Table 9.2:   The School System since 1964 (*Das Schulsystem in der Bundesrepublik bis 1964: Schularten oder Schultypen*)

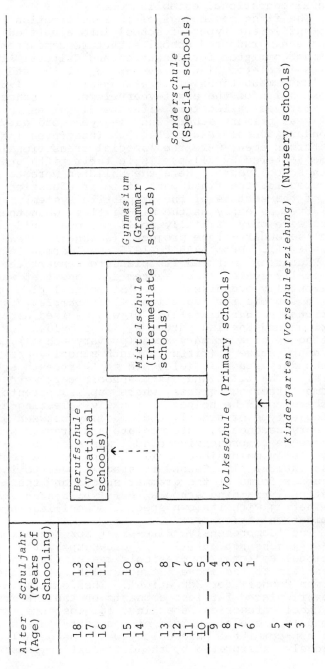

Source: Adapted from Winkeler, 1981, p.29.

general educational establishments.

The first beginnings of a transformation of the self-sufficient types of school into a unified corporate, graduated school structure came from the 'German Committee for Education and Cultural Affairs' in its 'Skeleton Plan' (*Rahmenplan*) (1959) and in its 'Recommendations' (*Empfehlungen*) (1962, 1964). An extension of the eight-year elementary school by one year was called for, with sub-divisions into four-year primary school and five-year ordinary secondary school (*Hauptschule*). Integrated into this arrangement were the 'special transitional forms' entered by all pupils in their fifth and sixth school years. Here the children were to be prepared for the final part of their education in one of the sectors of the tripartite system.

Even as early as the mid-sixties, when these plans were only partially realised, one could speak of a 'secondary-stage project' (*Sekundarstufen-konzeption*). From 1965 to 1975 the 'German Council for Education' matured its plans to convert the vertically-scaled shool system into one that was horizontally organised. The 'Structural plan of the German Council for Education' (*Strukturplan des Deutschen Bildungsrats*) (1970) was devised after American and English patterns. It provided for the setting up of a primary area (primary school), a secondary stage I (fifth to tenth school years) and a secondary stage II (eleventh to thirteenth school years). The fifth and sixth school years were to become 'steering' grades, where pupils, parents and teachers could be helped in finally selecting a suitable type of school, and mobility between ordinary secondary, intermediate and grammar schools - where no comprehensive school was available - was to be fully maintained until the end of the tenth class (*Abitur I*). Secondary stage II was to include the upper forms of the grammar school and the vocational training schools (*berufsbildenden Schule*), terminating with its own special school-leaving examination (*Abitur II*).

The 'Comprehensive Blue-print for Education' (*Bildungsgesamtplan*) (1973), drawn up by the 'National Regional Commission', was similar in its essentials to the above 'Structural Plan' of the 'German Council for Education'. The Commission, however, placed far less emphasis on the integration of school categories, speaking, for instance, of secondary 'levels' instead of secondary 'areas'. Such non-committal phraseology was consequently variously interpreted by the different regions.

Those controlled by the SPD (Social Democrats) laid more stress on integration as exemplified by the comprehensive school, while CDU (Christian Democrats) controlled regions tended to favour the traditional system of separately classified schools.

(b) Categories and Trends

In spite of the attempts contained in the 'Structural Plan' to foster integration, the secondary education sector in the Federal Republic instead of developing into a unified whole has become a conglomeration of the most diverse types of school, which as before are, for the most part, scaled vertically. The decision as to which type of school is suitable has to be made during the fourth school year, and restricted mobility between the schools makes this decision practically irrevocable. Not without significance is the fact that, since the sixties, numbers in the more advanced all-round schools (intermediate and grammar schools) have soared. This is due to the fact that whereas a transfer back into the ordinary secondary school is quite easily done, a reverse transfer into the advanced schools can only be made with difficulty. Nation-wide averages of pupils in the same grade, with the schools they attend, are:

Table 9.3: Distribution of Secondary Pupils by Type of School

1960		1980
c. 66% ⟵———	*die Hauptschule* (secondary modern schools)	———⟶ c. 45%
c. 14% ⟵———	*die Realschule* (intermediate schools)	———⟶ c. 25%
c. 20% ⟵———	*das Gymnasium* (grammar schools)	———⟶ c. 30%

Source: Wolf, 1980/81.

At the present time secondary stage I consists of the ordinary secondary schools and special schools (up to class 9), the intermediate schools (up to class 10) and the grammar schools (up to class 10). There is a routine preliminary stage - a phase of acclimatisation to the school - and then

the ordinary secondary and intermediate schools set
about providing vocationally-orientated education,
while the grammar schools pave the way towards
higher studies. The grammar school curriculum is
correspondingly more academically orientated. Such
a high percentage of pupils - in urban areas up to
80 per cent - are attending the more advanced
schools that the ordinary secondary school is
becoming something of a residual 'dumping ground'.
In order to try and raise its general standing, some
regions are now experimenting with model schemes in
which stronger emphasis is placed on vocation-
orientated training (vocationally orientated
practical courses) in the ordinary secondary school.
In the special schools, which are classified
according to the type of disability involved, there
are courses which can lead to the '*Abitur*' for the
physically handicapped. Usually, however, most
disabled children end their schooling at the ninth
school year. At present an intensive drive towards
the reduction of numbers in differentiated special
schools and in favour of increased integration into
the normal schools is under way. Courses in the
intermediate schools can lead to the 'Intermediate
Certificate' (*mittlere Reife*) at the end of the
tenth class.

Secondary stage II develops out of secondary
stage I. The grammar school, providing an all-
round education, leads in three years to the 'Higher
Certificate' (*Abitur*). At the moment, a 'reformed
upper school' characterised by the range of specialisation facilities which it offers (basic and
proficiency courses as required) is being tried out.
However, it does seem that here the interests and
aptitudes of the pupils are very much overshadowed
by even stronger drives towards academic performance.

Schools providing vocational training are
extensively organised and vary in character from
region to region. Basically one can differentiate
between the following types: part-time vocational
schools, full-time vocational and continuation
schools, advanced and very advanced technical or
trade schools (*Berufschule, Fachschule*, etc.).
Everyone who, after the nine-year school period, is
either receiving basic vocational training or is
actually in work is obliged to attend a three-year
course at a part-time or full-time vocational
school. The teaching here is primarily directed
towards preparation for jobs and either takes place
on one or more weekdays, or in continuous spells
during working time. The vocational school is

expected to work in close collaboration with
employers and may only release their trainees when
the course of study has been completed. Full-time
vocational schools run courses lasting from one to
three years and, like other vocational schools, give
compulsory periods of training. Here expert
instruction leading to qualifications in one or more
vocational skills is given. Continuation schools
offer specialist theoretical instruction which can
either run parallel with or follow on from the
vocational training. Being full-time establishments
their one to three-year courses can lead to the
'Technical Intermediate Certificate' (*Fachschulreife*)
corresponding to the 'Intermediate Certificate'
(*mittlere Reife*). Technical schools (*Fachschulen*),
whether full or part-time, run their own
independent professional courses, and provide fuller
specialist instruction combined with a more general
training. The upper grades of the technical schools
are linked with those of the intermediate schools,
and their full-time practical and theoretical
courses can, in two years, lead to the 'Technical
Higher Certificate' (*Fachhochschulreife*).
     Table 9.4 gives a simplified outline of the
present education system in the Federal Republic
(omitting the tertiary areas).

TERTIARY AND OTHER AREAS OF HIGHER EDUCATION

(a) Colleges and Universities
The founding of universities in the Federal Republic
dates back in some cases to the Middle Ages, but
their collective tradition rests mainly on the neo-
classical reforms instigated by Wilhelm von Humboldt
at the beginning of the nineteenth century. The
principles then advocated included those of academic
freedom for university teachers and students, of
co-ordinated teaching and research, and also the
right of the incumbent of a university chair
(*Ordinarius* or departmental head) to wield
administrative autonomy in academic matters. During
the National Socialist period these principles were
undermined and the universities were placed under
massive restrictions; but immediately afterwards the
old tradition, which aimed at the cultivation of an
academic élite, was revived. It soon became clear,
however, that this aim was incompatible with those
of a democratic industrial society. As a result
the university gradually began to turn away from the
'corps d'élite' ideal, becoming more like a

Table 9.4: Outline of Present Education System

Alter (Age)	Schuljahr (Years of Schooling)	Bereich (Cycle)	Schulart (Type of Institution)
19	15 14	Tertiär-bereich (Tertiary cycle)	Hochschulen (Colleges) Universitäten (Universities) Fachhochschulen (Technical Colleges) Fachschulen (Technical Schools) Hochschulreife (Matriculation Certificate) Fachhochschulreife (Higher College Certificate)
18 17 16	13 12 11	Sekundarbe-reich II (Secondary Cycle II)	Gymnasium (Oberstufe) (Grammar Schools) (Upper Phase) Fachoberschule (Technical High Schools) Berufsfach-schule (Vocational High Schools) Berufsschule (Vocational Schools)
15 14 13 12 11 10	10 9 8 7 6 5	Sekundarbe-reich I (Secondary Cycle I)	Gymnasium (Grammar Schools) Realschule (Intermediate Schools) Hauptschule (Secondary Schools) Sonderschulen (Special Schools) Gesamt = schule (Comprehensive Schools)
9 8 7 6	4 3 2 1	Primar-bereich (Primary Cycle)	Grundschule (Primary Schools)
5 4 3		Elementarbe-reich (Nursery Cycle)	Kindergarten (Vorschulerziehung) (Nursery Schools)

Source: Adapted from Peisert and Frammheim, 1979, p.17.

preparatory training establishment for the
professions and making itself accessible to a
continually expanding section of the community.
Outside the old established universities other
higher educational institutions, such as art
colleges, teacher training colleges, theological
colleges and technical colleges were aspiring to
equal status with the universities. Since the
beginning of the seventies several universities have
combined with other higher educational institutions
to form the so-called 'Comprehensive Institutions
for Higher Education' (*Gesamthochschule*).

A survey over the whole area of higher
education since 1950 can be broken down as in
Table 9.5.

Table 9.5: Higher Education: Numbers of
Institutions by Type

	1950	1960	1970	1975	1977	1982
Universitäten (Universities)	31	33	40	49	50	55
Kunsthochschulen (Art Colleges)	18	25	27	26	26	22
Päd. Hochschulen (Teacher Training Colleges)	78	77	32	33	31	12
Theol. Hochschulen (Theological Colleges)	16	17	14	11	11	11
Fachhochschulen (Technical Colleges)			98	156	136	97
Gesamthochschulen (Comprehensive Institutions)				11	11	9
Total	143	152	211	266	265	206

Source: Westdeutsche Rektorenkonferenz, 1982/83.

However, it is not only the number of colleges and
universities that has increased. The numbers of
those studying at this time have also been growing
rapidly. Whereas, under the National Socialists,
student numbers decreased from 121,000 (1932/33) to
56,000 (1938/89), the rise occurring in the Federal

Republic since 1950 is as follows:

Table 9.6: Higher Education: Numbers of Students by Type of Institution (students in thousands)

	1950	1960	1970	1975	1977	1982
Universitäten (Universities)	112	217	350	552	605	781
Kunsthochschulen (Art Colleges)	5	8	11	15	15	19
Päd. Hochschulen (Teacher Training Colleges)	10	33	59	79	69	19
Theol. Hochschulen (Theological Colleges)	5	3	2	2	2	3
Fachhochschulen (Technical Colleges)	40	68	112	145	165	224
Gesamthochschulen (Comprehensive Institutions)				43	56	75
Total	172	329	534	836	912	1121

Source: Statistisches Bundesamt, 1982.

This more than five-fold increase is not only the expression of a growing interest in the fields of scholarship and learning but it also indicates a new evaluation of higher education and its place in our society.

Because of changes in the function of higher educational institutions from that of 'non-related' research work to one geared to vocational research and teaching programmes, and also because of the large numbers of students, it became clear that a constitutional restructuring - whether of the professorial university or of other college-type complexes - was essential. In the older universities, the departmental head made decisions with regard to teaching and research and also to budgetary and staffing problems. He also had control over the conferment of degrees and over the right of a qualified member of staff to give lectures (*Habilitation*). As a result of reforming activities, however, the monopoly exercised by the

departmental head has, since the sixties, been
breaking up; even more so since the student protests
of 1968/69. The most important decisions are no
longer the prerogative of the Chair or Faculty
(professorial body) but of the so-called Departmental Boards (*Fachbereich*), where professors, students,
academic colleagues (lecturers, assistant lecturers,
etc.) and non-academic colleagues (e.g. library
staff, caretakers) are all represented. All have a
vote, though in varying degrees of precedence. The
Departmental Board Committee or Council takes
decisions itself in some cases, or it may hand over
items of business to the Senate for further
ratification. The latter deals with research and
teaching matters, budgetary items, examination
arrangements, staffing problems, student admissions
and general facilities. The so-called Grand Senate
or Convention is mainly responsible for the basic
organisation of the institute and is also authorised
to elect the Principal or Chancellor (*Rektor*). This
election takes place every four years.
        Of course, the increasing influence wielded by
the state has restricted the extent to which colleges
and universities are self-governing. Now that
building and research projects are progressively
costly and require more and more financial support
from the state, both the regional and, latterly, the
national government demand a greater say in higher
educational affairs. This is done through executive
bodies which are authorised to deal mainly with
co-ordination and planning.
        The 'Conference of Education Ministers' (KMK)
(at the regional level) and the 'Parliamentary
Committee for Cultural Affairs' (on the national
level) have been working ever since the founding of
the Federal Republic on the standardisation of
examination methods and organisation. Over the same
period of time the 'West German Rectors' Conference'
(*Westdeutsche Rektorenkonferenz*) - an authoritative
body combining the more influential higher
educational institutions - has been trying to bring
about unanimity in questions of planning and policy,
as well as representing higher educational interests
at national and international levels. Since 1957 the
'Council for the Arts, Sciences and Research'
(*Wissenschaftsrat*) has been responsible for planning
the support given to academic and research
programmes, and also acts as an intermediary between
higher educational institutes and regional and
national administrations. The Federal Ministry for
educational and cultural affairs - set up in 1970 -

is able to intervene in general questions of
higher education and research should they exceed
the competence of the regional government. Finally,
the 'National Regional Commission for Educational
Planning and the Advancement of Research' has, since
1970, acted as intermediary when problems arise
affecting both regions and nation jointly.

The present economic recession has brought any
further development and extension within the area of
tertiary education to a standstill.

(b) Other Training Centres and Further Education

Apart from colleges and universities, there are
other training centres offering professional
qualifications, such as technical schools and
advanced technical colleges, which also come into
the category of higher education. These cater for
the business and technological occupations. In
this area, too, economic restraints have slowed down
expansion for several years now.

By further education we mean the resuming of
institutionalised learning following an already
completed educational course, or subsequent to some
kind of job-experience. A rapidly changing
industrial society such as ours, together with the
pressures of a contracting labour market, make a
rapid acquisition of new knowledge and skills
imperative for many occupations. The role of
further education has, therefore, increased in
importance. Usually it takes place in conventional
institutions (schools, technical schools), and the
authorities responsible for its upkeep and expansion
include the state, the regions, local communities
and other independent bodies.

IMPLICATIONS FOR ECONOMY AND SOCIETY

At the end of the nineteen-fifties and during the
early sixties the Federal Republic joined in the
international debate then in progress on educational
economics. Education, it was discovered, was a
crucial factor in raising the gross national product,
as well as being a compensatory element in the lives
of those who were disadvantaged, either individually
or socially. Manpower and social-demand
initiatives, together with schemes specific to
regional and local circumstances in the field of
educational economy and planning, were openly
discussed and progressively improved upon.

Spokesmen in this vigorous debate included the
representatives of the Bâle (Basel) school,
Gottfried Bombach and Peter Widmaier, as well as
Friedrich Edding, Armin Hegelheimer, Georg Picht
and Ralf Dahrendorf. As a result an unprecedented
drive towards modernisation was set in motion.

From the mid-sixties onward, all regions in
the Federal Republic were dissolving the single-
class rural school and creating systems of classes
on an age-group basis. As illustration of this we
can take the case of Bavaria, which previously had
over 7,000 elementary schools under its jurisdiction.
This number was reduced after 1969 to 3,000. It was
claimed that this measure was the 'biggest change in
school organisation in the educational history of
Bavaria'[1]. The concentration of elementary schools
in sparsely populated rural regions made a cost-
intensive school transport system necessary. Today,
however, this school transport system has brought
with it the unpleasant side-effect that school-work
often comes on top of hours of travelling. As a
result pupils have to cope with something far in
excess of the adult 40-hour week. This arouses more
and more criticism. In principle, the modernising
impulse in educational organisation has been well
received, as has the school-building programme.
In rural areas the types of institute now pre-
dominating are the focal-point school (*Mittelpunktschule*) and the education centre. Schools of
differing kinds are brought together in large
building-complexes. It is expected that the spatial
proximity will ensure full usage of laboratories,
gymnasiums and language-laboratories as well as
facilitating the transfer from one kind of school
to another.

In addition to the realisation that the
economic standard of the country can only be
maintained when as many people as possible are
educationally well qualified, the overall sociological need for the changes taking place in the
sixties and seventies also became apparent.
Extensive research disclosed far-reaching
inequalities between town and country. The
discrimination against the 'Catholic working-girl
from the country' was proverbial; in other words,
the inequalities existing between people of
different religion, sex or social level would have
to be ironed out, if the country's Basic Law was to
be taken at all seriously. A particular problem
was the small number of 'deferred' school-leavers,
who for many years comprised only 5 per cent of each

year's intake. This, in comparison with other
countries of the European Community was very low,
and all experts were agreed that it should be raised
to at least 15 per cent. These results and the
implied warning-signals were taken very seriously,
and for once politicians, scientists, industrialists
and economists found themselves in unusual agreement
with the parents themselves that a major change was
necessary. Following a great deal of educational
propaganda, generous efforts in providing the means
and the opening of higher-grade schools, the
educational standards of children and young people
were raised between the years 1965 and 1976 to an
altogether unprecedented level. Hellmut Becker, one
of the 'grand old men' on the German cultural scene,
summarised the results in this way:

> Twice as many young people are reaching the
> 'Intermediate Certificate' as in 1965, and
> four times as many are attaining the
> 'Higher Certificate' at technical schools
> or colleges. At the same time the number
> of ordinary secondary school pupils leaving
> without a certificate, that is to say those
> who have absolutely nothing tangible to show
> for their schooling, has fallen by a third.
> The opening of educational establishments
> for the formerly disadvantaged groups has
> also made progress. Today, the chances of
> a 20-year-old working-class child born in
> 1958 reaching a university or college is
> approximately six times greater than it was
> for a similar child born in 1948[2].

These reforms were only possible against a
background of secure economic growth, and for more
than 15 years the gross national product showed an
average increase of 4 per cent per annum; indeed in
regions such as Baden-Württemberg it reached 5 per
cent. Apart from a short-term recession in 1967/68,
this increase persisted until 1973, the year of the
so-called 'oil-shock'. It was not only that the
end of the sixties and beginning of the seventies
saw a broadening of the range of educational
facilities in quantitative terms, even if this
persists as the outward and visible effect of that
time, but much more so could one observe a striving
towards qualitative changes; for example, in the
equalisation of living standards throughout the
whole of the German Federal Republic and a levelling-
out of the enormous variations between town and

274

country, and between the individual regions.
These endeavours were exemplified in the
extensive research programmes which included
experimental models within the education system.
The state and the regions carried out a programme
that was to involve all levels of education, from
schools to universities and colleges. Assistance in
the realms of forward-planning for the future
development of the system was to come from the fact
that educational strategy and policy could be
co-ordinated and rationalised on a federal basis,
with guaranteed economic investment. The immediate
antecedent of this programme, which has now been in
progress since 1971 was the agreement of the KMK to
experiment with the whole-day school and with
comprehensive schools, following suggestions put
forward by the 'Education Commission of the German
Education Council'.
The significance of the combined national-
regional programme can only be assessed when one
realises that since the Düsseldorf Agreement of the
KMK in 1965 experimental work in education was
practically nil. The Hamburg Agreement of the KMK
(Conference of Education Ministers) of 1964, which
for the first time allowed experimental work in this
field, deviated very little from the three-tiered
structure of the German school system. Indeed, the
whole national and regional endeavour - not to speak
of any future development - was at that time
regarded with pessimistic scepticism. However, none
of this can alter the fact that it was only with the
introduction of the national modernisation programme,
that the cultural backsliding and general educational
stagnation brought about by the National Socialists
was finally overcome. The importance of an up-to-
date education system for the maintaining and
developing of a democratic culture and sound economy
has been generally recognised by the people as a
whole since about 1970, and in more recent times is
undisputed.
How much in earnest these endeavours were, can
be judged from the rapid rate of increase in the
number of teachers. In 1950 there was a total of
179,100 teachers in the Federal Republic, a total
which rose slowly to 242,500 by 1975. Then, in that
year, an upward trend out of all proportion to
previous increases sent the numbers up to 422,000,
and in 1982 it has been calculated that 565,000 full-
time professional teachers are working in our
schools. School staffs have not only been greatly
enlarged but their members are significantly better

paid than in the fifties and sixties. Comparable
percentage rates of increase were to be found in the
colleges and universities[3]. These figures related
to a national population of about 60,000,000. These
figures become even clearer when one examines the
situation of a single region, of which Baden-
Württemberg, with a population of about 9,000,000,
can serve as an example. In 1960 a sum of DM 0.788
billion was earmarked in the regional budget for
schools and higher educational institutions, the
overall budgetary capacity at that time being about
DM 3,930,000,000. By contrast, in 1980 an estimate
of DM 8,483,000,000 was made in the budget for the
same purpose. The overall budgetary capacity
amounted to DM 30,234,000,000. Expressed as percentages the results are as follows: in 1960, 20.5
per cent of the budgetary capacity was earmarked for
educational purposes; in 1980 the rate was about 28
per cent.

How this affected those people employed in the
education service can be seen from the absolute
figures given here. The budget of 1965 allowed for
43,965 places for the school sector and 21,339 for
the higher education sector. By 1980 the former had
been increased to 94,730 and the latter to 33,805.
If the figures for 1965 are taken as being 100 per
cent, this corresponds to an increase to 214.6 per
cent in the school sector and an increase to 158.4
per cent in the higher education sector. The rate
of increase in the schools was disproportionately
greater, since the increase in the overall number of
places in all areas of the budgetary forecast lay at
around 165.8 per cent. A final look at developments
from another angle may make the points clearer. In
1956 approximately 20,000 students successfully
passed the state examination or obtained their
diplomas in German higher education institutions.
From this one can calculate that by 1985 between
about 80,000 and 90,000 graduates will pass out of
these institutions yearly. This process will
probably reach its peak in 1990, when - according to
the prognostications - approximately 120,000
graduates are expected to pass out of higher
education institutes[4].

POLICIES COMPARED AND CONTRASTED

In the Federal Republic at the beginning of the
education boom there was, as we have already
mentioned, full agreement on all important points.

All the political factions united to modernise the
elementary schools, to secularise them, to ensure
that compulsory education did not come to an end
before the ninth school-year, to basically revise
the curriculum in all types of school, to raise the
number of successful school-leavers in the
intermediate and grammar schools and to bring about
a co-ordinated inter-regional decision-making
procedure. All these goals were achieved within a
few years, and insuperable difficulties only arose
in connection with the co-ordination process. The
'National-Regional Commission' - founded in 1970 -
was therefore asked to produce an overall education
plan in which the Federal Chancellor (*Bundeskanzler*)
hoped to find 'a long-term synchronisation of
developments, improvements and reforms in the
education system as a whole, and a forward-planning
of the requirements within the employment sector for
qualified staff'[5]. This plan was submitted in 1973.
It became clear, however, that the desired
synchronisation of education and employment sectors
was not forthcoming, because the corresponding
forecasting and management agencies were lacking.
For example, it became apparent that the systematis-
ation of educational statistics in the Federal
Republic had been culpably neglected. Even now
this deficiency has not been made good. What an
overall system of educational statistics would be
like, and what function it ought to assume 'in the
area of tension between politics, administration,
science and the general public' has up to now
remained unclarified[6]. Nevertheless, this first
overall plan for education had, at least once,
formulated a binding commitment to the collective
aims and ideals of the late sixties which we have
already described.

By 1973, however, political unanimity had
collapsed, and it then became clear that the German
prediliction for grand solutions did not lie within
the realms of practical politics. The educational
system could not force itself to switch over, in
the short term, from the traditional tripartite
structure to that of open-grading after the pattern
of the 'Comprehensive School'. Two principal
factors contributed to this:

(a)   in the wake of the first oil crisis of
       1973 a prolonged economic stagnation set
       in, which put an end to any further large-
       scale investment and programming in the
       area of education;

277

(b)   furthermore, it was apparent that, for the
most part, the mind of the general public
was unreceptive to, or felt overtaxed by,
modern concepts expressed in difficult
sociological terminology. The education
of children and young people remained, as
always, no concern of the people but
degenerated into an affair for experts,
who themselves offered widely contradic-
tory opinions and ideas. This has
resulted since that time in an
educational-political polarisation between
the so-called 'A regions' (SPD/FDP -
Social Democrat Coalition) and 'B regions'
(CDU/CSU - Christian Democrat Coalition),
while shared goals and achievements have
been pushed further and further into the
background.

In particular, there were two main points of
conflict: disagreement over the 'horizontalising' of
the school system, and a fundamental cultural
controversy in the matter of what was actually
taught.

(1)   Whereas the socialist-liberal-controlled
regions decided unequivocally in favour of the open-
graded school (*Stufenschule*), and wanted, on a
national basis, to expand the four-year primary
school (which in many ways resembled the comprehensive school) to include an 'orientation' grade
covering the fifth and sixth school-years, the
CDU/CSU-controlled regions argued for a continuation
of the vertically-scaled school system. This
reflects in any case a traditional conflict, which
has cropped up with wonderful regularity since the
first German Republic in 1918.
    In Hesse, in particular, the 'orientation'
grade has been fully implemented, as also in Lower
Saxony, Berlin, Hamburg and Bremen. The situation
is quite different south of the Main, where, in
general, the school-spanning 'orientation' grade is
not to be found. Pupils are transferred to one of
the three higher types of school immediately after
the fourth school-year, although it is still
possible to transfer from one to the other without
any great difficulty during the following two years.
Even here, though, experiences of the procedure
seem to be quite ambivalent, since down-grading
appears to be the rule while up-grading is the

rather rare exception.

The tug-of-war situation with regard to the school-spanning 'orientation' grade applies also to the circumstances surrounding the comprehensive school. It is true that the experimental programme put forward by the 'Council for Education', which we mentioned earlier, has been carried out in all the regions. There are, however, immense differences between them. Whereas great numbers of comprehensive schools have been safely established north of the Main, the experimental programme in the south of the country could be scrapped during the next few years. Baden-Württemberg, in particular, seems unwilling to grant the same rights to this type of school as are enjoyed by the others - much against the wishes of numerous parents. Consistent with this situation is the argument that has broken out about the recognition of the comprehensive school's final examination. For years there has been a bitter struggle to give the same recognition to certificates of proficiency issued by comprehensive schools as is accorded to the traditional type of school, thus giving pupils the freedom, if they so wish, to enter upon some form of higher education. The cabinet under Chancellor Schmidt in September 1982 took an almost resigned tone, when it stated 'that the reciprocal agreement announced by the regions in 1978 concerning the mutual recognition of final qualifications and certificates awarded by schools as well as the teachers' certificate, and concerning the right of parents to decide upon the type of education for their children after the primary school, has not yet been published'[7]. In other words, children attending a comprehensive school in the north of the country are still not able to change over to a tripartite type of school in the south without any difficulty. And teachers who have been educated and obtained their qualifications in the northern regions are either refused teaching posts in the southern regions, or they must undertake further courses of study and examinations before being accepted. The Main is turning more and more into a cultural frontier inside the Federal Republic.

In passing, it should be mentioned that agreement between the regions to bring in a tenth compulsory school year for all pupils is still pending. In North-Rhine-Westphalia (*Nord-Rhein-Westfalen*), the largest region in the country, this is taken for granted; as opposed to Baden-Württemberg, where new school legislation at present under discussion abides by the nine-year general elementary school system.

A similar difference of opinion exists in connection with the so-called 'reformed upper school'. On 7 July 1972 the KMK decided that, by the school year 1976/77 at the latest, the eleventh to thirteenth classes of the grammar schools should be changed in favour of a system of subject-courses. The intention was to replace the standard age-group classes by the following type of organisation: an introductory phase lasting six months or a year, followed by a system of courses leading up over four half-year periods to the *Abitur*. This course system would allow for basic and advanced courses geared to individual subjects. In addition to this, a distinction would be made between compulsory and optional courses, and the three main fields of study would each be related to a compulsory subject group, as follows: (1) languages, literature and art, (2) community studies and social sciences, and (3) mathematics, science and technology. Religion and sport would be additional subjects. The combination of optional and compulsory courses would have to recognise more distinctly the requirements of our industrial society than had hitherto been the case in the traditional grammar school, as well as answering the needs of the individual pupil. Methods of study would be taught as much as the subjects needed for professional activities or training[8]. The reformed upper school has been introduced into all the regions of the Federal Republic, beginning with Berlin (1973/74) and ending with Baden-Württemberg and Bavaria (1977/78). After initial agreement over this plan it has recently come in for some hard criticism from the more conservative educational politicans. The main bone of contention is the so-called 'compulsory area'. Here the objection is that instruction in German and mathematics is insufficiently emphasised under this open system. Baden-Württemberg has been the first region to draw the logical conclusion and has directed that these subjects be made obligatory in the school curriculum.

(2) Apart from the question of organisation - i.e. whether the schools should be horizontally or vertically structured - one can discern even further divergences in policy, the contents of education being as vigorously fought over as its organisation. The so-called 'Hesse Basic Guide-Lines' (*Hessischen*

Rahmenrichtlinien) marked the beginning of this development. In 1972/73 the Ministry of Education and Culture (*Kultusministerium*) in the region of Hesse attempted to introduce new curricula which quite obviously meant a discontinuation of the hitherto accepted cultural tradition. In its place, those responsible wanted to bring in socially controversial material. In particular, a spotlight would be thrown on the capitalist development in the country's economic system which would reveal both its actual and its presumed injustices. Pupils would be required to take a stand in reforming society. This triggered off violent resistance. In the many years of conflict that followed, not only politicians and educationalists took part but also conservative parents' associations, as well as influential sections of the German press, both progressive and conservative. This controversy is going on even today. Far from subsiding it has spread beyond the borders of Hesse into all regions of the Federal Republic - with the result that the educational awakening of the sixties has been reversed, step by step.

Leading the field in the counter-reforming movement are the conservatively-controlled regions of Bavaria (*Bayern*) and Baden-Württemberg. At the instigation of the former Minister of Education in Baden-Württemberg, Wilhelm Hahn, a congress on 'Courage to educate' (*Mut zur Erziehung*) was held in the Academic Centre (*Wissenschaftszentrum*) in Bonn-Bad Godesberg on 9 and 10 January 1978. It was a stormy outburst and one which is still remembered even today. One of the organisers, Nikolaus Lobkowicz, for many years Chancellor (*Rektor*) of Munich University, outlined its aims thus:

> The organisers of this conference proceed from the conviction that we find outselves at the end of a ten - or, more strictly speaking, perhaps a fifteen year development - in which a disastrous educational experiment has been embarked upon in many western democracies, not least in the Federal Republic. In this experiment, academically furbished up ideologies count for more than experience; a trend set by a few intellectuals is more important than intelligence, let alone wisdom; an emancipation from almost everything that constitutes the realities of life is joyfully proclaimed as reform; and the whole area of education from the family to the university

threatens to transform itself into an
instrument whereby - once again in the name of
a so-called last chance to reach final
salvation - human realities become unhinged ...
   The title of this symposium is 'On
Education", and on this we wish to say two
things. First, that we do not address ourselves to those bigots who, in their opinion,
have discovered and monopolised the true
principles of up-to-date, progressive and
emancipated education, but to those who have
for many years been made uncertain by the
ideological fanfares; those who wait for a
liberating word telling them that the tested
insights of tradition, the normal order upon
which society is built and from which they -
perhaps not particularly well - live and the
rules of parliamentary democracy, especially in
the field of education, are worth rediscovering,
defending and following.
   Secondly, we wish to say that today one
needs courage and, above all, encouragement in
order to leave the false road into which we
have allowed ourselves to be driven, and to
strike out upon new paths, which will include
most of what is old and tried[9].

There are plenty of emulators and fellow-
campaigners, among which Education Ministers Maier
(Bavaria) and Mayer-Vorfelder (Baden-Württemberg)
are particularly prominent. Speaking from positions
of influence they stress the future necessity to
press the 'ability principle' harder in German
schools. Egalitarianism in education is no longer
the aim. It is much more a question of admitting
the 'actual fact' that native ability is variable,
and that the education of an élite must take its
place beside that of the rank and file. Another
important principle in this educational policy is
that of the pre-eminence of character training over
the imparting of knowledge. Schools ought to work
much more towards the inculcation of discipline,
industry, courtesy, reliability and adaptability.
The unspoken thinking behind this is that in
economically and politically unstable times, the
school, through its educating function, must make
its contribution towards maintaining democratic
values. In other words, it has to co-operate in
integrating children and young adults into the state
and community. This demand has been activated by
certain administrational and practical directives.

The roles of school governors, and of school heads and principals, are to be strengthened, while in the school curricula the call is 'back to basics'. For example, in the primary school there is a retreat from the scientifically and sociologically based 'Integrated Studies' in favour of a revival of the 'local knowledge' principle of the nineteen-fifties. Musical instruction is expected to place more emphasis on 'class singing' - where possible using the good old folk-songs. The new mathematics is to be replaced by so-called 'plain arithmetic'. The teaching of German will once more include nineteenth or twentieth century classics. Works of social criticism such as those by E. Fried or even by B. Brecht are now frowned upon or, in some cases, even removed from the reading lists.

In summarising, one comes to the following conclusions: today, the Federal Republic of Germany is divided into two major camps, each having an influence on discussion and action in the field of educational policy: the Social-democrat controlled regions which, in spite of social difficulties, adhere to their programmes of modernising and democratising in an open-structured education system; the Christian-democrat controlled regions which are attempting to revert ('roll back') to the nineteen-fifties, and accordingly advocate a scaled and graded education system.

POLICIES INVOLVED AND THEIR SIDE-EFFECTS

It has long been a feature of the German education system that it was geared more or less to the demand of the labour market. In other words, the ordinary secondary school (*Hauptschule*) laid the foundations of the whole system, by catering for the majority of the population, i.e. those who were expected to earn their living in the manual and industrial occupations and in the lower-paid jobs. Those intended for later training as engineers and middle-grade jobs generally, attended the inter-mediate schools. This group was a good deal smaller. The grammar school was expected to prepare children for top management and other élite occupations in the community. Consequently in the nineteen-fifties, for instance, only a mere 5 per cent of a single school age-group were admitted to this type of school. Because of the educatonal upswing of the last fifteen years, however, the traditional system, so delicately balanced over

decades, finds itself in an extremely critical
situation. The distributing mechanism is no longer
working properly. The numbers of students continue
to rise without being able to fulfil their
traditional prospects and expectations. There is
the problem of overcrowding. Whereas in 1969 only
14.3 per cent of a single age-group entered higher
education, this figure now stands at 20 per cent.
The expansion of colleges and universities has not
kept in step with this development. They are
designed to accommodate only a total of 750,000
students and yet today there are 1.1 million people
studying in universities and other educational
institutions. This number is expected to rise to
1.5 million by the end of the century. This becomes
even more of a problem when official policy declines
to recognise the need for adequate facilities and
staff. One side-effect of the loosening of
educational policies is that these policies have
found themselves in fundamental dilemma to which
there appears to be no present solution. Helmut
Becker describes it thus:

> If only 3 or 4 per cent of one age-group enters
> higher education then no competition is to be
> feared in the post-*Abitur* period; if 50 per
> cent or more enter higher education, however,
> a contradiction arises between the hierarchical
> structure of the vocational system and the
> strongly democratised structure of the
> education system. Up to now this contradiction
> has not been resolved in the Federal Republic.
> In the United States, when 50 per cent of an
> age-group attend some form of higher education
> (in California 90 per cent), the link between
> education and élitist pretensions ceases to
> exist. In Germany we have begun to democratise
> education without being willing to rid ourselves
> of the élitism. This and other unresolved areas
> of tension are influencing more and more
> strongly the discussion on educational reform
> taking place in the seventies[10].

Shortly before its fall from power, the
national government under Helmut Schmidt demanded
that the German education system should, as quickly
as possible, free itself from its one-sided bias
towards higher education. This was expected to come
about by means of preferential treatment and
financing of vocational training, accompanied by a
series of weighty re-orientation measures. In

addition, the final qualifications in vocational
training were to be regarded as equal to those in
higher education and must be accorded the same
prestige. Were all this to be carried out it would
be of signal importance, especially for the many jobs
maintained by the state itself. These posts are
only offered on strict career principles which
relate to the level of school or college
qualifications. Someone applying for a post with
only a vocational qualification is assigned to a
less important position and, in the face of the
rigid career procedure, can rarely push up into
positions for which a good, formal, final
qualification is a pre-condition. Whether this
traditional structure can really be altered is
extremely doubtful, since the present occupants of
posts, those with university or college
qualifications, are resisting drastic changes.
Probably they will be successful, too, because a
high proportion of these people are to be found in
the legislative institutions - in the national and
regional governments, for instance.

For one particular professional group, an
academic training is having at the moment extremely
negative consequences. These are the teachers.
They are specifically trained to meet the needs of
the schools and, from the point of view of trade,
crafts and industry, are unemployable in any other
way. Although there is always a need for teachers
in the education service, jobs for trained teachers
are increasingly diminishing in number as state
funds are expected to become less available for
personnel than for investment. At present, there
are approximately 30,000 unemployed teachers in the
Federal Republic, and the numbers are expected to
rise dramatically over the coming years. The Kiel
Institute for World Economy has calculated that by
1990, at least 150,000 teachers will be unemployed.
The problems involved here can only be solved if,
in the long run, the training of teachers in the
country is made less specialised, i.e. more basic
and general in nature. The first phase of courses
in universities and teacher-training colleges will
have to lead to broader, more useful basic
qualifications. More specialised professional
training would be introduced into the second phase.
At the same time undergraduates and students will
have to be made aware that an academic education
will not automatically secure a high income, as
used to be the case.

The new governing coalition of the CDU/FDP in

Bonn under Chancellor Helmut Kohl accepts this
assessment in principle but wants to bring more
immediate pressure on pupils and students, in order
to coerce them into rethinking their future careers.
The coalition has therefore already decided to do
away with a large part of the state financial aid
for school-children, and has also stipulated that
student grants will henceforth only be available as
repayable loans. It is hoped that, from 1984, the
saving gained from these measures will amount,
nationally and regionally, to more than DM 3 billion.
If these plans are realised it will mean that the
'working-class child' is going to suffer particular
disadvantages. The former State Education Ministry
once put out the following statement in this
connection:

> The BAFÖG (State Support for Education) system
> in schools is for the direct benefit of those
> families who come into the lower-income
> category. 80 per cent of the parents of
> state-aided school-children draw a net income
> of less than DM 2,000 per month, 50 per cent
> draw less than DM 1,500 and 25 per cent less
> than DM 1,000. In 1980 a total of about
> 490,000 pupils were state-aided, of which
> 170,000 attended all-round schools and 305,000
> attended vocational schools, while 15,000 made
> use of the facilities provided by the 'second
> road to education'[11].

If the aid to these children is done away with,
it means that the families concerned will lose up
to a third of their income. Parents will be forced
to send their children out to work at the earliest
possible opportunity - inasmuch as there are any
jobs to be had.
Another undesirable side-effect is making
itself felt in the educating of foreign working-
class children. It is exceptionally difficult for
them to come up to the standards expected of them
by this country's education system. Only a few
succeed in completing a formal course of education.
In 1979 there were 551,600 foreign children in the
all-round schools and 75,900 in vocational schools.
Altogether, a total of 627,500 foreign children took
advantage of West German educational opportunities.
Of these 46 per cent were Turkish, 13 per cent
Italian, 10 per cent Yugoslavian, 9 per cent Greek,
4 per cent Spanish and 3 per cent Portuguese[12].
The Federal Republic of Germany is hardly in a

position to draw upon previous experience in the
problems of assimilating foreigners. There is, for
instance, no colonial tradition to fall back on.
It is therefore not surprising that the difficulties
of integrating foreign working-class children into
the German education system are on the increase,
particularly in the areas where they are concentrated such as Cologne, Frankfurt, Stuttgart and
Munich, and in Berlin and the Ruhr area. Already
there are classes, particularly in primary and
ordinary secondary schools, in which German children
are in the minority. It is no longer a question
here of how to integrate foreign children into
German classes but rather the reverse: how can
German children preserve their own national
identity? Of course this is not yet the norm. The
problem, however, is being increasingly aggravated
by the fact that the German birthrate has fallen
drastically, while that of foreigners has lurched
upwards to a high level. Up to now, all efforts on
the part of the authorities have had little effect.
The training of teachers, in particular, has not
kept up with these developments. Certainly it is
possible to enrol for supplementary courses of
study; in a few regions one can even form special
study-groups and the like. One has to recognise,
however, that both the training facilities (in
language and culture of the countries of origin) as
well as the necessary funds are just not available.
The new Bonn government has made it plain that it
will intensify its efforts to raise the proportion
of immigrant workers returning to their countries
of origin. This means that no more cost-intensive
measures, such as might possibly have helped to
overcome this critical situation, will be taken in
future. In addition, there is the very real
difficulty that the largest immigrant group, namely
the Turks, show little willingness to be assimilated
into the German cultural background. On the
contrary, orthodox Moslems are careful to bring up
their children by the tenets of the Koran and also,
unfortunately, in the doctrines of their new
political right-wing. The Turks confide too little
to the Germans about their methods and customs of
transmitting information for a radical change to be
brought about here. So, in the last analysis,
everything conspires to prevent a resolving of the
problem and to encourage its destabilising effects
on the community. In the case of the other ethnic
groups the situation appears to be less dramatic.
Immigrants from the EEC countries, in spite of many

differences, belong to the common European tradition
of thought and behaviour.

Although people everywhere are becoming somewhat resigned to the apparent impossibility of
finding a solution to this problem, many and
repeated attempts to change the situation are always
being made. For instance, the National Institute
for Vocational Training - an administrative body
largely responsible for the development of
vocational education - has initiated numerous
academic and practical training programmes to try
and make headway in this field. At the moment, a
project is in progress in many parts of the country,
which is concerned with training foreign children as
skilled workers and craftsmen. In collaboration
with local governments it aims at attempting to
familiarise people, particularly instructors in the
schools and the heads of firms and factories, with
the idiosyncrasies of youngsters from other
countries. If just a minimal amount of
educational, psychological and sociological
expertise could be applied to the training, then the
imparting of the necessary technical, mathematical
and practical knowledge and skills could be
successfully accomplished. But how far these
isolated initiatives could one day meet the needs
of all foreign working-class children is a matter
for scepticism, taking into account the difficult
economic situation and the present political climate.

NATIONAL AND LOCAL DICHOTOMIES

The German education system is characterised by
regional idiosyncrasies and local specialities, and
one can hardly attach any importance to dichotomies
here. In conclusion, therefore, the main
differences between the regions ought to be given
in summary. Bearing in mind, then, that every
generalisation is at the same time a rather crude
over-simplification, one can make the following
statements:

(1) A cultural conflict exists between regions
with a strong Prussian-social-democratic tradition,
and regions which have a long Catholic tradition and
are also permeated with influences of either
Hapsburg or French origin. The first group, to
which regions such as Berlin, Hamburg, Bremen,
Lower Saxony, North-Rhine-Westphalia and Hesse
belong, regard education as a key factor both in
procuring better and fairer opportunities within the

community and in achieving a greater degree of
self-fulfilment. As opposed to this the second
group, to which regions such as Rhineland-Palatinate
(*Rheinland-Pfalz*), Baden-Württemberg, Saarland and
Bavaria (*Bayern*) belong, emphasise the necessity of
adjusting the school and higher education systems to
the needs of the economy.
 (2) These differences are reflected exactly in
the kind of values and hopes that are placed in the
education system. Whereas the first group greatly
values qualities such as creativity, the safe-
guarding of the individual's right to freedom and a
critical, inquiring attitude to society and the
state, the second group have decided in favour of
traditional values, such as orderly conduct and the
willingness to conform - in short, in favour of
'Law and Order'.
 (3) Of course, the first group has no desire
for a radical alteration in the traditional school
system, but it does regard the comprehensive school
as an essential alternative, and as an enrichment of
the range of state education. The second group, on
the other hand, rejects the comprehensive school
absolutely. Present experiments on these lines are
likely to be discontinued within the next few years
unless parents put up a resistance to such attempts.
 (4) The former advocate the scientifically
orientated curriculum. Only in this way do they see
the chances of future industrial development being
sustained. The latter - Baden-Württemberg in
particular - want to return to the old school
subjects and disciplines. For them, analytic-
cognitive learning has no central role to play in
school work. Instead there should be an emotional
identification with nation, home and local
tradition. They wish to return to '*Heimatkunde*', to
reading, writing and plain arithmetic. Expressed in
terms of recent trends in America it is 'Back to
Basics'.
 (5) The first group wishes to maintain at
least the present level of development in the field
of higher education, even if this does involve a
multitude of problems. The second group places
greater emphasis on the development of vocational
schooling even in the tertiary area. For example,
they are founding vocational colleges of their own,
are extending practical engineering courses and are
closing down institutes of higher education wherever
they are thought to be unnecessary. In Baden-
Württemberg at the moment the teacher training
colleges have been particularly hit by this. Of

nine existing institutions two will be closed by
1984. At the present time the debate as to whether
this is enough is flaring up again, and one must be
prepared for further closures.

(6) The former regions wish to continue aiding
so-called working-class children by means of
generous grants. The latter regions, on the other
hand, want the opposite in order to stop the rush
into higher education, and so as to balance the
employment and education sectors in the traditional
way. The rigid German qualifying system is expected
to be extensively maintained.

At the present time it looks as though the
conservative arguments may prevail.

Readers with no background knowledge may like
to be reminded that West Germany is a *federal*
country, with political and educational responsibility divided between the Federal Government in
Bonn and the regional Ministries in each region
(Baden-Württemberg, Bavaria, Hesse, etc.).
Education is mainly the responsibility of the
regional ministries. Broadly speaking they are
responsible for
- school building policy
- the financing and content of teacher training
- school curricula
- the appointment of teachers
- the maintenance costs of colleges and universities
- the appointment and remuneration of university and
  college staff.

The Federal Government has in contrast
negligible influence. Even where it can act, it can
as a rule do so only in concert with the regional
ministries. As a result of Article 91a of the
German Constitution the Federal Government finances
50 per cent of university building and initial
equipment expenses. In addition, it provides
considerable funds for general and specialist
research. It has a certain limited influence on
further vocational education.

That this unequal division of responsibilities
has not led to a complete regionalisation of
education is due on the one hand to the
co-ordination of policy between the individual
regional ministries (excluding the federal
ministry) in the Permanent Conference of Education
Ministers and on the other hand to concerted efforts
to create national co-ordination bodies. These,
however, are as a rule greatly hindered in their

work by particular regional interests and sometimes
even have to be disbanded (German Committee for
Educational and Cultural Affairs, German Council for
Education). In conclusion one can say that the
strength of the German education system lies in its
differences at the regional level rather than its
similarities at the federal level.

NOTES

    1. A.O. Schorb, *Entwicklungen im Schulwesen
eines Flächenstaates am Beispiel Bayern* (Reinbek,
1980), p.779.
    2. H. Becker, *Auf dem Weg zur lernenden
Gesellschaft* (Stuttgart, 1980), p.132.
    3. Projektgruppe Bildungsbericht (Project-
Group Educational Report), *Bildung in der Bundesrepublik Deutschland - Daten und Analysen* (2 vols,
Reinbek, 1980), p.54 *et seq.*
    4. *idem*, p.90.
    5. J. Raschert, *Bildungspolitik im
kooperativen Föderalismus. Die Entwicklung der
länderübergreifenden Planung und Koordination des
Bildungswesens der Bundesrepublik Deutschland*
(Reinbek, 1980), p.113.
    6. H. Köhler, *Amtliche Bildungsstatistik im
Wandel* (Reinbek, 1980), p.1271.
    7. *Dienst für Kulturpolitik* (4 October 1982),
p.5.
    8. P. Lohe, K. Reinhold, H.-D. Haller, *Die
Reform der gymnasialen Oberstufe und ihre
Verwirklichung in den Ländern der Bundesrepublik
Deutschland* (Reinbek, 1980), p.1177 *et seq.*
    9. N. Lobkowitz *et al.*, *Mit zur Erziehung*
(Stuttgart, 1978), p.7.
    10. Becker, *op. cit.*, p.24.
    11. *DPA - Dienst für Kulturpolitik* (4 October
1982), p.2.
    12. Presse- und Informationsamt der Bundes-
regierung, *Gesellschaftliche Daten 1982* (Freiburg,
1982), p.80.

OTHER USEFUL REFERENCES

Arnold, R. and Marz, F. (1979), *Einführung in die
     Bildungspolitik. Grundlagen, Entwicklungen,
     Probleme*, Stuttgart.
Bund-Länder-Kommission für Bildungsplanung (1976),
     Bildungsgesamtplan, Bonn.

Derbolav, J. (1977), *Grundlagen und Probleme der Bildungspolitik*, Munich.

Der Bundesminister für Bildung und Wissenschaft (1976), *Hochschulrahmengesetz*, Bonn.

Führ, C. (1979), *Das Bildungswesen in der Bundesrepublik Deutschland - Überlick*, Weinheim.

Klink, J.-G. (ed.) (1972), *Aktuelle Bildungsprogramme*, Bad Heilbrunn.

Lange-Quassowski, J. (1979), *Neuordnung oder Restauration? Das Demokratiekonzept der amerikanischen Besatzungsmacht und die politische Sozialisation der Westdeutschen: Wirtschaftsordnung - Schulstruktur - Politische Bildung*, Opladen.

Pakschies, G. (1979), *Umerziehung in der britischen Zone 1945-1949*, Weinheim/Basel.

Peisert, H. and Framheim, G. (1979), *Das Hochschulsystem in der Bundesrepublik Deutschland. Funktionsweise und Leistungsfähigkeit*, Stuttgart.

Roloff, E.-A. (1979), *Schule in der Demokratie - Demokratie in der Schule Eine exemplarische Einführung in Theorie und Praxis der Schulpolitik*, Stuttgart.

Schweizer, G. (1979), *Veränderte Qualifikationsanforderungen des ökonomischen Systems in ihrer Relevanz für gesellschaftlich organisierte Bildungsprozesse*, Cologne.

Statistische Bundesamt (1982), *Statistische Jahrbuch 1982 für die Bundesrepublik Deutschland*, Stuttgart.

Westdeutsche Rektorenkonferenz (1982/83), *Übersicht über die Studienmoglichkeiten und Zulassungsbeschrankungen für Studienanfänger an den Hochschulen der Bundesrepublik Deutschland im Wintersemester 1982/83*.

Winkeler, R. (1981), '*Der Sekundarbereich. Begriff - Entwicklung - Struktur*' in W. Twellmann (ed.), *Handbuch Schule und Unterricht*, vol.2, Düsseldorf, pp.27-42.

Wolf, A. (1980/81), unpublished lecture notes, Winter term 1980/81.

Zedler, P. (1979), *Einführung in die Bildungsplanung*, Stuttgart.

Ten

CONCLUSIONS

J.R. Hough

It is not the intention here to summarise all the
often complex analyses comprised in the individual
country essays, which the constraints of space alone
would not permit, but rather to endeavour to
emphasise some of the main similarities and contrasts
between educational policies in the seven countries.
    It is again necessary to commence with
theoretical and conceptual questions: inevitably
these appear throughout the book, in every chapter,
and are often crucially important for an appreciation
of the development of educational policy. The coverage of conceptual and theoretical questions by Grant
Harman in Chapter Two can be viewed as setting the
scene for what follows, from a number of points of
view. For example, his discussion of the different
uses and meanings of the word *policy*, and of the
need to relate these to particular contexts and
policy processes, find echoes throughout the
remainder of the book.
    The *constitutional and legal framework* of a
country must dominate any discussion of policy,
educational or otherwise, at central (national)
government level: thus, of the seven countries only
in France, Japan and Sweden can the central government exert full control over the educational sector.
Australia, the USA and West Germany being federal
countries have constitutions which prescribe the
roles and powers allotted to the centre as compared
with the component states (or territories, or
länder); in each of these three countries education
is primarily a matter for the sub-federal level and
was, constitutionally, not intended to come within
the authority of the national (federal) government.
Often for practical purposes educational policy is
determined below the level of the component states,
as in the case of the USA's school boards, each

293

responsible for a school district, which may vary in size from one small school to some millions of pupils.

The United Kingdom is an exception, in this as in a number of other respects, in that the central government has supreme law-making and administrative authority but in the case of educational policy it chose to hand much of its power over to the 104 local education authorities. In each of these four countries, however, the constitutional position as outlined above has not prevented considerably change taking place over time in *the central/local relationship* in connection with educational policy. However clearly it might have been thought that the respective federal and state (and sub-state) roles had been specified on paper, in practice there has been a clear tendency for national (or federal) governments to develop a greater interest in education and to seek a closer involvement in the formation and development of educational policy. The reasons often lay in some mix of finance (education has become a very expensive business, consuming very large sums of money and often more significant as a proportion of public expenditure than any other sector), social policy (as with the desegregation of schools in the USA), perceived economic need (as with the national need for more technologists and engineers, perhaps especially in West Germany), and direct concern about school curricula and educational standards (as in the UK, West Germany and elsewhere).

If educational policy is at its most disaggregated in the USA, it is most centralised in France where, for example, all teachers are directly employed by the Ministry of National Education. In France, especially since the advent to power of the socialist government, there has been a trend towards delegation of some, usually fairly limited, policy-making powers to more local levels, as has also been the case in Sweden. In Japan local administration of the school system is well established at the level of units of local government but increasingly the Ministry of Education, Science and Culture in Tokyo wishes to influence the education sector to follow and benefit from the latest international trends.

Pre-primary level education means different things in different countries: to age 5 in the UK, to 6 in France, to 6 or 7 in West Germany. In all countries there is a clearly established trend for higher and higher proportions of children to have some pre-school experience in a semi-educational

setting, whether this is called nursery, kindergarten or crèche.

Formal instruction may be given, as in France,
or activities may centre on educationally-related
play, as in most other countries. In France and
the USA nearly 100 per cent of children have such
an experience in the year or two immediately
preceding the commencement of formal schooling but
elsewhere take-up is lower. In France policy now
aims at dramatic increases in the percentage of
two-year-olds in some such semi-educational establishment whereas in many parts of the UK it is
forbidden by law to leave children in such a
setting under the age of 3. There could scarcely
be a greater policy contrast. In all countries
greater percentages of children from middle-class
homes are liable to have such experiences than
children from working-class homes, which may be
contrary to aims expressed in terms of educational
equality.

Much of the discussion regarding *primary schools*
relates to teaching styles and 'progressive' teaching
methods, in which the UK is often seen as having
taken the lead. Shipman shows, however, that the
extent of change was in reality remarkably limited.
Similar trends towards more 'child-centred'
approaches to teaching in primary schools are
apparent in every one of the other countries and
always gave rise to an opposition which displayed
entrenched views and was often extremely vocal.
Everywhere there was concern that language (the
mother tongue) and mathematics should seem interesting and relevant to young children and also that
standards of achievements should not fall. Especially
in Sweden, but also in France and West Germany, it
has become increasingly common for children to
commence learning a foreign language (usually
English) whilst at primary school, whereas this
happens only in a minority of schools in the UK (the
language always being French) and in even fewer in
Australia or the USA.

Educational policy at *secondary school level*
has, over long periods of time, been dominated by
the question of *re-organisation on comprehensive
lines*, especially in France, Sweden, the UK and West
Germany, but also to some extent in Australia.
Secondary schooling in the USA has traditionally
been on comprehensive lines, at least as regards the
public or state schools, and when Japanese education
was being re-organised after the Second World War it
was deliberately modelled on the American pattern.

Amongst the other countries it was in Sweden that the earliest and fullest implementation of the comprehensivisation principle was to be found, dating as far back as 1950; as Marklund shows, the principle was extended up to and including the tertiary level, thus apparently achieving full democratisation of education. In France, on the other hand, the Haby reforms involved the postponement of differentiation between pupils, in terms of the institutions they attended, to the later secondary years.

In Germany only the northern länder, with their socialist-liberal governments, introduced comprehensive schools and it has become increasingly difficult for either pupils or teaching staff to transfer from one type of school system to the other: '*The Main is turning more and more into a cultural frontier inside the Federal Republic*'. In the UK most, but not quite all, of the LEAs adopted the comprehensive principle but with such a bewildering variety of patterns of schooling that one recent volume, having described schooling systems in several other countries, for the UK merely put a large question-mark[1]. When some Conservative-controlled LEAs could resist the demands of Labour central governments to go comprehensive, and when the Courts of Law at times supported the recalcitrant LEAs, this threw new light on the central-local relationship. A similar backlash against comprehensive reform took place in West Germany (very strongly), Australia and France.

In all seven countries the situation in such combined or one-track schools was complicated by (i) the existence of separate, private, schools, and (ii) the question of streaming versus mixed-ability teaching, the combined effect of which was that it was by no means universal for children of a wide range of abilities and from very differing socio-economic backgrounds to be taught together in the same classroom. In every one of the countries policy has always accepted the existence of *private, usually fee-paying, schools*, often with strong religious affiliations. Such schools were least evident in Sweden and most evident in France, where they provided the education of over 20 per cent of the secondary age range. In both France and the UK church-related schools could opt for either closer or less close integration with the state school system with the financial arrangements varying accordingly. In the USA increased participation in private schools occurred with the desegregation of

public schools in the wake of the 1954 decision of
the US Supreme Court in *Brown v. Board of Education*
which Guthrie and Bodenhausen describe as '*among the
most significant in the history of the nation*'.
Here education policy was clearly being used for
purposes of social equality and to eliminate racial
injustice but the parents involved in the 'white
flight' could opt out of the consequences as far as
their own children were concerned. The new socialist
government in France promised (threatened?) major
changes to the status of private schools, particularly those in receipt of public funds, but after
over two years in office was still discussing the
problem.
  The question of whether children within any one
school should be streamed, setted, or banded, i.e.
in any way *differentiated into separate classes by
ability*, arose in all the countries at some time and
sometimes gave rise to confusion in policy terms.
In the USA for example,

> *Either by design or de facto students will
> generally be tracked by the time they reach
> secondary schools. Indeed this system of
> academic streaming or segregation may have
> begun in the junior high, and critics of
> American schooling assert that it begins,
> even if subtly, in the elementary years.*

In Sweden, however, '*until the end of their compulsory schooling, students are kept together in
undifferentiated classes*' and the same is broadly
true of France, at least as regards the earlier
secondary years. In the UK this remained a question
for the individual headteacher to decide although
the LEA was increasingly liable to exert pressure,
explicitly or implicitly, towards mixed ability
classes.
  School curricula, timetabling and calls for
'*Back to Basics*' (the slogan used in West Germany)
have occurred prominently in policy discussions in
most of the countries. In West Germany (particularly
the southern, Christian-democrat controlled regions),
the UK (particularly after the return to power of the
Conservative government in 1979), France (in the
post-Haby period), Japan (in the third official
revision of curricula from 1977 onwards), Australia
and Sweden, governments have come to take closer
interest in detailed curriculum reform in the light
of changing economic and social needs. It is, however, necessary to recall the widely differing

national contexts: at the time of writing it remains true that such a question as, for example, offering a *second* foreign language, would largely not arise in the USA, would in France be decided by the Minister himself, would in Japan be a matter for the local government unit, and in the UK would still be for the individual headteacher to decide in his or her own school.

Policy relating to *post-school education* has in each country resulted in a wide variety of institutions catering for differing ability ranges, interests, and type and duration of courses. With the exception of France, where the most able students typically seek entry to the *grandes écoles*, in each country the universities take the most able students, have the most generous levels of resourcing and have secured for themselves a large measure of independence from official control. They have been largely free to pursue their own specialisms and develop their own courses and only in the last decade has there been serious concern about the students' future careers, the needs of the national economy, and graduate unemployment. Criticism perhaps reached a peak in Japan where the universities came to be dubbed 'leisure centres'. In the USA and Japan public and private universities co-exist side by side but elsewhere they are semi-autonomous institutions within the public sector (despite the way the latter term is often used in the UK to refer to LEA-funded institutions such as the polytechnics). If it is in France that there has been achieved the greatest integration of higher education with national economic planning, it is in Sweden that the 'comprehensive' principle has been most successfully applied: entry standards have been varied and lowered and within institutions students from differing educational backgrounds and on widely differing courses of study will now mix freely. A similar trend may be discerned, although to a far less extent, in West Germany.

In all the countries *further education* colleges or institutes offer technical, vocationally-orientated courses, both full-time and part-time and in recent years educational policy has come to take far more interest in what was often seen previously as a 'Cinderella' or rather under-privileged area. This has been one further aspect of the closer integration over time of educational output with economic need. Rather paradoxically, it was once mass unemployment came to dominate job markets, especially for young people, that much

larger numbers of students were recruited on such
training courses. In each of the countries there
has been some uncertainty as to whether policy
relating to such courses should continue to aim at
training for jobs which may not exist, or for
enforced leisure, or for some mix of both. By the
1980s, with mass unemployment in all the countries
predicted to last for the remainder of the twentieth
century, some young people leaving some schools or
colleges were having to face up to the fact that
they might never have a regular job.
    The educational systems in all the seven
countries broadly coped well with the massive
expansion of education that took place approximately
in the period of thirty years from 1945, as a result
of the combination of 'baby booms' with much
increased social demand for education, including
higher education. The school-leaving age was raised
to around 16 in most countries (15 in Tasmania and
some parts of the USA) but in West Germany and in
California around 100 per cent of 17-year-olds and
even 18-year-olds continued in full-time education
or training of some kind. Thereafter, apparently
quite suddenly, reduced birth rates and reduced
rates of staying on into post-compulsory education
brought new problems of *contraction* and retrenchment,
with which educational policy coped, and is still
coping, much less well. At the same time the years
of high economic success and quite rapidly rising
standards of living, especially in Japan, West
Germany and France but also in the other countries
and even (more slowly) in the UK, gave way to
economic stagnation and depression. There followed
less generous funding for the national education
sector and much heart-searching as to where
financial cuts could or should be made. This
situation occurred in every one of the seven
countries but was perhaps at its most acute in the
UK.
    In such a brief summary it is not possible to
do justice to the many complex strands of
educational policy that are covered within the
individual country essays. Some, indeed, have not
been mentioned here at all - sex equality, for
example, or policy relating to handicapped students.
Nor is it possible adequately to capture here the
local national ethos, as with Australia's apparent
preoccupation with its geographical isolation, the
close adherence to international trends in Japan,
the emphases in Sweden and the USA on equality and
democracy respectively, the north-south divide in

West Germany, the (still) overwhelming centralisation
in France, or the quite perplexing central/local
relationship in the UK.   In particular the conceptual
and theoretical issues set out so lucidly by
Dr Harman throw much light on policy developments in
the various countries and show the cumulative and
on-going nature of the processes involved.   In his
concluding words: '*Sometimes education policies are
openly and deliberately terminated, but more commonly
policies are repeatedly adjusted, modified, refined
or replaced with other policies.*'
     If the issues with which educational policy
will have to deal in the later 1980s may at the time
of writing seem clear - especially relating to
financial constraint, the demands of technological
change, mass unemployment, greater equality of
opportunity, and concern over educational standards -
it is far from clear how policy in each of the
countries will deal with such complex problems,
either in terms of establishing priorities or in
terms of the inherent conflicts which seem certain
to arise between contrasting and competing aims.
It is hoped that the present volume, in throwing
light on questions of educational policy over the
recent period, will also be of some assistance in
the elucidation of such issues in the future.

NOTE

     1.   E.J. Nicholas, *Issues in Education: A
Comparative Perspective* (Harper & Row, 1983), p.35.

Professor David Beswick is Director of the Centre for the Study of Higher Education, University of Melbourne.

Ms Judith Bodenhausen is Research Associate at the School of Education, University of California, Berkeley.

Professor James Guthrie is Professor of Educational Administration and Evaluation and Chairman of the School of Education, University of California, Berkeley.

Dr Grant Harman is Reader at the Centre for the Study of Higher Education, University of Melbourne.

Dr J.R. Hough is Reader in Education and Economics in the Department of Education, Loughborough University.

Dr Shogo Ichikawa is Director of Research Department II at the National Institute for Educational Research, Tokyo.

Professor Sixten Marklund is Professor at the Institute for International Education, University of Stockholm.

Professor Marten Shipman is Head of the Department of Education, University of Warwick.

Dr W. Schwark is Rector of the Pädagogische Hochschule, Freiburg.

Dr A. Wolf is Professor at the Pädagogische Hochschule, Freiburg.